Fenians, Freedmen, and Southern Whites

CONFLICTING WORLDS
New Dimensions of the American Civil War
T. Michael Parrish, Series Editor

Fenians, Freedmen, and Southern Whites

Race and Nationality in the Era of Reconstruction

Mitchell Snay

Louisiana State University Press
Baton Rouge

Published with the assistance of the V. Ray Cardozier Fund

Published by Louisiana State University Press
Copyright © 2007 by Louisiana State University Press
All rights reserved
Manufactured in the United States of America
Louisiana Paperback Edition, 2010

Designer: Michelle A. Neustrom
Typeface: Tribute
Typesetter: Newgen

Library of Congress Cataloging-in-Publication Data

Snay, Mitchell.
   Fenians, freedmen, and southern Whites : race and nationality in the era of Reconstruction / Mitchell Snay.
     p. cm. — (Conflicting worlds)
   Includes bibliographical references and index.
   ISBN 978-0-8071-3273-9 (cloth : alk. paper)
     1. Reconstruction (U.S. history, 1865–1877) 2. Nationalism—United States—History—19th century. 3. Political culture—United States—History—19th century. 4. Ethnicity—Political aspects—United States—History—19th century. 5. Fenians—History. 6. Irish Americans—Politics and government—19th century. 7. Freedmen—United States—Political activity—History—19th century. 8. Whites—Southern States—Politics and government—19th century. 9. United States—Race relations—Political aspects—History—19th century. 10. Southern States—Race relations—Political aspects—History—19th century. I. Title.
   E668.S66 2007
   973.8—dc22

2007007924

ISBN 978-0-8071-3716-1 (pbk. : alk. paper)

The paper in this book meets the guidelines for permanence and durability of the Committee on Production Guidelines for Book Longevity of the Council on Library Resources. ∞

Portions of this book in an earlier form were published in "The Imagined Republic: The Fenians, Irish American Nationalism, and the Political Culture of Reconstruction," *Proceedings of the American Antiquarian Society* 112, part 2 (2002): 291–313. Used by permission.

For Liz
I am my Beloved's, and my Beloved is mine.
—Song of Songs 6:3

Contents

Acknowledgments   ix

Introduction   1
1. The Context of Republican Reconstruction   18
2. The Political Culture of Countersubversion   50
3. Nationality and Class: The Land Question   81
4. Ethnic and Racial Nationalism   114
5. Civic Nationalism   139
Conclusion   171

Bibliography   177
Index   209

Illustrations follow page 80.

Acknowledgments

Writing this book was not an easy task, so my expressions of gratitude to the institutions and individuals that helped me along the way are sincere and heartfelt.

The financial awards I received were not only invaluable sources for research travel and writing time but welcome affirmations of my project. For their support, I wish to thank the American Antiquarian Society (Joyce Tracy Fellowship), Denison University (R. C. Good Fellowships), the Gilder Lehrman Institute (Fellowship in American Civilization), the Filson Historical Society, the Irish American Cultural Institute (Irish Research Fund), the National Endowment for the Humanities (summer stipend), and the North Caroliniana Society (Archie K. Davis Fellowship).

Writing about both the North and the South during Reconstruction forced me to travel far and wide in search of primary sources. I am grateful to the following libraries and archives for their help in facilitating this research: the Alabama Department of Archives and History, the American Antiquarian Society, the Columbia University Rare Book Room, the Denison University Library, the East Tennessee Historical Society, the Filson Historical Society, the Florida Historical Society, the Georgia Department of Archives and History, the Georgia Historical Society, the Hargrett Rare Book and Manuscript Library at the University of Georgia, the Historical Society of Pennsylvania, the Louisiana State University Archives, the Mississippi Department of Archives and History, the Newberry Library, the New York Historical Society, the North Carolina Division of Archives and History, the Ohio Historical Society, the Philadelphia Archdiocesan Historical Research Center, the South Caroliniana Library, the South Carolina Department of Archives and History, the Southern Historical Collection at the University of North Carolina, and the Tennessee State Library and Archives. For their special service and support, I would like to thank in particular Ann Watson and Mary Prophet at Denison, Ann Webster and Nancy Bounds at the Mississippi Department of Archives and History, and Caroline Sloat, Phillip Lampi, Dennis Laurie, and Russell Martin at the American Antiquarian Society.

Conversations with other historians are perhaps the most pleasant part of writing history. This book benefited immeasurably from the help of teachers, colleagues, and friends. Two former mentors from my graduate school days, David H. Donald and Morton Keller, offered encouraging words at the project's inception. Because his muster is so hard to pass, Michael O'Brien's interest in my inquiry became an important milestone in the journey from idea to completed manuscript. Eric Foner generously shared his advice, insights, and sources on Reconstruction. For the portions of this book that were initially sketched out in conference papers, I am grateful for the commentary of Michael Les Benedict, David Carlton, Russell Duncan, Wayne K. Durrill, Robert F. Engs, J. Matthew Gallman, and Jay Mandle. Presentations at the American Antiquarian Society, the Ohio Seminar for Early American History, the Filson Historical Society, the Southern Intellectual History Circle, and the Global Studies Seminar at Denison University gave me the opportunity to present my work in progress. Michael W. Fitzgerald and J. Mills Thornton III each gave the entire manuscript a close and helpful reading that significantly improved the final product. Over the course of many years, conversations with Michael Perman, Randall Miller, Ted Tunnell, Mark Smith, Mark W. Summers, and Lacy Ford helped me think about the dynamics of Reconstruction. Rebecca and Doug Rutledge generously opened their bookstore and themselves to a struggling writer and an addicted bibliophile.

It was Ray Arsenault who first suggested that the Ku Klux Klan might merit a new look by comparing it with such groups as the Fenians. He thus deserves credit for much of the shape of this book. Ray's support and friendship continue to be one of the great boons of my professional career. The other members of my Brandeis circle—Jim and Lois Horton, Stephen J. Whitfield, and Jama Lazerow—may not have contributed directly to this project, but the models of humanity and scholarship they present continue to inspire. I cherish the intellectual support and personal friendship I have received from Diane Miller Sommerville over many years.

At various times in the writing of this book, Heather Cox Richardson cajoled, questioned, edited, advised, sustained, and inspired. Thanks to cell phones, her company on those long rides to and from Dayton taught me much about the mysteries of Reconstruction and writing about the past. She retained faith in this study when it was slipping away from its author. This book—and I—are far better for knowing her.

Mike Parrish is the ideal series editor. Throughout the long process from grant proposals to book, he was persistent in his support, bibliographic advice, editorial assistance, and encouragement. It has also been a pleasure to work with Rand Dotson of LSU Press and Sylvia Frank, formerly with LSU Press, and copy editor Derik Shelor.

The time in which this book occupied my professional life witnessed the loss of some very important people to me. My former adviser from graduate school, Marvin Meyers, did not live to see his student's second book. While I often wish for his guidance, his teachings remain with me as I continue to aspire to the kind of incisive historical thinking he personified. During the time of this project, I also lost both my parents. Yet their love, support, and respect remain imbedded inside me, there to call upon in times of need. My remaining and adopted family—Abby, Ed, Ben, Jen, Arnie, Sue, Ernie, David, Jack, Larry, Emily, Tony, William, Daniel, Jeremy, Lauren, Juliana, and the Doodle—deserve mention for reminding me that life, unlike writing, need not be a solitary endeavor.

There can be little doubt that in many ways my son, Elliott, took time and energy away from my immersion in the history of Reconstruction. Yet he has given me much in return, far in excess of what he took away. On road trips to forts and battlefields, we shared the excitement of discovering history together. He was with me on a cold and rainy day in Ontario when we stumbled onto the site of the Battle of Ridgeway. It is indeed possible that those countless hours reading about Pokeweed Public School and telling stories about Twin Springs Camp made me a more creative writer. What will never be in question are the myriad of ways in which being his father has been the great joy of my life.

At every stage and in every way, my wife, Liz, has contributed to the creation of this book. She made sure I had a study in which to put the books I bought and write the one I was writing. On many research trips, she sent me what I needed and kept a light burning in the window until I returned. In words spoken and unspoken, she demanded that I persevere in my life's vocation, face its toughest challenges, and live up to my potential. More important, our marriage has taught me that there is nothing more important in life's journey than traveling together. For these and countless other reasons, I dedicate this book to Liz, my beloved and my friend.

Fenians, Freedmen, and Southern Whites

Introduction

Ridgeway, Ontario, 1866

The Fenians, the American branch of an Irish revolutionary movement aimed at national independence and the establishment of an Irish republic, had become increasingly militant in the immediate aftermath of the Civil War. One faction, led by Thomas W. Sweeny and William R. Roberts, believed that a blow for Irish independence could be struck by assaulting Canada. In 1866, an attack was imminent. General John O'Neil, a native of Ireland who had gained military experience in the Union army, would lead the invasion. On Thursday, May 31, O'Neil took command of a Fenian army of about eight hundred men that had assembled in Buffalo, New York. At midnight, he sent an advance party across the Niagara River into Ontario. The main force of the Fenian army, emboldened by flags adorned with gold harps and sunbursts, crossed over into Canada a few hours later. Their immediate target was the small village of Fort Erie, a town of about three hundred residents. It capitulated with little resistance and the Fenian flag now flew on British territory. "We have taken up the sword to strike down the oppressors' rod," proclaimed Sweeny, "to deliver Ireland from the tyrant, the despoiler, the robber."[1]

Canadian authorities were alarmed. "The soil of Canada has been invaded," declared Governor-General Charles Stanley Monck, "not in the practice of legitimate warfare, but by a lawless and piratical band,

---

1. The description of the Fenian invasion in this and the following paragraphs has been drawn from W. S. Neidhardt, *Fenianism in North America* (University Park: Pennsylvania State Univ. Press, 1975), chapter 8. Margaret E. Teal, ed., "The Battle of Limeridge: Stories and Legends of the Fenian Raid, June 2, 1866, at Ridgeway, Ontario" (1976; reprint, Ridgeway, Ontario: Bertie Historical Society, 1982), contains interesting anecdotes collected and preserved by local residents. There is an informative exhibit on the Fenian raids at the Fort Erie Historical Museum in Ridgeway, Ontario.

in defiance of all moral right, and in utter disregard of all the obligations which civilization imposes upon mankind." Two companies from the Queen's Own Rifle Regiment were rushed to the Niagara frontier, where they were joined by scores of volunteers from the area surrounding Fort Erie. U.S. officials in Washington, with the tense state of Anglo-American relations on their minds, closely followed events unfolding on the Canadian border. General George Meade, the hero of Gettysburg three years before, wrote to the secretary of war that "the long and much talked of effort has seriously been begun." In the next few days, the opposing armies maneuvered for battle while the best-laid plans of each were going awry. Gunboats from the U.S. Navy that had been rushed to the scene prevented additional supplies from reaching O'Neil. Confused Canadian military authorities had sent a force to the town of Ridgeway, a small village containing a flour mill, a few stores, twenty houses, and two taverns, to the west of Fort Erie. There, Lieutenant-Colonel Alfred Booker sat with a poorly prepared and strategically misplaced Canadian militia to meet the Fenian army.[2]

The morning of Saturday, June 2, dawned exquisitely. "It was a beautiful day," recalled one of the Canadian participants, "—the trees were clothed with the tender, delicate foliage of early summer, and the fields were green with young crops." But for the Canadians, the natural beauty of the day would be stained by bloodshed. Booker had mistakenly thought that the Fenians had gathered in a cavalry formation. To repel the impending assault, he formed his men in a defensive "Form Square." When the cavalry charge failed to materialize, Booker's men were caught in a vulnerable tactical position and were cut down by Fenian fire. One Canadian soldier was shot in the head, the bullet piercing his forehead and breaking his bone at the back of the skull. Booker retreated and the bold band of Fenian warriors claimed victory at the "Battle of Limestone Ridge."[3]

---

2. Neidhardt, *Fenianism in North America*, 60; George Meade to Edwin Stanton, June 2, 1866, Andrew Johnson Papers, 2nd Series, vol. 6, 1813-4-5, Library of Congress, Washington, D.C. I am indebted to Professor Michael Vorenberg for providing me with a copy of this letter.

3. Neidhardt, *Fenianism in North America*, 65.

The Fenian triumph, however, was short-lived. O'Neil soon found himself enveloped by a numerically superior Canadian force that had been rushed to the battle. Attempting to withdraw, many of his men were captured by two American gunboats positioned to intercept the Fenian retreat. To make matters worse, President Andrew Johnson had issued a Proclamation of Neutrality, which further isolated the Irish American nationalists. The Fenian invasion of Canada—a rearguard attack on England's tyrannical grip upon Ireland—had failed.

Yet all was not lost. Patrick O'Reilly, a Fenian volunteer from Buffalo wounded in the raid, took refuge in a nearby farmhouse, where he was treated by a young woman who hid him and later helped him escape. He returned months later and eloped with his female accomplice. If he had failed to free Ireland, O'Reilly had at least conquered the farmer's daughter. The Battle of Ridgeway had other qualities of the burlesque. One Canadian volunteer, eager if inexperienced, mistook a cow for a Fenian scout and killed it. In the midst of the battle, a Fenian officer grabbed the rifle of a Canadian soldier, boasting that it would never shoot another Fenian. As the officer smashed the gun against the rocks, it accidentally misfired and killed him.

But to the Canadians, the Fenian invasion festered bitterly for years. Seven Canadians had been killed, two others died later from their wounds, and their national defense had been humiliated. The Fenian invasion of Canada alerted watchful Americans to the depth of Irish American nationalist sentiment after the Civil War. The Fenian movement had demonstrated its intent to use force to create an independent Irish republic.

Bullock County, Alabama, 1867

More than a thousand miles south of Canada lay the Black Belt of Alabama, a region of rich cotton-growing lands that had been at the heart of the antebellum plantation South. Bullock County, at the eastern end of the Black Belt, typified the Reconstruction cotton South. The population of the county was three-fourths African American. Planters and former slaves were negotiating a troubling postwar world of physical destruction, a new free labor system, a federal tax on cotton, a dearth of credit, and political upheaval. Racial struggles over land and labor erupted during Reconstruction. Consequently, Radical Republicans were active in organizing the freedmen.[4]

Into this volatile setting came George Shorter, a black adventurer from Montgomery. His background remains obscure. According to one northern newspaper, Shorter was one of the blacks who had been sent from "a Northwestern State to organize a black government for Alabama." He claimed to have had such orders from Wager Swayne, assistant commissioner of the Freedmen's Bureau in Alabama. With the help of the local Union League, the Republican-sponsored organization to mobilize African American voters, Shorter established what was essentially a de facto black government in the Bullock County town of Perote. It adopted a constitution and established a list of crimes and punishments. According to the Mobile *Times,* the Union Leaguers formed "a code of laws to govern the negro population, opened a court officered and organized, arresting by night all blacks who opposed their unlawful proceedings."[5]

The events at Perote confirmed the worst white fears of Reconstruction. Apprehension spread that the African American government established in Bullock County would soon launch what seemed essentially like a program of ethnic cleansing. According to the editor of the distant *Irish Citizen* of New York, blacks who gathered at the county seat were "threatening a general rising and extermination of the whites and taking possession of the country." A storekeeper in nearby Eufaula heard one freedman say that they "would take them from the cradle up." When Shorter arrested one of the League members over a financial disagreement, the man sought help from civil authorities. A confrontation between two rival governments, the local Bullock County administration and the one inaugurated by Shorter, was brewing as white planters and blacks from other Union Leagues poured into Perote. The arrival of U.S. Army troops from Montgomery finally restored order. Shorter

---

4. Cecil E. McNair, "Reconstruction in Bullock County," *Alabama Historical Quarterly* 15 (spring 1953): 82, 107; Michael Fitzgerald, *The Union League Movement in the Deep South: Politics and Agricultural Change during Reconstruction* (Baton Rouge: Louisiana State Univ. Press, 1989), 45, 124, 153–155.

5. Pittsburgh *Catholic,* December 28, 1867; Fitzgerald, *Union League Movement in the Deep South,* 156–157.

and other black leaders were arrested, though Shorter escaped from jail and disappeared from the area. The "Perote disturbances," as they were called, showed that, like the Fenians, African Americans in the Reconstruction South saw political self-determination and ethnic autonomy as a desirable and indeed feasible aspiration.[6]

Meridian, Mississippi, 1871

Since it had begun its campaign of terrorism in 1867, the Ku Klux Klan had often used members from neighboring counties to carry out its plans in order to escape detection and prosecution. By early 1871, Klan violence had gotten so bad in western Alabama that many blacks were fleeing into Lauderdale County, Mississippi. To apprehend alleged violators of labor contracts, Alabama Klansmen began pursuing freedpeople across state lines into the railroad center of Meridian. In late 1870, two black county supervisors were murdered. The situation had become so dangerous that three black leaders from Meridian—William Dennis, Warren Tyler, and Aaron Moore—went to Jackson to seek help from the Republican state administration. When they returned, they addressed a meeting of freedmen in Meridian on the night of March 4, 1871. After their rally, a fire of mysterious origins broke out in a store owned by the brother of the Republican mayor of Meridian. Local blacks refused to help put out the conflagration, claiming it was a "white man's fire." The next day members of both races filled the streets of Meridian, armed and ready for battle.[7]

To help defuse the situation, the sheriff in Meridian arrested the three black leaders for giving "incendiary" speeches. Racial tension

6. *Irish Citizen*, December 14, 1867; Fitzgerald, *Union League Movement in the Deep South*, 157; *Tri-Weekly Austin Republican*, December 5, 1867; Fitzgerald, *Union League Movement in the Deep South*, 158. See also Pittsburgh *Catholic*, December 14, 1867.

7. The outline of events in this and the following paragraphs was pieced together from Allen W. Trelease, *White Terror: The Ku Klux Klan Conspiracy and Southern Reconstruction* (Baton Rouge: Louisiana State Univ. Press, 1971), 290–293; William C. Harris, *The Day of the Carpetbagger: Republican Reconstruction in Mississippi* (Baton Rouge: Louisiana State Univ. Press, 1979), 396–398; Vernon Lane Wharton, *The Negro in Mississippi, 1865–1890* (1947; reprint, New York: Harper and Row, 1965), 188–190; and James W. Garner, *Reconstruction in Mississippi* (1901; reprint, Baton Rouge: Louisiana State Univ. Press, 1968), 349–350.

moved from the streets into the courtroom. The black defendant Warren Tyler challenged the testimony of a white witness, James Brantley, who then angrily approached Tyler with a stick. What happened next remains unclear. White Democratic witnesses claimed that Tyler took out a gun and shot at Brantley. The bullet meant for Brantley missed him but hit the courtroom judge in the head, killing him. Whites began shooting, hitting and mortally wounding another black defendant, Bill Dennis. Tyler managed to escape the building. The Klan then seized control of Meridian, taking justice into its own hands. They apprehended Tyler and killed him. They later found the wounded Dennis and cut his throat. Another injured black leader was taken from the Meridian jail and lynched. Aaron Moore's home was burned to the ground and a black Baptist church was destroyed.

On Monday, the Ku Klux Klan completed their coup in Meridian. Conservative whites gathered and demanded that the Republican mayor resign, giving him twenty-four hours to leave the state. The whites in Meridian then appointed a committee of public safety to take over the job of law enforcement. Under Klan justice, three more African Americans were lynched. Perhaps as many as thirty more blacks were hunted down, killed, and their bodies mutilated. B. F. Moore, a Republican circuit court judge, claimed that "the whites have committed, & applauded outrages committed which History must hand down as only equaled by the most uncivilized of the Human Race."[8]

The common thread in these stories is a struggle for ethnic autonomy and political self-governance. After the Civil War, Irish Americans, southern whites, and African American freedpeople developed a consciousness of being a separate people and fought for a place in the American body politic. Examined collectively, they suggest that Reconstruction can be profitably explored from the perspective of nationalism.[9]

---

8. Harris, *Day of the Carpetbagger*, 398.

9. For introductions to Irish American nationalism in the nineteenth century, see Gilbert Osofsky, "Abolitionists, Irish Immigrants, and the Dilemmas of Romantic Nationalism," *American Historical Review* 80 (October 1975): 889–912; Thomas N. Brown, *Irish-American Nationalism, 1870–1890* (Philadelphia: J. B. Lippincott, 1966); and Eric Foner, "Class, Ethnicity, and Radicalism in the Gilded Age: The Land League in Irish-

The era of the American Civil War and Reconstruction occurred in an age of nationalism. In Europe, German and Italian national unification movements triumphed while Hungarians and Poles fought for their independence. Nationalism emerged within the United States as well. While the Confederacy marked a short-lived and ultimately unsuccessful experiment in southern nationalism, a new American nation was forged by the Civil War. The demands of mobilizing northern society for total war strengthened the centralizing and standardizing tendencies in American life. The Union, through the fiery crucible of war, was transformed into a transcendent symbol of American nationhood. Indeed, historian David Potter suggested in 1968 that nationalism could explain the larger significance of the Civil War. From a global perspective, he argued that a new link between nationalism and liberalism was the enduring legacy of the American Civil War. For decades, few historians followed Potter's lead in investigating the connections between nationalism and the Civil War era.[10]

Yet since 2000, a number of books on this long-neglected subject have appeared. Melinda Lawson and Susan-Mary Grant, for example, have traced the construction of a national identity in the North. For southern whites, Anne Sarah Rubin has shown how a southern national identity persisted after the Confederacy ceased to exist as a nation. In his Pulitzer Prize–winning *A Nation under Our Feet,* Steven Hahn suggests how the processes of community building and political activism created a sense of a nation among rural blacks in the nineteenth-century South.

America," in *Politics and Ideology in the Age of the Civil War* (New York: Oxford Univ. Press, 1980). The best general volume on the Klan remains Trelease, *White Terror,* but see also Stanley F. Horn, *Invisible Empire: The Story of the Ku Klux Klan, 1866–1871* (1939; reprint, Cos Cob, Conn.: John E. Edwards, 1969). The fullest work on the Union Leagues is Fitzgerald, *Union League Movement in the Deep South,* but see also Steven Hahn, *A Nation under Our Feet: Black Political Struggles in the Rural South from Slavery to the Great Migration* (Cambridge, Mass.: Belknap Press of Harvard Univ. Press, 2003).

10. See Eric J. Hobsbawm, *The Age of Capital, 1848–1875* (New York: Scribner, 1975), chapter 5; David M. Potter, *The South and the Sectional Conflict* (Baton Rouge: Louisiana State Univ. Press, 1968), 281; David Herbert Donald commented in 1978 that the history of American nationalism "has been surprisingly neglected by historians" (*Liberty and Union* [Lexington, Mass.: D. C. Heath, 1978], 273); Eric Foner, *Reconstruction: America's Unfinished Revolution, 1863–1877* (New York: Harper and Row, 1988), 18–34.

By demonstrating the relevance of nationalism to the Civil War era, these and other studies encourage further inquiries into the subject.[11]

Unlike southern whites and blacks, Irish Americans are seldom mentioned in Reconstruction histories. When the nationalist Fenians are lucky enough to appear, they are typically cited as one of several issues that strained Anglo-American relations in the late 1860s. "Though the movement was too pathetically feeble to justify official sympathy," wrote William A. Dunning in his 1907 survey of the period, "the support which enabled it to assume even the little dignity it attained was traceable to the popular resentment against England." By joining the Fenians with freedpeople and southern whites, this study seeks to suggest their central relevance to the dynamics of nationalism during Reconstruction.[12]

Two concepts from the theoretical literature on nationalism are useful to this inquiry. Of particular applicability is the distinction between civic and ethnic nationalism. Civic nationalism can be said to exist where primary loyalty is given to common citizenship in a national state governing a specific territory. This definition comes close to describing American nationalism after the Civil War, one forged primarily by northern Republicans and their white Unionist allies in the South during and after the conflict. The destruction of slavery and the rise of a nation state gave special focus to the question of citizenship. What would be the status of former Confederates and freedmen? What rights did such groups as African Americans, immigrants, and women possess? More fundamentally, what did it mean to be American? The Republican Party's commitment to the federal protection of equal rights, made evident in such legislation as the Civil Rights Act of 1866 and the Fourteenth Amendment, encouraged a variety of groups to press for answers

---

11. See Melinda Lawson, *Patriot Fires: Forging a New American Nationalism in the Civil War North* (Lawrence: Univ. Press of Kansas, 2002); Susan-Mary Grant, *North over South: Northern Nationalism and American Identity in the Antebellum Era* (Lawrence: Univ. Press of Kansas, 2000); Anne Sarah Rubin, *A Shattered Nation: The Rise and Fall of the Confederacy, 1861–1868* (Chapel Hill: Univ. of North Carolina Press, 2005); and Hahn, *A Nation under Our Feet.*

12. William A. Dunning, *Reconstruction, Political and Economic, 1865–1877* (1907. Reprint, New York: Harper and Row, 1962), 160.

to these questions. By focusing on questions of freedom, citizenship, and suffrage, Reconstruction ideology channeled nationalist impulses into civic terms of political enfranchisement. In addition, the Republican emphasis on color-blind equality limited expressions of national identities based solely on ethnicity or class. Finally, postwar partisan politics tended to absorb the separatist efforts of Irish Americans, freedmen, and southern whites into the two-party system.[13]

In contrast to civic nationalism, ethnic nationalism might be defined as a condition where the underlying loyalty in a state is attached to a specific group of people based on the perceived awareness of singular inherited characteristics, such as language, customs, and history. Among the three groups under study, the Fenians provide the clearest case of nationalist aspirations along the lines of ethnicity. However, the rise of racial consciousness among both southern whites and blacks also might be seen as expressions of ethnic nationalism.[14]

13. Some recent works include Patrick J. Kelly, *Creating a National Home: Building the Veterans' Welfare State, 1860–1900* (Cambridge, Mass.: Harvard Univ. Press, 1997); Barbara Young Welke, *Recasting American Liberty: Gender, Race, Law, and the Railroad Revolution, 1865–1920* (Cambridge: Cambridge Univ. Press, 2001); Elizabeth Sanders, *Roots of Reform: Farmers, Workers, and the American State, 1877–1917* (Chicago: Univ. of Chicago Press, 1999); Gaines M. Foster, *Moral Reconstruction: Christian Lobbyists and the Federal Legislation of Morality, 1865–1920* (Chapel Hill: Univ. of North Carolina Press, 2002); and Richard Franklin Benzel, *Yankee Leviathan: The Origins of Central State Authority in America, 1859–1877* (Cambridge: Cambridge Univ. Press, 1990). An interesting essay on the potentials of political science theory on state development for American history is Richard R. John, "Governmental Institutions as Agents of Change: Rethinking American Political Development in the Early Republic, 1787–1835," *Studies in American Political Development* 11 (fall 1997): 347–380. The implications of John's argument for the Civil War era merit further study. Steven Hahn's "Class and State in Postemancipation Societies: Southern Planters in Comparative Perspective," *American Historical Review* 95 (February 1990): 75–98, recognizes the power of the state. I am indebted to Heather Cox Richardson for sharing with me a draft of her essay "North and West of Reconstruction: Studies in Political Economy," in *Reconstructions: New Perspectives on the Postbellum United States*, ed. Thomas J. Brown (New York: Oxford Univ. Press, 2006).

14. On ethnic nationalism, see John Hutchinson and Anthony D. Smith, eds., *Nationalism* (New York: Oxford Univ. Press, 1994), 3–10, 43; Liah Greenfeld, *Nationalism: Five Roads to Modernity* (Cambridge, Mass.: Harvard Univ. Press, 1992), 12–13; and John Hutchinson and Anthony D. Smith, eds., *Ethnicity* (New York: Oxford Univ. Press, 1996), 275–277. James McPherson uses a similar distinction in his "Was Blood Thicker Than

Another useful concept from the social sciences, the notion of "proto-nationalism," also helps in understanding nationalism during Reconstruction. Political scientist Walker Connor defines a proto-nation as "groups of people who appear to have all of the necessary prerequisites for nationhood but who have not as yet developed a consciousness of their sameness and commonalty, nor a conviction that their destinies are interwound." The idea of proto-nationalism is especially useful to historians, for it is implicitly dynamic, suggestive of an evolutionary process. Yet a concept with the term "proto" runs the danger of seeing any expression of ethnic identity as the first stage in an inexorable movement toward ethnic nationalism. Situations in which ethnic nationalism does not occur are as historically significant as when and why it does.[15]

Looking at Reconstruction from the perspective of nationalism reveals the continuing importance of republicanism in American political discourse. This "grammar" of society and politics, rooted in the Jeffersonian, Jacksonian, and antebellum periods, framed the efforts of southern whites and blacks and Irish Americans at self-governance and identity formation. My approach to Reconstruction then highlights the continuities between pre– and post–Civil War America. From the vantage point of nationalism, Reconstruction appears as a period as much grounded in the past as it was a harbinger of the future. It also seems possible that the confrontation of republicanism with the national question exposed its increasing irrelevance in a world of intensifying class, ethnic, and racial conflict.

In July of 1867, the editor of the *Irish People* of New York commented that Reconstruction was "the order of the day everywhere, from Egypt to Alabama, and from Japan to Canada. Every race and nation is now agitated by it in some form or other." His comment anticipated the recent

---

Water? Ethnic and Civic Nationalism in the American Civil War," *Proceedings of the American Philosophical Society* 143 (March 1999): 103.

15. Walker Connor, *Ethnonationalism: The Quest for Understanding* (Princeton: Princeton Univ. Press, 1994), 114. See also Anthony D. Smith, ed., *Nationalist Movements* (London: Macmillan, 1976), 6–7; and Wilson Jeremiah Jones, ed., *Classical Black Nationalism: From the American Revolution to Marcus Garvey* (New York: New York Univ. Press, 1996), 6–8.

historiographic trend of viewing American Reconstruction in a transnational perspective. For example, historians have placed emancipation and its consequences in the wider context of a worldwide process of capitalist development. Attempting to explain the transition from slavery to freedom in America, they have found similar struggles over land and labor in the British West Indies, Cuba, and Brazil. This book places Irish Americans, African Americans, and southern whites in a comparative framework, providing a promising lens for studying the dynamics of nationalism during Reconstruction. Its centrality to this book merits some brief explanation.[16]

Several factors justify placing Irish Americans, southern whites, and freedpeople in a comparative context. First, all three groups worked

16. *Irish People*, July 6, 1867. The seminal study remains Hobsbawm, *The Age of Capital*. For the United States, see David Montgomery, *Beyond Equality: Labor and the Radical Republicans, 1862–1872* (1967; Urbana: Univ. of Illinois Press, 1981), especially page x. More recent relevant books include Amy Dru Stanley, *From Bondage to Contract: Wage Labor, Marriage, and the Market in the Age of Slave Emancipation* (New York: Cambridge Univ. Press, 1998); and Sven Beckert, *The Monied Metropolis: New York City and the Consolidation of the American Bourgeoisie, 1850–1896* (New York: Cambridge Univ. Press, 2001). Class relations are becoming more central to studies of the postwar North. See especially Foner, *Reconstruction*, chapters 10 and 11. For other efforts to link class to politics, see Richard Schneirov, *Labor and Urban Politics: Class Conflict and the Origins of Modern Liberalism in Chicago, 1864–97* (Urbana: Univ. of Illinois Press, 1998); and John B. Jentz and Richard Schneirov, "Chicago's Fenian Fair of 1864: A Window into the Civil War as a Popular Political Awakening," *Labor's Heritage* 6 (winter 1995): 4–19.

The literature on the transition from slave to wage labor is quite extensive. See the important statements by Armstead L. Robinson, "Beyond the Realm of Social Consensus: New Meanings of Reconstruction for American History," *Journal of American History* 68 (September 1981): 276–297; Julie Saville, *The Work of Reconstruction: From Slave to Wage Laborer in South Carolina, 1860–1870* (New York: Cambridge Univ. Press, 1994); and Joseph P. Reidy, *From Slavery to Agrarian Capitalism in the Cotton Plantation South: Central Georgia, 1800–1880* (Chapel Hill: Univ. of North Carolina Press, 1992).

An older but seminal essay on the comparative history of emancipation is C. Vann Woodward, "The Price of Freedom," in *What Was Freedom's Price?*, ed. David Sansing (Oxford: Univ. Press of Mississippi, 1978). Important newer works include Peter Kolchin, *A Sphinx on the American Land: The Nineteenth-Century South in Comparative Perspective* (Baton Rouge: Louisiana State Univ. Press, 2003); and Frederick Cooper, Rebecca Scott, and Thomas Holt, eds., *Beyond Slavery: Explorations of Race, Labor, and Citizenship in Postemancipation Societies* (Chapel Hill: Univ. of North Carolina Press, 2000).

through similar semi-secret, fraternal, paramilitary societies. The Union Leagues, which began during the Civil War to support the northern war effort and wartime Reconstruction, spread to the South after the war and mobilized African Americans to fight for their political rights and economic security. Formed in large part to resist the Leagues, the Ku Klux Klan used intimidation and violence to maintain the political and economic hegemony of southern whites. There are suggestive similarities among these three groups. Both the League and Klan, for example, employed elaborate rites of initiation and secret passwords common to fraternal organizations in the nineteenth century. There are other points of connection as well. Fenians could be found in the South as well as the North, especially in such urban areas as Savannah, Charleston, Portsmouth, and Nashville. New Orleans boasted seven circles, with almost eight hundred members. The Fenians, the Union Leagues, and the Ku Klux Klan were also paramilitary in structure and activities. Most importantly, all three groups were chronologically rooted in the era of Reconstruction. Although the Union League of America was officially established during the Civil War, the movement flourished primarily in the South in 1867 and 1868. The Klan began in 1866 and was active until crackdowns by state and federal authorities in the early 1870s. The Fenian movement was founded in the United States in 1859 but reached the height of its activities and influence between 1865 and 1867.[17]

Contemporaries often drew analogies between two of the three groups. Several Fenian leaders, for example, saw similarities between the English domination of Ireland and Radical Reconstruction in the South. John Mitchel, editor of the New York *Irish Citizen* and a prominent Irish American nationalist, was struck by the similar condition of the Irish and southern whites. He compared parish priests in Ireland with southern editors. Irish Catholics who openly expressed their faith were likened to *"Southern gentlemen who would not take the ironclad oath."* What lay behind the tyranny in both Ireland and the American South to Mitchel was the sinister hand of the Anglo-Saxon. "Confisca-

---

17. David Herbert Donald, Jean Harvey Baker, and Michael F. Holt, *The Civil War and Reconstruction* (New York: Norton, 2001), 614; David T. Gleeson, *The Irish in the South, 1815–1877* (Chapel Hill: Univ. of North Carolina Press, 2001), 71–72.

tion, disfranchisement, and civil extinction" would be the ultimate result of despotism, whether in Ireland or the former slaveholding states of America.[18]

White southerners also saw the analogy between Ireland and the South. The Charleston *Daily Courier* insisted that the problem of Ireland "is precisely that which now exists at the South. The legislation has been one of dominion rather than of equality." Colonel J. P. Thomas of South Carolina maintained that the South was "contending for that right to direct our own affairs which the people of Ireland have for centuries struggled to obtain." Even apologists for the Ku Klux Klan found legitimacy in the recent history of Ireland. Speaking before a hearing of the Ku Klux Klan Committee in South Carolina, former U.S. senator James Chesnut Jr. explained that "such associations naturally arise under all despotic governments, and the more despotic the governments may be the greater will be the number and violence of such bodies." Ireland was one of the nations Chesnut cited as precedent.[19]

Yet some Fenian leaders saw otherwise. Thomas Lavan, in an address to the Irish in Ohio, called any likeness between Ireland and the South "a parallel between light and darkness—Heaven and Hell."

---

18. *Irish Citizen*, April 11, 1868. See also the New York *Freeman's Journal and Catholic Register*, March 19, 1867. For further evidence of Fenian comments linking the struggles of Ireland and the South during Reconstruction, see the *Irish Citizen*, April 18, 1868, and the letter by "A Claremouis-Man" in the *Irish People*, February 16, 1867. The conservative New York lawyer George Templeton Strong once commented that "Celtocracy is as bad as a niggerocracy" (Allan Nevins and Milton Halsey Thomas, eds., *The Diary of George Templeton Strong*, 4 vols. [New York: Macmillan, 1952], 4:538).

19. Charleston *Daily Courier*, April 2, 1867; Charleston *Daily News*, November 6, 1868. For additional evidence linking the cause of Irish freedom with that of the South, see J. G. de Roulhac Hamilton, ed., *The Papers of Thomas Ruffin*, 4 vols. (Raleigh: Edwards Broughton Printing Company, 1920), 4:45; *Southern Observer*, June 29, 1867; Macon *Daily Telegraph*, July 7, 1866; *Messenger and Advertiser* (Troy, Alabama), July 5, 1869; and U.S. House of Representatives, *Testimony Taken by the Joint Select Committee to Inquire into the Condition of Affairs in the Late Insurrectionary States*, 13 vols. (Washington, D.C.: Government Printing Office, 1872), cited hereafter as KKK Hearings. KKK Hearings, Georgia, vol. 1, page 132. See also Galveston *Weekly News*, March 1, 1867, quoted in Laurensville *Herald*, July 21, 1871; J. G. de Roulhac Hamilton, ed., *The Papers of Randolph Abbott Shotwell*, 2 vols. (Raleigh: North Carolina Historical Commission, 1931), 2:239; and Kevin Kenny, *Making Sense of the Molly Maguires* (New York: Oxford Univ. Press, 1998), 21.

Michael Scanlon, editor of the liberal *Irish Republic* of Chicago, dismissed any resemblance between the oppression of the two groups: "Let us hear no more of Ireland and the South. The South drew the sword for the maintenance of the vilest kind of slavery; Ireland draws the sword for Liberty." Several Fenian leaders drew a comparison between African American and Irish American struggles for freedom. Scanlon, for example, argued that the true allies of the Irish were the freedmen of the South. "Like ourselves," he explained, "the poor African has become the victim of the great plunderer and enslaver of mankind." Other Fenians followed Scanlon's reasoning. "We can never expect to accomplish any great object without being consistent," explained the Emmet Circle of Blairstown, Iowa, "and for us to claim liberty for Ireland while denouncing the liberation of the negroes, is a species of inconsistency too intolerant and palpable to pass the scrutiny of any intelligent people."[20]

Black leaders as well noted the similarities between the struggles of African Americans and Irishmen. Former abolitionist and activist Henry Highland Garnet of New York assured the readers of the *Irish Republic* that "the black men who are true to themselves are with you, heart and hand, in your just struggles for liberty and independent nationality." The editors of the black New Orleans *Tribune* saw the natural affinity between freedmen and Fenians as well: "We said several times that having devoted our energies to the cause of general liberty, our wishes were for the independence of all nationalities, and the liberal progress of all nations. We, therefore, desire the success of the Fenians in the great work of regenerating old Ireland, and extending to that country the benefit of a Republican or popular government, according to the form of true democratic institutions."[21]

There are thus compelling reasons to bring together Irish Americans, southern whites, and freedpeople in a comparative study of nationalism during Reconstruction. Yet sound comparative history needs

---

20. Cleveland *Morning Leader*, October 6, 1866; *Irish Republic*, May 18, 1867; June 29, 1867; July 6, 1867. See also the Washington *Chronicle*, quoted in *Tri-Weekly Austin Republican*, November 21, 1867.

21. *Irish Republic*, August 24, 1867; New Orleans *Tribune*, September 23, 1866.

to recognize differences as well as similarities. Most obvious of these was the bitter conflict between southern whites and African Americans over political rights and class interests. Freedpeople understandably tended to embrace Republican nationalism while those southern whites who opposed Reconstruction ignored or rejected it. In addition, the Fenians were unique among the three groups in struggling for the independence of Ireland, a foreign country. There was no real material basis for their struggle in the United States. Finally, there were crucial dissimilarities between the Fenian movement and the black struggle for equality. The Fenians tended to speak in terms of liberty, while southern African American leaders were more concerned with civil equality. A long and persistent history of Irish antipathy toward American blacks further distanced the two groups from each other. Keeping these caveats in mind, comparative history can create new ways to understand the nationalist aspirations of Irish Americans, freedpeople, and southern whites during Reconstruction.

Other movements for political self-determination might well have been included in this study. Reconstruction also witnessed the rise of an independent movement for women's suffrage. For members of the National Woman Suffrage Association, such as Elizabeth Cady Stanton and Susan B. Anthony, true equality demanded that women as well as African American men should be granted the right to vote. The Plains Indians, who fought relentlessly in the 1860s and 1870s for their lands and even their existence against the encroachment of white settlers in the West, furnish another example of ethnic or racial separatism. Early forms of the Ghost Dance ritual appeared among western Indians in 1870, calling for a revitalization of Native American communities in the face of white aggression. Other fraternal organizations, such as the Grand Army of the Republic and the Grange, also had political goals.[22]

22. On women's suffrage during Reconstruction, see Ellen Carol DuBois, *Feminism and Suffrage: The Emergence of an Independent Women's Movement in America, 1848–1869* (Ithaca: Cornell Univ. Press, 1978); Frederick Hoxie, ed., *Encyclopedia of North American Indians* (Boston: Houghton Mifflin, 1996), 223. On Native Americans during the post–Civil War era, see Dee Alexander Brown, *Bury My Heart at Wounded Knee: An Indian History of the American West* (New York: Holt, Rinehart, and Winston, 1970). Stuart McCon-

Any student of the Reconstruction South soon confronts the prejudiced nature of many of the sources. In particular, accounts of African American and Union League political activities tended to reflect the bias of the author. A sympathetic Republican editor, for example, would stress the orderliness and peaceful nature of a black political assembly, while a hostile Democratic editor would describe the same gathering as a threatening and disorderly crowd. In many cases, our knowledge of Union League activities comes from hostile white sources who were not above manufacturing information that would discredit freedpeople. In addition, valuable local studies of Mississippi Reconstruction often rely on "eyewitness" accounts not only critical of Reconstruction but compiled several decades after 1877. Finally, southerners were often careful to couch their public remarks in ways that would not incur the wrath of northerners. Hence, different views often appear in personal correspondence. By being attentive to the context in which the sources appear, I have tried to the best of my abilities to avoid taking biased evidence at face value.[23]

The structure of this book has been designed to highlight the comparisons among the Fenians, freedpeople, and southern whites and relate them to the theme of Reconstruction nationalism. The first chapter introduces the three main groups and their relationship to the politics of Reconstruction. Chapter 2 focuses on the political culture of countersubversion shared by the Fenians, the Union Leagues, and the Ku Klux Klan. The next three chapters examine the construction of a national identity for African Americans, Irish Americans, and southern whites. Chapter 3 looks at the importance of land and its use in the

---

nell, *Glorious Contentment: The Grand Army of the Republic, 1865–1900* (Chapel Hill: Univ. of North Carolina Press, 1992), and Solon Buck, *The Granger Movement: A Study of Agricultural Organization and Its Political, Economic, and Social Manifestations, 1870–1880* (Cambridge, Mass.: Harvard Univ. Press, 1933), discuss these other postwar societies.

23. Kevin Kenny acutely recognizes a similar problem in studying the Molly Maguires: "Quite simply, none of the surviving evidence is neutral, nor was it ever so; it demands an ideological reading, which not only searches for the outlines of a credible factual narrative about the Molly Maguires, but also inquires into the social origins and the ideological impact of descriptions written about them by their enemies and detractors" (*Making Sense of the Molly Maguires*, 21).

creation of collective identities. Chapter 4 sets forth the possibilities and limitations of ethnicity as a basis for a nationalist identity for the three groups. The last chapter of the book shows how civic nationalism became the dominant paradigm by which each group forged its collective identity.

1
The Context of Republican Reconstruction

Reconstruction was in essence a political process. State governments in the South were reorganized and African American males were given the right to vote. National Republicans sought to create and sustain a party organization in the South, efforts resisted at every turn by southern Democrats and Conservatives. Reconstruction politics was thus the fundamental context in which Irish Americans, southern whites, and freedpeople sought political self-determination and a collective ethnic identity. It was perhaps the strongest factor uniting these three groups, providing each with a common set of ideas and languages that both encouraged their aspirations and set limiting contours to those ambitions.[1]

The politics of Reconstruction also provided the framework in which those secret paramilitary societies that were so instrumental to freedmen, southern whites, and Irish Americans—the Union League, the Ku Klux Klan, and the Fenians—emerged. The League was an essentially political organization with the purpose of mobilizing the votes of newly enfranchised freedmen to erect a viable Republican Party in the South. To thwart the political goals of the Union Leagues, the Ku

---

1. Writing from a Post-Revisionist perspective, recent historians of the Reconstruction South have appropriately broadened their definition of politics to include labor insurgency and gender relations within southern households. Indeed, the Union Leagues and the Ku Klux Klan were agents in a class and racial struggle for political, social, and economic power. Yet this effort to broaden the definition of the "political" has perhaps diminished the centrality of electoral politics to Reconstruction in the South. Important statements of this trend include Eric Foner, *Reconstruction: America's Unfinished Revolution, 1863–1877* (New York: Harper and Row, 1988), Michael Fitzgerald, *The Union League Movement in the Deep South: Politics and Agricultural Change during Reconstruction* (Baton Rouge: Louisiana State Univ. Press, 1989); Julie Saville, *The Work of Reconstruction: From Slave to Wage Laborer in South Carolina, 1860–1870* (New York: Cambridge Univ. Press, 1994); and Steven Hahn, *A Nation under Our Feet: Black Political Struggles in the Rural South from Slavery to the Great Migration* (Cambridge, Mass.: Belknap Press of Harvard Univ. Press, 2003).

Klux Klan acted as an arm of the Democrats and Conservatives who saw themselves as victims of political despotism imposed by Radical rule. To a lesser extent than with the Union Leagues and Ku Klux Klan, Reconstruction politics was also influential in shaping the American Fenian movement. In the late antebellum period, Irish American votes were especially important to the Democratic Party in northern cities, such as New York, Philadelphia, and Boston. The power of ethnic politics persisted in the immediate postwar era. In seeking the electoral support of Irish Americans, both Democrats and Republicans had to pay close attention to the rise of Fenianism.

The dominant factor that determined the influence of Reconstruction on the process of identity formation was the Republican Party. Founded as an antislavery third party during the 1850s, the Republicans cemented their power in American life during a successful Civil War that abolished slavery and established the supremacy of the Union. As postwar Reconstruction began in 1865, Republicans were united in their commitment to the final abolition of slavery and securing the fruits of emancipation for former slaves and their party. Yet by 1866, intraparty conflict and deep divisions over Reconstruction policy split the party into radical and moderate factions. By 1867, the Radicals, in compromise with moderates and conservatives, framed a new Reconstruction policy that divided ten former Confederate states into military districts under military control, gave voting rights to blacks while disfranchising some former Confederate whites (temporarily, as it turned out), and protected the rights of citizenship and suffrage through two amendments to the U.S. Constitution. It was this political world created by Radical Reconstruction in which the Union Leagues, the Ku Klux Klan, and the Fenians operated. Participation in partisan politics helped define the collective identity of freedpeople and Irish Americans. To counter their disfranchisement, many southern whites turned to Klan violence to influence elections. Reconstruction politics then served to channel separatist impulses along civic rather than class or ethnic lines.[2]

---

2. Important works on the Republican Party during Reconstruction include Hans Trefousse, *The Radical Republicans: Lincoln's Vanguard for Racial Justice* (1968; reprint, Baton Rouge: Louisiana State Univ. Press, 1975); Michael Les Benedict, *The Compromise of*

The Republican Party was the primary means of black political enfranchisement in the Reconstruction South. African American freedpeople tied their aspirations for freedom and citizenship to the political organization that had been a driving force for emancipation. It was the freedmen, along with selected northern and southern whites, who made up the basis of the Republican Party in the South. Their connection to the Republican Party was thus instrumental in their quest for political autonomy. In stating the principles of his newspaper, the editor of the black *Freeman's Standard* announced that his would be "an organ of the colored and all other Loyal citizens of the State of Georgia, and as a supporter of the Government of these United States and a fearless advocate of the rights of the people and principles of the Republican Party." A convention of freedmen in Mobile similarly proclaimed themselves "a part of the Great National Republican Party of the United States, and of the State of Alabama." Prominent black leaders during Reconstruction recognized the Republicans as their best chance to gain civil rights. "It is the only party," insisted a convention of Alabama freedmen, "which has ever attempted to extend our privileges, and as it has in the past always been trying to do this, it is but natural that we should trust it for the future." In a campaign speech delivered at Aberdeen, Mississippi, in 1869, an African American spokesman told his listeners that the Republicans were "the party that promises equal rights to all without regard to race, color, or previous condition."[3]

As one of the main avenues through which freedmen sought political participation, the Union League was also deeply devoted to the Republican Party. Its values were clearly set forth in the constitution of the national organization: "to preserve Liberty and the Union of these United

---

Principle: Congressional Republicans and Reconstruction, 1863–1869 (New York: Norton, 1974); David Montgomery, *Beyond Equality: Labor and the Radical Republicans, 1862–1872* (1967; reprint, Urbana: Univ. of Illinois Press, 1981); and Heather Cox Richardson, *The Death of Reconstruction: Race, Labor, and Politics in the Post–Civil War North, 1865–1901* (Cambridge, Mass.: Harvard Univ. Press, 2001).

3. *Freeman's Standard* (Savannah), February 15, 1868; *Alabama Beacon*, May 18, 1867, quoted in Montgomery *Daily State Sentinel*, May 21, 1867; quotation in *Weekly Mississippi Pilot*, November 27, 1869. For African American attacks on the Democratic Party, see the Mobile *Nationalist*, June 21, 1866, and the *Weekly Mississippi Pilot*, November 27, 1869.

States; to maintain the Constitution thereof, and that of this State, and the supremacy of the laws of the United States, to sustain the existing Administration in putting down the enemies of the Government, and thwarting the designs of traitors and disloyalists, and to protect, strengthen and defend all loyal men, without regard to sect, condition, or party." Union Leagues in the South adopted these goals. "The object of this Council," stated the Deep River Union League of North Carolina, "shall be to preserve Liberty and the Union of the U.S. to maintain the Constitution thereof and the Supremacy of the laws to elect honest and reliable Union men to all offices of profit or trust in National State and Local Government and to secure equal civil and political rights to all men under the Government." A Galveston League upheld the major Republican principle that "loyalty shall govern what loyalty has preserved." Union Leagues across the South endorsed Republican efforts at Reconstruction. Leagues of north Alabama, meeting in convention in 1867, gave "our cordial and entire sanction to the action of Congress for the restoration of Union and to the wise and just principles of the Republican Party." Some Union Leagues expressed their specific support for Radical Reconstruction. A writer to the Athens *Republican* claimed that Congress was "the conservators of our nationality, peace, and prosperity." Banners at a Union League rally in Franklin, Tennessee, conveyed such messages as "Andy can't Control Congress" and "Vote the Radical Ticket." The close identification between the Leagues and Republican Reconstruction would help funnel black proto-nationalism into civic channels.[4]

The Union Leagues in the Reconstruction South were essentially a political arm of the Republican Party. A quick glance at the state leaders of southern Union Leagues reveals the links between white League leadership and Republican politics. In North Carolina, Governor William W. Holden was also the president of the state Union League. A former

---

4. Union League Constitution, page 4, Rare Book and Manuscript Library, Columbia University, New York, New York; "Minute Book, 1868, Deep River Union League," Joel Romulus Welborn Papers, Perkins Library, Duke University, Durham, North Carolina; San Antonio *Daily Express*, December 27, 1868; Montgomery *Daily Mail*, April 17, 1867, quoted in Athens (Tennessee) *Republican*, July 12, 1867; Savannah *Daily News and Herald*, July 13, 1867.

Unionist during the Civil War, Holden was also prominent in the Heroes of America. White Republican E. W. M. Mackey was speaker of the South Carolina House of Representatives and a League official. William Markham, president of the state Union League in Georgia, had a prewar career as a Whig mayor and Atlanta railroad promoter. Northern-born Republican General H. H. Thomas was a secretary to Governor William G. Brownlow in Tennessee. Valentine Dell, editor of the Fort Smith *New Era*, allied with the Fishback faction of Unionists in Arkansas. H. C. Dibble, the Union League representative of Louisiana, was a federal judge who later opposed Henry Clay Warmoth. The close connection between League and party leadership is understandable since the Union Leagues were considered instrumental in the creation of a Republican voting base in the South.[5]

The association between the Union Leagues and Republican politics was widespread in the Reconstruction South. "The Union League organization," stated Republican U.S. senator Willard Warner of Alabama, "was simply a political organization." A South Carolinian testifying before the 1871 congressional hearings on the Ku Klux Klan explained similarly that the Loyal League was a political organization for mobilizing black voters. An African American journal from New Bern, North Carolina, termed the Union League a "Great Political Society." As the Leagues began to spread with the advent of Congressional Reconstruction, one Virginia newspaper assumed that the purpose of the League "was to accomplish some political end."[6]

At its annual meeting in 1869, the Union League of America affirmed its role in spreading Republicanism to the South: "[T]he League was actively pushed into the South, for the double purpose of resisting Rebel outrages, and of laying the foundation for a truly Republican policy, when it should be adopted by Congress." Union Leaguers in the South

---

5. The Union Leagues in Tennessee, for example, were associated with the Radicals (Thomas B. Alexander, *Political Reconstruction in Tennessee* [1950; reprint, New York: Russell and Russell, 1968]). The list of state leaders can be found in the Wilmington *Daily Post*, October 15, 1867.

6. Warner, quoted in KKK Hearings, Alabama, vol. 1, page 35; KKK Hearings, South Carolina, vol.1, page 77; *National Savings Bank*, January 1, 1868; Richmond (?) *Register*, quoted in *American Union* (Harrisonburg, Virginia), July 6, 1867.

joyfully accepted this task. To a correspondent to the Charleston *Daily Republican,* the Union League "deals with a man's devotion to Republicanism, and love for the union, under the sanctity of an oath." Council No. 9 of the U.L.A. in Georgetown, South Carolina, affirmed that "the onward progress of communities and States depended upon the continued and constant success of the great political party that we are identified with." Supporting the Union Leagues in his address to some citizens of North Carolina, T. A. Byrnes insisted that the Republican Party "has gloriously maintained and vindicated the doctrine of the equality of American citizenship, the development and progress of this nation, and the responsibility of a dissolution of the government or country."[7]

As part of the political machinery of the Republican Party, Union Leagues in the South garnered support for Radical Reconstruction. The movement blossomed with the advent of Congressional Reconstruction in the spring of 1867. Congress passed two Military Reconstruction Acts in March that divided the ten unreconstructed southern states into five military districts, ordered military commanders to register voters for elections to constitutional conventions, and in the process enfranchised black men over twenty-one. The state League in Georgia noted correctly that it was "not until the passage of that Law that they assumed the character of political agencies." In March 1867, a meeting of blacks in Raleigh called upon "the colored People of the State to form themselves into Leagues, and organize for the work before them." In May, freedmen in Mobile urged the establishment of Union Leagues in every county. Significantly, the expansion of League activity in 1867 increased the number of African American members. The *Southern Watchman* of Augusta, Georgia, reported in March of that year a "meeting composed of five hundred freedmen under the auspices of the Union League . . . A few whites participated." Essie Harris, a black man from North Carolina, recalled that there were only three or four whites in his League.

7. *Proceedings of the National Council of the Union League of America at its Sixth Annual Session, held in the City of Washington, D.C., on Tuesday and Wednesday, March 2d and 3rd, 1869* (n.p., 1869), 9; Charleston *Daily Republican,* August 24, 1870; August 27, 1869; T. A. Byrnes, *Address to the Citizens of the 16th Senatorial District* (n.p., n.d.), 3. See also Rev. James Lynch to Thomas Tullock, July 9, 1867, Robert C. Schenck Papers (microfilm), Rutherford B. Hayes Memorial Library, Fremont, Ohio.

On the other hand, a meeting of the Union League in Autauga County, Alabama, in June 1867 reported between twelve hundred and fifteen hundred members, "most of whom are white."[8]

Southern white conservatives saw the Union Leagues as political in more negative terms. To opponents of Congressional Reconstruction, the Leagues were tools of the Republican Party to fasten black suffrage on the South. As the Republicans began to rally black voters after the passage of the Reconstruction Acts of March 1867, the Richmond *Whig and Public Advertiser* warned its readers about a "secret political society or league" created by Radical Republicans "to coerce the whole negro vote." The Savannah *Daily News and Herald* concurred that the formation of the Loyal League was a "political scheme in pursuance of the policy which had inaugurated the war, which was to obtain through the negroes and renegade whites, the political control of the Southern states." Henry L. Benning of Georgia told a congressional committee that the Union Leagues were an organization for the purpose of influencing votes. James Boyd of Alamance, North Carolina, told a similar committee that the Leagues were composed principally of black Republicans. To the Natchez *Democrat,* the idea that the Union Leagues existed to support Radical Reconstruction should be "obvious to even an obtuse mind."[9]

---

8. Circular, Grand Council Chamber, Henry P. Farrow Collection, Hargrett Rare Book and Manuscript Library, University of Georgia, Athens, Georgia; Raleigh *Daily Standard,* March 12, 1867; *Southern Watchman,* May 8, 1867; E. Merton Coulter, *William G. Brownlow, Fighting Parson of the Southern Highlands* (Chapel Hill: Univ. of North Carolina Press, 1937), 353; Roberta F. Carson, "The Loyal League in Georgia," *Georgia Historical Quarterly* 20 (June 1936): 126; KKK Hearings, Alabama, vol. 1, page 8; *Southern Watchman,* March 27, 1867; KKK Hearings, North Carolina, page 97. See also San Antonio *Daily Express,* December 29, 1868; *Daily State Sentinel,* June 4, 1867.

9. Richmond *Whig and Public Advertiser,* April 2, 1867; Savannah *Daily News and Herald,* April 24, 1868; KKK Hearings, Georgia, vol. 1, page 189; Johnny W. Barnes, "The Political Activities of the Union League of America in North Carolina," *Quarterly Review of Higher Education among Negroes* 20, no. 4 (October 1952): 143; Natchez *Democrat,* April 6, 1867. For other contemporary views, see the Richmond *Enquirer and Examiner,* July 21, 1868; KKK Hearings, Mississippi, vol. 1, page 16; and Edward Randolph Hopkins, "Some Reminiscences of Lowndes County History," page 18, Ms.Z461f, Mississippi Department of History and Archives, Jackson, Mississippi.

The Union Leagues were indeed instrumental in mobilizing the newly enfranchised freedmen to support the Republicans. With the passage of the Reconstruction Acts of 1867, African American males could vote for the constitutional conventions to be held in the former Confederate states. The Union League directed its attention to these elections. "Most of the Leagues in the Country," a Republican leader wrote, "will meet between now and Monday and take some action towards a new Convention in which the will of the people will be expressed." In October of 1867, Tallahassee Republicans held a meeting of the League to nominate delegates to the Florida constitutional convention. There was apparently a Loyal League in every black community in the 1867 elections for delegates to the Mississippi constitutional convention. Once these conventions were held, Union Leaguers worked for the ratification of these new Reconstruction constitutions. "The Constitution must be ratified," urged the state meeting of the North Carolina Union Leagues in February 1868: "We must elect loyal members of Congress, and loyal state and County officers. All our past labors have been directed to this end." One angry southerner thought that the North Carolina Leagues, by "all kinds of villainy," helped the Republicans ratify the 1868 state constitution.[10]

As Republican governments were being established in the South, the Union Leagues helped enlist black voters to build a party base in each southern state. "To this end," urged the editor of the Jonesboro, Tennessee, *Union Flag*, "Union Leagues should be organized in each civil district of the county." Calling attention to "the imperative necessity for a better organization of the party," a Mississippi editor suggested the Leagues "as one of our most efficient means." Democratic opponents as well noted the connection between the Union Leagues and the Republican Party. The conservative Mobile *Advertiser and Register* worried

---

10. William Fowler to Leonidas Campbell Houk, July 10, 1868, Leonidas Campbell Houk Papers, McClung Collection, Lawson McPhee Library, East Tennessee Historical Society, Knoxville, Tennessee; Fernandina (Florida) *Courier*, October 24, 1867; Charles Madison Bacon, "A History of Hinds County, Mississippi during Reconstruction, 1865–1875" (Master's thesis, Mississippi College, 1959), 32; quoted in *Loyal Georgian* (Augusta), February 15, 1868; William Hauser quoted in *Central Georgian*, May 13, 1868. See also Mattie Thomas Thompson, *History of Barbour County, Alabama* (Eufaula, Ala.: n.p., 1939), 194.

that the appearance of Union Leagues indicated the creation of "a Radical party" across the state. As part of the Republican Party machinery, the Union League was especially active in mobilizing voters before elections. "The U.L.A. ought to be in every neighborhood in the State before the election," implored the editor of the Raleigh *Tri-Weekly Standard:* "It is one of the best agencies yet devised to unite the loyal men and ensure an individual vote for Liberty and Union." A Virginia editor told his readers that the Leagues were "a powerful political agency if properly wielded, and will exert a tremendous influence in the coming Elections South." The president of the Union League in York County, South Carolina, recalled that his League "was doing its most powerful work, as it was drawing nigh to election day."[11]

As political organizations, the Union Leagues performed functions similar to those of urban political machines in the North. Among these was the endorsement of candidates for political office. At the first meeting of the Deep River Union League in Guilford County, North Carolina, the Council decided "to select candidates for Township No. 17 offices at next meeting." Union Leagues in Marshall and Blount counties in Alabama nominated William H. Smith for governor in 1867. In Abbeville Court House, League members petitioned Governor Robert K. Scott on a vacancy in the South Carolina State Senate. Union Leagues endorsed Republican candidates such as Henry P. Farrow, who ran for governor in Georgia in 1868. League membership could be helpful in establishing the Republican credentials of office seekers for Radical governments. For instance, the loyalty of an aspirant for an office in the North Carolina Railroad was affirmed since he was "a true Member of the U.L. of A." Conversely, the Union Leagues warned party officials of untrustworthy candidates. The League in Ashe County, North Carolina, sent a petition signed by thirty-two members urging the governor not to make certain political appointments since "we know them to be

---

11. Jonesboro (Tennessee) *Union Flag,* April 5, 1867; Vicksburg *Republican,* January 7, 1868; Mobile *Advertiser and Register,* quoted in Natchez *Democrat,* April 23, 1867; Raleigh *Tri-Weekly Standard,* May 9, 1867; *American Union* (Harrisonburg, Virginia), September 7, 1867; KKK Hearings, South Carolina, vol. 1, page 37.

vowed enemies to the republican party." Members of a Union League in Charleston similarly urged the appointment of a trial justice, warning the governor that his opponent had been "odious to republicans as city detective."[12]

The Union Leagues were also useful in the dispensing of political patronage, a central strategy for building up Republican regimes in the South. The patronage functions of the Union Leagues are illustrated in the papers of William W. Holden, Republican governor of North Carolina during Reconstruction and president of the state Union League. During his one-year term as president, Holden provided strong centralized Republican leadership to the state League. League councils across North Carolina offered their political advice to Holden. The Enfield Union League in Halifax County, for example, backed a candidate for the Board of Registration, explaining to the governor that "the whole of the said Council is opposed to the said Hinton occupying that position." The Union League in Wilkes County sent Holden names for justices of the peace. In the heavily Republican city of Wilmington, the League petitioned Governor Holden concerning positions as police and inspectors of fuel for the town. One Union League even asked the governor to remove the voting disabilities of one James Harrington because he was "a member of Holden Council U.L.A. . . . and has voted with the Republican party and rendered other valuable services therein."[13]

---

12. "Minute Book, 1868, Deep River Union League," Joel Romulus Welborn Papers, Duke University, Durham, North Carolina; *Daily State Sentinel,* May 30, 1867; J. H. Hollinshead to Robert Scott, December 12, 1870, Robert Scott Papers, South Carolina Department of Archives and History, Columbia, South Carolina; McBaron Timoney to John E. Bryant, January 28, 1868, Bryant Papers, Duke University, Durham, North Carolina; J. A. Sechrest to W.H.H. (?), July 3, 1868, James Henry Harris Papers, North Carolina Division of Archives and History, Raleigh, North Carolina; Petition of the Union League Council to William H. Holden, July 4, 1868, Harris Papers; W. H. Mishaw to Robert Scott, May 5, 1870, Robert Kingston Scott Papers, Ohio Historical Society, Columbus, Ohio. See also W. E. Connelly to W. H. Smith, September 20, 1867, Swayne Papers, Alabama Department of Archives and History, Montgomery, Alabama, and the notice about the Brownlow Council of the U.L.A. in the August 19, 1868, Knoxville *Whig.*

13. William C. Harris, *William Woods Holden: Firebrand of North Carolina Politics* (Baton Rouge: Louisiana State Univ. Press, 1987), 223; C. Mayo to William W. Holden, Holden

One of the most important functions of the Union Leagues was political education, perhaps best illustrated in the records of the Union League of Maryville, Tennessee. A Unionist area in eastern Tennessee during the Civil War, Maryville was a center of black political activism during Reconstruction. In early 1867, freedmen met there to endorse black suffrage and the candidacy of Republican William G. Brownlow for governor. The local newspaper, the Maryville *Republican,* was edited by two African Americans. The town also boasted four black aldermen. The Union League of Maryville engaged in the kinds of political activity common to Union Leagues across the South: issuing certificates to delegates to the state Republican convention, electing delegates to the county Republican convention, and collecting money to send out a canvasser for elections. The Maryville Union League also devoted a good deal of its time to political education. This function became clear at their meeting of January 29, 1867, when they voted to elect one member to address the League at each meeting. In September, the League agreed to a course of lectures when no other important business was pending. At one gathering they heard about the "depreciation of the National Currency by the Democratic Party." At another, the League debated the currency question before Congress. In February of 1868, League members heard "a noble address in regard to the impeachment of Andrew Johnson." In later years, members of the Maryville League discussed such topics as the payment of railroad bonds and separate statehood for East Tennessee. By endorsing candidates, dispensing patronage, and educating voters, the Union Leagues performed valuable services for the Republican Party in the South.[14]

Governor's Papers, North Carolina Division of Archives and History, Raleigh, North Carolina; Petition to William W. Holden, [1868], Correspondence 1868, Holden Governor's Papers; John Dawson to William W. Holden, Holden Governor's Papers; N. M. McLeod [?] to William W. Holden, Holden Miscellaneous Papers, 1852–1930.

14. Thomas B. Alexander, *Political Reconstruction in Tennessee* (1950; reprint, New York: Russell and Russell, 1968), 205; Coulter, *William G. Brownlow,* 329; Minutes of the Maryville Union League, February 14, 1867; March 25, 1867; May 16, 1867; January 29, 1867; September 12, 1867; September 3, 1867; September 24, 1867; February 27, 1868; June 4, 1868; and January 14 [?] 1869, McClung Collection, East Tennessee Historical Society, Knoxville, Tennessee.

The League faced the particular challenge of reaching a mass of voters most of whom had been rendered illiterate by slavery. To this purpose, the Union Leagues turned to oral means of communication. "Most of the negro population who are grown," argued native white Radical Robert Flournoy of Mississippi, "were slaves a few years ago, and there are but few of them who can read. Documents which you may send never reach them. The only way in which they can possibly be reached is by oral communication, in other words, by gathering them together." John E. Bryant, head of the Georgia Equal Rights Association, explained that in rural areas the freedpeople usually gathered on the Sabbath after church services. Since as many as two or three thousand people attended these meetings, he arranged to have the *Loyal Georgian* read to them. One of the most common and successful means of oral communication for the Union Leagues were the dialogues published by the Republican Party and distributed throughout the South during Reconstruction. Often called the "Loyal League Catechism," these dialogues presented the main principles of Republican ideology though a conversation between a white Republican and a freedman. Henry McNeill Turner, a black minister who organized for the Republican Party in 1867, enthusiastically endorsed this means of political education. "The rule adopted," he explained to party leaders in Washington, D.C., "was to read the dialogues in the country churches, societies, leagues, clubs, ball, picknics [*sic*] and all other gatherings by one man in the rear of the audience and the other standing up in the pulpit or some other suitable place. I have ordered the dialogue read in the meetings until our people know it by heart and can recite it from memory." At a Methodist church in Macon, Georgia, Turner himself took part in one of these readings. When his partner read the other part of the dialogue, "the house would ring with shouts."[15]

15. KKK Hearings, Mississippi, vol. 1, page 89; Henry M. Turner to Thomas Tullock, July 9, 1867, Robert C. Schenck Papers (microfilm), Rutherford B. Hayes Memorial Library, Fremont, Ohio; Henry M. Turner to Thomas Tullock, July 9, 1867, Robert Schenck Papers. See also Henry Turner to Thomas L. Tullock, July 23, 1867, Robert Schenck Papers. The Union League dialogue is reprinted in Walter L. Fleming, ed., *Documentary History of Reconstruction: Political, Military, Social, Religious, Educational, and Industrial, 1865–1906* (1907; reprint, New York: McGraw-Hill, 1966), 2:13–19.

The politics of Reconstruction was also essential to the political needs and collective identity of southern whites. In contrast to the freedpeople and their Union Leagues, conservative whites defined themselves in *opposition* to Republican Reconstruction. Their self-image as a conquered people was a persistent theme in their writings. In the immediate aftermath of the Civil War, most southerners acknowledged their military defeat. Citizens of Pulaski County, Georgia, conceded in July 1865 that they were a "subjugated people." Ironically, southern whites exercised their widest degree of political power over the freedmen during this early period of presidential Reconstruction. The portrayal of southern whites as a conquered people emerged with much greater force with the beginning of Congressional Reconstruction in 1867. "The conquerors have prescribed their terms to the conquered," lamented the *Southern Watchman,* "and they leave us little or no volition in the matter." A newspaper in Crystal Springs, Mississippi, considered the condition of the South under Military Reconstruction "even worse than Egyptian bondage." This self-representation as a conquered people provides the most useful guide to understanding how the struggle over Reconstruction shaped the formation of a collective southern white identity. Throughout the late 1860s, southern whites launched incessant attacks on Republican Reconstruction, with the goal of undermining the legitimacy of Radical governments and restoring white political hegemony. In this way, Republican governance proved instrumental in helping southern whites redefine their values and shape a new collective identity.[16]

Many southerners saw northern Republicans as a revolutionary party. At the beginning of Congressional Reconstruction, the Natchez *Democrat* noted that the Republican Party was organizing "with that rapidity of action which usually characterizes the movements of revolutionary organizations." In attempting to define "Radicalism," an Arkansas Democratic editor feared that the Republican Party was "now a few steps removed from anarchy, in its utter disregard of all law and precedent, the only right recognized being that of might." Conserva-

---

16. Macon (Georgia) *Daily Journal and Messenger,* July 1, 1865; *Southern Watchman,* March 27, 1867; May 15, 1867; *Southern Argus,* August 1, 1869.

tive southern whites drew analogies between Republican Reconstruction and the excesses of the French Revolution. The Mobile *Daily Advertiser and Register* referred to Republicans as "Jacobin tyrants." One frightened southerner spoke in fear of a "reign of Terror," explaining that "The party of Robespierre, Danton, and Marat has set the example in history, and there is no greater truth than that history repeats itself." Several southerners observing Republican legislatures drew on this analogy. A Kentuckian who witnessed the debate over the Fourteenth Amendment in the House of Representatives compared the scene to the French Revolution. In Mississippi, former fire-eater Albert Gallatin Brown saw "the disembodied spirit of Danton Marat and Robespierre Stalking in the Senate Chamber." Since many of the above comments came from personal correspondence, the metaphor of the French Revolution served not only to discredit Republican Reconstruction but to express the seemingly real fears of a world being turned upside down.[17]

Southern whites insisted that the imposition of Radical Reconstruction on the South amounted to military oppression. "The Southern States," maintained the Milledgeville *Recorder*, "were never before divested of everything and placed under military despotism." The Reconstruction Acts, according to one Texas newspaper, were "so framed as to make the military officer of each district a complete dictator." Looking back from 1869, an Arkansas editor complained that the Radicals in the South had "stifled free speech, muzzled the press, trampled on the Constitution, suspended the writ of *habeas corpus*, quartered troops in the States without their consent, taxed the people without the correlative

---

17. Natchez *Democrat*, April 16, 1867; *Southern Standard*, July 3, 1869; Mobile *Daily Advertiser and Register*, February 7, 1868; A. C. Garlington to A. B. Springs, Springs Family Papers, Southern Historical Collection, University of North Carolina, Chapel Hill, North Carolina; J. Proctor Knott to the Rev. James Croitt [?], February 10, 1869, Filson Historical Society, Louisville, Kentucky; A. G. Brown to Jonathan Tarbell, September 28, 1867, Miscellaneous Manuscripts, New York Historical Society, New York, New York. For further analogies of the Republicans to the French Revolutionaries, see Josiah Turner to his wife, July 8, 1870, Turner Papers, Southern Historical Collection, University of North Carolina, Chapel Hill, North Carolina; The Griffin (Georgia) *Star*, quoted in the Macon *Daily Telegraph*, July 6, 1866; Florence (Alabama) *Journal*, July 4, 1866.

right of representation, passed *ex post facto* laws, and showed a perfect disregard of all fundamental laws and precedents."[18]

White conservatives contended that Radical Reconstruction would create a dangerously centralized government in the United States. As early as 1866, the Macon *Daily Telegraph* warned that the Republicans "would inaugurate a centralized despotism over these States." That same year an Alabama editor concluded that the national government had already "been converted from one of limited powers into a consolidated Empire." After the passage of the Reconstruction Acts of March 1867, a lawyer from Petersburg, Virginia, agreed that the United States had passed "from a Confederation, to consolidated Nationality." The result would be an oppressive cultural hegemony: "We as the weaker party must *perforce* adapt ourselves, or else be moulded by the hand to power, to suit the exigencies of the new dispensation. We will be *Yankeeised* [sic]." Later that year, a Texas editor told his readers that the goal of Radicals was to "overthrow the Government, and ride over a prostrate Constitution to the goal of unlimited despotism."[19]

The creation of a centralized government with despotic powers, many southern whites feared, would overturn the Constitution as they understood it. The Mobile *Daily Advertiser and Register* saw Radical Reconstruction as a contest between liberty as embodied in the Constitution and "the power of despotism to annihilate that Constitution on the other." To the Charleston *Daily Courier,* Reconstruction had revolutionized the Constitution of 1787. "Congressional usurpation and repeated violations of the Constitution," declared the Pineville Democratic Club of Marengo County, Alabama, "have justly excited the alarm of all lovers of political and social order and happiness, and well-nigh destroyed the old landmarks of the government, as established by its framers." The Raleigh *Daily Sentinel* agreed that the Reconstruction Acts marked

---

18. Quoted in *Alabama Beacon,* April 20, 1867; Galveston *Weekly News,* March 1, 1867; *Southern Standard,* June 19, 1869. For further comments on Reconstruction as military despotism, see the Mobile *Daily Advertiser and Register,* February 18, 1868.

19. Macon *Daily Telegraph,* July 3, 1866; Demopolis (Alabama) *New Era,* May 18, 1866; John Lyon to A. B. Springs, August 15, 1867, Springs Family Papers, Southern Historical Collection, University of North Carolina, Chapel Hill, North Carolina; Austin *Daily State Gazette,* October 28, 1867.

"a radical change in the government itself, conferring powers upon the Congress over the internal police and regulations of the States, at war with the whole spirit and tenor of the Constitution." The centralization of power undermining the Constitution threatened states' rights, a creed that had long been a means of defending white supremacy in the South. To an Alabama editor, the architects of Radical Reconstruction were ignoring "the great principle of State Sovereignty." Indeed, states' rights were, according to the Austin *Daily State Gazette*, "the great preservative of political liberty, and, in fact, the only safety to the whole country."[20]

If Radical Reconstruction was unconstitutional, Republican political power was therefore illegitimate since it had not come from the consent of the governed. "I regard all of you," wrote Jonathan Worth to Republican governor William W. Holden of North Carolina, "as, in effect, appointees of the Military power of the United States—and not as deriving your powers from the consent of those you claim to govern." An Arkansas Democratic paper argued similarly that Republican governor Powell Clayton was not the governor of Arkansas but only the governor of the Radical Party. Through this kind of reasoning, the Montgomery *Mail* concluded that Reconstruction was a "despotic enactment of laws by illegitimate authority."[21]

The southern conservative assault on Reconstruction, with its rhetoric of constitutionality, despotism, and the usurpation of political authority, illustrates how the discourse of republicanism still cast a strong shadow in the post–Civil War era. Southern whites continued to think in terms of power as predatory, an idea rooted in the American Revo-

20. Mobile *Daily Advertiser and Register*, September 21, 1868; Charleston *Daily Courier*, March 29, 1867; Mobile *Daily Advertiser and Register*, September 25, 1868; Raleigh *Daily Sentinel*, March 6, 1867; *Alabama Beacon*, June 1, 1867; Austin *Daily State Gazette*, October 24, 1867. For similar comments, see the Charleston *Mercury*, quoted in the Mobile *Daily Advertiser and Register*, September 21, 1868; *Southern Watchman*, April 24, 1867; *Southern Standard*, February 13, 1869; and the Natchez *Democrat*, March 23, 1867.

21. Jonathan Worth to W. W. Holden, July 1, 1868, Holden Governor's Papers, North Carolina Department of History and Archives, Raleigh, North Carolina; *Southern Standard*, February 13, 1869; Montgomery *Mail*, quoted in Tuscaloosa *Independent Monitor*, October 9, 1867.

lution. "Tyranny is seldom or never fixed upon a free people 'at one fell swoop,'" warned the Austin *Daily State Gazette* in 1867: "Its approaches are gradual, and often veiled under pretended care for the public good." One southerner described the Republicans as a revolutionary party, "aggressive in its character," whose progress would be difficult to stop. It is not surprising, then, that southerners warned that the despotism of Radical Reconstruction would spread to the North. As the Charleston *Daily Courier* explained, "Power is ever encroaching. It goes on from point to point. Its spirit is that of unrest. And thus having crushed the commonwealth of the South, it also aspires to subjugate the liberties of the North." An Alabama editor agreed that "the chains forged for ten of the States will just as easily fit the limbs of the other twenty-six. The power that is daringly adequate to strike down local government in the great expanse of territory that reaches from the Potomac to the Rio Grande, is certainly able to repeat it north of the Potomac and west of the Ohio."[22]

Several key political institutions aided southern whites in their assault upon Radical Reconstruction. The first was the Democratic Party. Throughout the existence of the second American Party System, the Democratic Party had proved the most faithful to southern political values and racial creeds. During the Civil War, the Democrats maintained their principal tenets of states' rights, limited government, and white supremacy. The Democratic Party served as a well-entrenched weapon for southern white opposition to Republican Reconstruction. The editor of the influential Mobile *Daily Advertiser and Register* urged the South to act in concert with the Democratic Party, explaining that it was "the only living organization that is in the field to combat the demon of Radicalism. Its creed on national politics, too, is our creed, and principle, policy, safety, and duty, all conspire to bind the people of the South in bonds of the closest sympathy and alliance with this ancient party." A South Carolina editor informed his readers that the Democratic maga-

---

22. Austin *Daily State Gazette,* October 28, 1867; Charleston *Daily Courier,* April 1, 1867; Mobile *Daily Advertiser and Register,* February 14, 1868. See also A. C. Garlington to A. B. Springs, February 17, 1866, Springs Family Papers, Southern Historical Collection, University of North Carolina, Chapel Hill, North Carolina.

zine *Old Guard* contained "the grand old principles of truth and justice, under which we of the South were brought up." Southern white conservatives looked to the Democratic Party to continue to uphold southern racial values. "Its faith, its theory and its practices," explained the Richmond *Enquirer and Examiner,* "are fast anchored and deeply imbedded in the teaching of our forefathers, that THIS IS A WHITE MAN'S GOVERNMENT." A Texas editor noted that the Democrats were trying to keep the South free from the "degradation of negro equality and negro rule."[23]

The partisan press was a second means southern conservatives deployed in their fight against Reconstruction. Newspaper editors such as Francis W. Dawson of the Charleston *News and Courier* and John Forsyth of the Mobile *Register* were especially influential spokesmen for the cause of the white South. Some newspapers were particularly hostile to Radical Reconstruction. Edward Ryland Randolph, editor of the Tuscaloosa *Independent Monitor,* was especially vicious in his attacks on Republicans, black and white.[24]

Political clubs also aided the Conservative/Democratic campaigns against Republican Reconstruction. Clubs had a long tradition in American political history dating back to Democratic-Republican societies of the 1790s and "Clay Clubs" of the Age of Jackson. Political clubs were also active during the presidential election of 1860. "Wide Awakes," groups of young men who marched in military style to campaign for Abraham Lincoln, were staples in Republican campaigning in 1860. To answer the Wide Awakes, secessionists in the South formed "Minute

23. Mobile *Daily Advertiser and Register,* February 11, 1868; Laurensville (South Carolina) *Herald,* February 1, 1867; Richmond *Enquirer and Examiner,* July 2, 1868; Austin *Daily State Gazette,* October 26, 1867.

Useful in understanding the Second Party System in the antebellum South are J. Mills Thornton III, *Politics and Power in a Slave Society: Alabama, 1800–1860* (Baton Rouge: Louisiana State Univ. Press, 1978); William J. Cooper, *The South and the Politics of Slavery, 1828–1856* (Baton Rouge: Louisiana State Univ. Press, 1978); and William Freehling, *The Road to Disunion,* vol. 1, *Secessionists at Bay, 1776–1854* (New York: Oxford Univ. Press, 1990).

24. Mobile *Daily Advertiser and Register,* February 15, 1868; E. Merton Coulter, *The South during Reconstruction, 1865–1877* (Baton Rouge: Louisiana State Univ. Press, 1947), 289; William Warren Rogers Jr., *Black Belt Scalawag: Charles Hays and the Southern Republicans in the Era of Reconstruction* (Athens: Univ. of Georgia Press, 1993), 40.

Men" companies in South Carolina, Alabama, and Virginia. The "Roanoke Guards" rallied support for secession in Virginia. Secessionists were also represented by Southern Rights Associations, like the one founded by Edmund Ruffin in Prince George County, Virginia.[25]

Political clubs in the postwar South served as extra-party means for organizing Democratic voters. For example, there was a Pinevelle Democratic Club in Marengo County, Alabama. Seymour and Blair Clubs organized Democratic support during the presidential election of 1868. The city of Mobile, Alabama, illustrates the breadth and function of political clubs during Reconstruction. Mobile had a Constitutional Club and a Central and Auxiliary Constitutional Club, of which editor John Forsyth served as president. In 1868, John Mullaly, editor of the New York *Metropolitan Record,* lectured to the Mobile Central Constitutional Club. In this sense, these clubs served educational functions for whites much as Union Leagues did for African Americans. Representing a different social stratum, the White Draymen's and Cartmen's Democratic Club of Mobile was also active in the presidential campaign of 1868. Young Men's Democratic Clubs sprung up in the Reconstruction South, showing up in Whistler, Alabama, and Columbus, Mississippi. The Young Men's Democratic Club of Leon County, Florida, furnishes a good example of how these clubs functioned as political organizations. The club divided the white electorate into sections of fifty voters. Smaller circles of ten were entrusted with finding information on individual voters. Like the Klan and Union Leagues, the Young Men's Democratic Club of Florida used secret signs and passwords. There was a loose confederation of county clubs with similar constitutions. In the social disorder of the post–Civil War South, these political clubs could also be the nucleus for other social organizations. For instance, the chairman of the Democratic State Executive Committee of Mississippi

---

25. Emerson David Fite, *The Presidential Campaign of 1860* (1911; reprint, Port Washington, N.Y.: Kennikat Press, 1967), 227–229; Ollinger Crenshaw, *The Slave States in the Presidential Election of 1860* (1945; reprint, Gloucester: Peter Smith, 1969), 216, 251; William L. Barney, *The Secessionist Impulse: Alabama and Mississippi in 1860* (Princeton: Princeton Univ. Press, 1974), 208; Henry T. Shanks, *The Secession Movement in Virginia, 1847–1861* (1934; reprint, New York: AMS Press, 1971), 125; Crenshaw, *Slave States in the Presidential Election of 1860,* 145; Shanks, *Secession Movement in Virginia,* 41.

claimed that his party's organizations "may be useful alike for political, agricultural and social purposes."[26]

Yet the most notorious and perhaps most effective means southern whites used to recapture and maintain their political supremacy over the freedmen was the Ku Klux Klan. When Congress held its Ku Klux Klan hearings in 1871, many witnesses claimed that the essential intention of the Klan was political. Testimony from South Carolina is indicative of beliefs found throughout the Reconstruction South. David Carlin of Union County believed that the Klan in South Carolina was "an adjunct of a political party, with a view to effect political results." Those goals included an end to black political progress and the restoration of white supremacy. "Of course," explained former Unionist and governor James L. Orr, "the white element of the State is very much dissatisfied and mortified at the elevation of the colored man not only in terms of political equality, but of superiority in many respects." He explained to the committee that those persons selected for nocturnal visits by the Klan "have been those holding office in their respective counties, such as auditors, treasurers, county commissioners, school commissioners, &c." One witness testified that in Spartanburg, the Klan told one South Carolinian "that he must make a public renunciation of his republican principles or they will return and kill him." J. H. Goss from Unionville claimed that no white man in South Carolina could safely be a Republican.[27]

The Ku Klux Klan was an agent of racial oppression. In every way possible, the Klan was dedicated to keeping white supremacy the central theme of southern history. "They would learn me," explained a freed-

26. Mobile *Daily Advertiser and Register,* September 25, 1868; September 5, 1868; February 1, 1868; February 27, 1868; September 2, 1868. For a further listing of clubs in Mobile, see Mobile *Daily Advertiser and Register,* September 5, 1868; September 16, 1868; Hopkins, "Some Reminiscences of Lowndes County History," 20, Ms.Z461f, Mississippi Department of Archives and History, Jackson, Mississippi; William Watson Davis, *The Civil War and Reconstruction in Florida* (New York: Columbia Univ. Press, 1913), 561–562; *Weekly Panola Star,* May 9, 1868. On the existence of Democratic clubs in the North, see Alexander B. Callow Jr., *The Tweed Ring* (New York: Oxford Univ. Press, 1966).

27. KKK Hearings, South Carolina, vol. 1, pages 79, 6, 3, 27, 65. It should also be noted that the Klan was considered in other ways. See the comments of R. B. Carpenter, KKK Hearings, South Carolina, vol. 1, page 244.

man from Winston County, Mississippi, "when I met a white man on the road to lift my hat to him and let me know I was a nigger." Edward C. Holman of Holly Springs, Mississippi, believed that the Klan "do not like to see the negro go ahead." Because of their centrality to black aspirations during Reconstruction, schools were a target of particularly symbolic significance to the Klan violence. A Union military officer in Monroe City, Mississippi, claimed that "they appear to be opposed to public schools." In the fall of 1870, almost every schoolhouse in the area near Tuskegee, Alabama, was burned. The Klan was also a means of intimidating labor. "Sometimes colored people are working for part of the crop," explained Alfred Richardson of Clarke County, Georgia. "They work on till the crop is nearly completed and ready for gathering. Then a fuss arises between them and the employer, and they are whipped off—whipped off by these men in disguise." One South Carolinian spoke of the Klan in his state in terms of the "unsettled State of Affairs in this Country, antagonizing labour & Capital." Klan violence knew few boundaries in terms of race or gender. A railroad worker in North Carolina reported that the Klan attacked a young girl, then "while she was prostrate on the floor, one of them lit a match and burned the hair off from her private parts."[28]

Klan intimidation and violence targeted African American and Republican politics. A northerner living in the Black Belt of Alabama testified that "the object of the organization was to control the negro vote, and to defeat the republican party in obtaining offices." To W. J. Purman of Jackson County, Florida, the purpose of the Klan was "the murder of the leaders of the republican party in the State, and the intimidation

28. KKK Hearings, Mississippi, vol. 1, pages 489, 350; Ku Klux Klan Papers, Perkins Library, Duke University, Durham, North Carolina; see also KKK Hearings, Mississippi, vol. 1, pages 229, 467; Foner, *Reconstruction*, 428; KKK Hearings, Georgia, vol. 1, pages 12–13; A. B. Springs to Richard Clark Springs, May 5, 1868, Springs Family Papers, Southern Historical Collection, University of North Carolina, Chapel Hill, North Carolina; KKK Hearings, North Carolina, page 67. The class dimensions of Klan violence have become a more pronounced theme in Reconstruction historiography. See, for example, Foner, *Reconstruction*, 428–429; Fitzgerald, *Union League Movement in the Deep South*, 136, 207–213; and Hahn, *A Nation under Our Feet*, 265–288.

of other republicans, and in that way to obtain possession and control of the State government." A North Carolinian believed that the Klan worked "for the purpose of keeping the negroes and white republicans from voting." Lieutenant Governor Ridgely Powers of Mississippi claimed similarly that the "main object of the organization" was "to operate just previous to and during elections, in order to have an effect on colored voters." A freedman in Georgia was warned by the local Klan that "if he ever voted any other ticket besides the democratic ticket, they would kill him." In carrying out their missions of intimidation and terror, local Klans would often cross county and state borders. South Carolina Klansmen crossed the border for raids in North Carolina, while men from Georgia came to South Carolina. "They wanted dens from other settlements," explained a member of the Invisible Empire, "to go to the settlement where it was to be done; to change the thing so that they would not know them." One North Carolinian testified that even the oath was administered by someone from another county.[29]

The results of the efforts of the Ku Klux Klan to foil black Reconstruction politics remain chilling. Over one thousand people were killed in Louisiana during the months leading up to the presidential election of 1868. African American politicians suffered significantly. About 10 percent of the blacks who had participated in the 1867–1868 constitutional conventions were victims of Klan-sponsored political violence. Alabama Klan members murdered black legislator Richard Burke in 1870. White Republicans were also the target of Klan violence. In an open allusion harking back to slavery, an angry crowd in Tennessee seized a Confed-

---

29. KKK Hearings, Alabama, vol. 1, page 79; KKK Hearings, Florida, page 149; KKK Hearings, North Carolina, page 52; KKK Hearings, Mississippi, vol. 1, page 592; KKK Hearings, Georgia, vol. 1, page 4; KKK Hearings, North Carolina, pages 203, 313, 206; W. H. Phillips et al. to Robert K. Scott, August 19, 1868, Scott Papers, South Carolina Department of Archives and History, Columbia, South Carolina; KKK Hearings, North Carolina, page 205; Testimony of Eli Euliss, Holden Governor's Papers, North Carolina Division of Archives and History, Raleigh, North Carolina. For further evidence, see KKK Hearings, Mississippi, vol. 1, page 232, and Henry B. Whitefield to James Lusk Alcorn, April 6, 1871, Alcorn Governor's Papers, Mississippi Department of Archives and History, Jackson, Mississippi.

erate veteran who had voted the Republican ticket and put him up for sale. In North Carolina, State Senator John W. Stephens was assassinated in 1870. The Klan also attacked Republican meetings held throughout the South.[30]

To intimidate freedmen and white Republicans, the Ku Klux Klan employed an elaborate iconography that conveyed their political ideology and racial identity. In fact, the use of icons was a key element of the political culture of Reconstruction secret societies. J. H. Caldwell, a Methodist minister who became involved in Georgia Republican politics, explained in a letter to the New York *Times* how the Klan used icons: "Placards have been posted up at the doors of Union men containing their mystic letters and signs, with skulls, coffins, skeletons, crossbones, deadly weapons, and written sentences breathing out most terrible threatenings against them." C. D. Forsyth of Rome, Georgia, told a congressional investigating committee that the Klan left him a notice with "a parcel of hieroglyphics that I did not understand." At least one Republican newspaper saw in Klan symbolism an opportunity for political satire. "These Kabalistic Karacters," wrote the Richmond *Daily New Nation* in 1868, "have arrived in town at last. A wonderful combination of hieroglyphics are upon the posters. A friend suggests that, without a reference to the Sanscrit or Chaldee, he has come to the conclusion that these letters only mean Kilkenny Kats, and that if they are severely let alone, like the famous Kat story of our childhood there will be nothing left but tales."[31]

Perhaps best known of Klan iconography were the costumes. Victims of Klan violence remembered the long white robes and hats most often associated with the night riders, a feature that has persisted in popular culture to the present day. Yet as the Reverend A. S. Lakin of Alabama testified, the Klan did "not all wear the same uniforms at all times and in all places." Joseph Nelson, a freedman from Jacksonville, Florida, said the Klan in his area dressed in "cracker-fashion," with old white or

---

30. Allen Trelease, *White Terror: The Ku Klux Klan Conspiracy and Southern Reconstruction* (Baton Rouge: Louisiana State Univ. Press, 1971), 135; Foner, *Reconstruction*, 426; Trelease, *White Terror*, 175; Foner, *Reconstruction*, 427–428.

31. KKK Hearings, Georgia, vol. 1, pages 451, 43; Richmond *Daily New Nation*, March 31, 1868.

black hats pulled down over their faces. In North Carolina, Klansmen wore white and red uniforms. William Moss, a freedman from Spartanburg, South Carolina, recalled that the Klan had "horns and red stripes all about on them." A North Carolina victim of Klan violence recounted that Klan members "came up and poked their horns at me, like they was going to hook me."[32]

The primary function of Klan iconography was to intimidate political opponents. Virgil Lusk of North Carolina, perhaps a master of understatement, told a congressional investigating committee that a threat from the Klan "was something to think about." David Schenck reported that "by cabalistic signs, mottoes and advertisements, they struck terror into the hearts of blacks, threatening all manner of punishment even to assassination." The most pervasive and ominous symbol was the coffin. The Klan often put wooden coffins at the doors of their enemies. A Unionist in Newberry, South Carolina, had a casket marked "KKK" placed on his piazza. Coffins were also used on threatening letters. One Alabama Republican received a letter from the Klan with a picture of a coffin next to the signature of five men. Rice E. Harris, also of Alabama, got a note from "Moorsville Den, No. 6, K.K.K." with a depiction of his coffin. To call the Klan of Glasgow, Kentucky, into action, leaders issued the following order: "Spectres!!! Unsheath your daggers!! The Illustrious Coffin Maker of the Ghostly Brotherhood announces that the coffins of the doomed are ready and await their victims!" Other icons included two sticks with the word "Death" written on each one placed on the door of the intended victim. In Florida, Klansmen rode around with flags inscribed with three letter K's arranged as a star.[33]

32. KKK Hearings, Alabama, vol. 1, page 120; KKK Hearings, Florida, page 140; KKK Hearings, North Carolina, page 221; KKK Hearings, South Carolina, vol. 1, page 397; Ku Klux Klan Papers, Perkins Library, Duke University, Durham, North Carolina.

For some interesting comments on the meaning of costumes, see Georg Simmel, "The Sociology of Secrecy and of Secret Societies," *American Journal of Sociology* 11 (January 1906): 488. Gordon Wood also has some trenchant observations on the significance of masquerades to conspiratorial thinking ("Conspiracy and the Paranoid Style: Causality and Deceit in the Eighteenth Century," *William and Mary Quarterly* 39 [July 1982]: 422–423).

33. Virgil S. Lusk File, page 11, North Carolina Division of Archives and History, Raleigh, North Carolina; David Schenck, "Diaries," vol. 6, page 4, David Schenck Papers, Southern Historical Collection, University of North Carolina, Chapel Hill, North

In their arsenal of iconography, the Klan utilized superstition to intimidate and terrorize freedpeople. "The attempt at mystery," explained J. H. Caldwell of Georgia, "was of course intended to mystify, and to give it the appearance of something supernatural. It was intended evidently to operate upon the superstitious fears of the negroes." John H. Christy of Athens, Georgia, called the freedmen "very superstitious." The most common use of superstition was for Klansmen to present themselves as ghosts of the Confederate dead. "They tell the colored people," explained one editor, ". . . that the spirits of the departed rebel soldiers have returned to earth, and are demanding the rights which they failed to obtain by the rebellion." An Atlanta man heard a story of the Klan leaving bones suspended on an office door, intending them to be the bones of Confederate soldiers who had arisen from their graves to avenge the wrongs perpetrated on the South. Klansmen led a North Carolinian to believe "that they have been seven-years in the bone-yards at Richmond, and have come for vengeance." Stories of Klan vigilantism through the masquerade of dead solders often mentioned specific Civil War battles. In Clarke County, Georgia, Klan members told victims that "they were killed at Manassas and are just out of the grave." A Klansman from White County, Georgia, said he rose from the battlefield of Shiloh. Such references to the Civil War might well have served to intimidate freedpeople with implicit threats of paramilitary violence and to reinforce postwar racial boundaries by cementing southern whiteness to the experience of war and defeat.[34]

According to contemporaries, Confederate ghosts reincarnated as

Carolina; Testimony of John Long, Ku Klux Klan Papers, Perkins Library, Duke University, Durham, North Carolina; Thomas Slider to Robert K. Scott, August 2, 1868, Robert K. Scott Papers, South Carolina Department of History and Archives, Columbia, South Carolina; *Report of the Joint Committee on Outrages* (Montgomery: Jno. G. Stokes and Company, 1868), 62, 9; *Central Georgian*, June 10, 1868; A. McIntyre to Lt. James Ulis, July 23, 1868, Rufus Brown Bullock, Executive Department Correspondence, Georgia Department of Archives and History, Atlanta, Georgia; KKK Hearings, Florida, pages 221, 258.

34. KKK Hearings, Georgia, vol. 1, pages 433, 239; Memphis *Daily Post*, March 22, 1868; KKK Hearings, Georgia, vol. 1, page 432; KKK Hearings, North Carolina, page 17; KKK Hearings, Georgia, vol. 1, pages 10, 512, 195. For additional evidence, see also William Alburtus Day, "Book of Recollections and Miscellany," page 220, Southern Historical Collection, University of North Carolina, Chapel Hill, North Carolina.

Klan night riders possessed an insatiable thirst. "I heard of their drinking water," testified Letty Mills, a black woman from Walton County, Georgia, "and of their going in and telling about their bursting out of tombs and rising from the dead." Klan visits would often involve a ceremony of drinking several buckets of water, using a rubber pouch and a hose to trick the observer. Robert Philip Howell of Mississippi recalled that freedmen told "dreadful stories of having seen large bodies of men in white masks drinking buckets of water at their wells which they could hear *burning as it went down their throats.*" In Panola County, Mississippi, a Klansman made a freedman bring him some water, "saying that at the same time that he was very thirsty, as he had nothing to drink since he left Hell three days before." Other myths about the Klan included the belief that they had come from the moon and that if a Klansmen were shot, "the ball would bounce back and kill you."[35]

Republican Reconstruction was not as determinative of Irish American nationalism as it was for southern whites and blacks. Unlike the Ku Klux Klan and the Union Leagues, the Fenians did not owe their inception to the Civil War and Reconstruction. They were not at the center of the struggle for political power in the postwar South. Yet in several ways the politics of Reconstruction significantly shaped the Fenian movement in the United States. Partisan competition between Republicans and Democrats enhanced the potential power of the Irish American vote. In addition, the primacy of Anglo-American relations in postwar foreign policy drew the Fenians into electoral politics.

Irish American voters had been largely Democratic during the antebellum era. The receptivity of urban political machines to the immigrants and the suspicion of Whig-and Republican-enforced morality

---

35. KKK Hearings, Georgia, vol. 1, page 468; Julia C. Brown, "Reconstruction in Yalobusha and Grenada Counties," *Publications of the Mississippi Historical Society* 12 (1912): 236; Robert Philip Howell, "Memoirs," page 24, Southern Historical Collection, University of North Carolina, Chapel Hill, North Carolina; John W. Kyle, "Reconstruction in Panola County," *Publications of the Mississippi Historical Society* 12 (1912): 53; KKK Hearings, Georgia, vol. 1, page 365; KKK Hearings, North Carolina, page 89. See also Julia Kendel, "Reconstruction in Lafayette County," *Publications of the Mississippi Historical Society* 13 (1913): 240.

led the Irish into the Democratic camp. During Reconstruction, Irish American votes became more contested as Republicans saw cracks in the Democratic Party. Radical Republicans also saw opportunities to draw Irish votes in Anglo-American diplomatic difficulties. Many Fenians, for example, were angry with President Andrew Johnson and Secretary of State William Seward for their failure to support the June 1866 invasion of Canada.[36] In the presidential election of 1868, some Fenians championed the Republican Party. The New York *Irish People* endorsed Republican candidates Ulysses S. Grant and Schuyler Colfax. Republicans also received the support of Michael Scanlon and the *Irish Republic*. Irish American Republican Clubs were active in Chicago, Cincinnati, and Troy, New York. One Irish Republican meeting at the Cooper Institute in New York urged all Irishmen to support the Republican Party.[37]

Fenian leaders were divided in their attitudes toward Republican Reconstruction. Perhaps the most active critic of Reconstruction was John Mitchel, editor of the influential *Irish Citizen* of New York. As a loyal Democrat, Mitchel explained to his readers that the Democrats were "the party which champions right against power; the rights of independent communities against centralization; the right of individual citizens against proscription; the rights of America against the whole world." Throughout the late 1860s, Mitchel remained firmly attached to the Democrats and opposed any alliance between the Republicans and the Fenians. "The attempt to make Radical Republican voters out of the Irish citizen," he once wrote, "has not thriven hitherto, and probably will not thrive." Mitchel, reflecting the antebellum Democratic critique of Whiggery, warned his readers of the "Great Moral Ideas" of the Republican Party, like Sabbatarianism and their opposition to Catholic schools. He attacked Radical Reconstruction as expensive, an assault on minority rights, and misguided in its racial policy. Mitchel feared that

---

36. Jerome Mushkat, *The Reconstruction of the New York Democracy, 1861–1874* (Rutherford: Fairleigh Dickinson Univ. Press, 1981), 59, 94.

37. Mabel Gregory Walker, *The Fenian Movement* (Colorado Springs: Ralph Myles Publisher, 1969), 168–170; and Florence E. Gibson, *The Attitudes of the New York Irish Toward State and National Affairs, 1848–1892* (New York: Columbia Univ. Press, 1951), 219–221.

Republican philanthropy would "bring on a war of races, which can only end in the extirpation of the black people." In his role as a Fenian leader, Mitchel also castigated the Republicans for being vassals to Ireland's arch enemy, England. "Whatever doubt may hang over the professions of Democrats in this campaign time," he wrote in 1868, "there is *no* doubt that the Radical Party is the humble servant of Great Britain, and the natural enemy" of the Irish. He warned that the Republican administration would be weakened by Reconstruction in the South, making the United States less able to stand up to England and other world powers.[38]

John Mitchel also condemned Republican foreign policy. "We must look to party affiliations and party exigencies which control party men," the editor of the *Irish Citizen* explained, "and all politicians and statesmen are party men; and exert all our power in support of that *party* which is by necessity most hostile to England—in other words most truly American. Not to be enigmatical, we mean the Democratic Party." Mitchel considered the Radical Republicans "the meanest and most servile vassals of English opinion." Regarding American claims over damages inflicted by the British-built *Alabama* during the Civil War, a writer to the *Irish People* of New York agreed with Mitchel, suggesting that Secretary of State William Henry Seward was "fooled by the wily Tory premier."[39]

In contrast, Michael Scanlon and his *Irish Republic* of Chicago backed Republican Reconstruction. In the internecine conflicts within Fenian ranks, Scanlon had been a supporter of the William R. Roberts faction and an opponent of John O'Mahoney. (Perhaps partisan differences reflected this split in Fenian ranks). "The Democratic party had [used] the Irish people," Scanlon maintained, "so long, and laughed at them so often, that they began to think they could use them for their packing horses forever, on whose shoulders every ignorant and unprincipled

---

38. *Irish Citizen*, May 30, 1868; see also the resolution of an Irish meeting in Boston in the December 21, 1867, issue; *Irish Citizen*, November 9, 1867, May 9, 1868; January 18, 1868; November 2, 1867; April 18, 1868; September 3, 1868; August 15, 1868.

39. *Irish Citizen*, June 13, 1868; July 25, 1868; "W.M.C." in *Irish People*, March 9, 1867.

ruffian could ride into office." In 1867, Scanlon applauded the election of Radical Republican William G. Brownlow as governor of Tennessee. Unlike Mitchel, Scanlon supported Republican postwar expansionism. He insisted that the annexation of Caribbean islands "is inflicting greater and more lasting injury to the power and aristocracy of England, than a war between this country and her could possibly do." Other Republican spokesmen saw their party as ideologically suited to the Fenians. The party, explained the Minneapolis *Tribune,* "strives to inculcate the doctrine that the liberation of Ireland is to be accomplished only by the universal diffusion of the doctrines of liberty, and that the true interests of the Irish people are with the party of freedom and equal rights—the Republican Party." Similarly, a Texas Republican paper noted the inconsistency of the Irish support for the Democrats, "the only party in America that is anti-progressive and aristocratic in all its tendencies, a party which persistently opposes in the New World the very principles for which Irishmen contend in the Old." He looked forward to the day when Irish voters left the Democratic Party "and put themselves in harmony with the liberty-loving citizens of the United States."[40]

A third Fenian position was partisan neutrality. "It is high time, fellow countrymen that we show some independence in political matters," urged Thomas Lavan; "it is high time that we should no longer be the property, souls and body of a party that knows us only a few days before each election, but during the interregnum knows us not." The editor of the New York *Irish People* agreed: "We are not partizan [sic] in any form. In American politics, we fight for neither Republicans nor Democrats." In a lecture before the Fenian Brotherhood of New York in 1865, W. R. Roberts staked out a position of political neutrality. He admitted that Fenians as individual citizens would have their partisan preferences, but the idea that the Fenians as a body were dedicated to one party he called "a wicked and malicious falsehood." Fenian leaders recognized that both parties would try to court the Irish American vote but remained skeptical about either party's commitment to the Irish cause. "For the next three or four weeks," John O'Neil wrote to a fellow Fe-

40. *Irish Republic,* August 24, 1867; August 10, 1867; *Irish Republic,* 488; *Irish Republic,* October 5, 1867; *Daily Austin Republican,* August 25, 1868.

nian, "the politicians of the Country will be loud in their professions of love for Ireland, and desire to see her free."[41]

Some Republicans suspiciously detected partisan motives in political decisions. In 1867, Congressman William E. Robinson from Brooklyn moved to impeach Charles Francis Adams, American minister to Great Britain. The Republican Cleveland *Morning Leader* hinted strongly that this motion was an attempt to keep the Irish firmly in the Democratic camp. A year earlier, it saw in the effort to remove the U.S. district attorney from the northern district of New York a political move to strengthen the vote for Democratic gubernatorial hopeful John T. Hoffman. The Republican editor warned that the "Fenian eye must be exceedingly *filmy* if it does not penetrate this *filmiest* of gauze-looms."[42]

Because any attack on England could further the cause of Irish independence, Fenians in the United States closely followed the course of Reconstruction diplomacy. Some became interested in postwar efforts to expel the French-sponsored Emperor Maximilian from Mexico. Sensing a connection between establishing republics in Ireland and Mexico, General Sweeney even considered establishing Irish colonies there. But primarily, Fenians focused on the often tense diplomatic relations between England and the United States after the Civil War. They recognized that their own role in international diplomacy could be advantageous to them. Fenianism, noted the Pittsburgh *Catholic,* "is now the menace by means of which the United States impose on England more than one decision by which her interests or her self-esteem may have to suffer." John Mitchel was characteristically more direct. The United States, he argued, could hold up the Fenians "before the eyes of England, by way of inducing her to be more compliant in the diplomatic discussions which are going on between London and Washington; just as a man holds a bull-dog by the collar, sure that he can let him slip against his enemy, or else drive him back to his kennel." The Republican

---

41. Quotation in Cleveland *Morning Leader,* October 6, 1866; *Irish People,* April 20, 1867; W. R. Roberts, *Lecture by W. R. Roberts, Delivered Before the Fenian Brotherhood of New York, at Cooper Institute, on Wednesday, Sept. 27th, 1865* (New York: J. Croft, 1865), 25; John O'Neil to Francis Gallagher, October 6, 1868, Fenian Brotherhood Papers, Philadelphia Archdiocesan Historical Research Center, Philadelphia, Pennsylvania.

42. Cleveland *Morning Leader,* November 22, 1867; November 5, 1866.

Cleveland *Morning Leader* also sensed that the Fenians would be "a new cause for uneasiness in England."[43]

As Irish Americans, most Fenians were naturally hostile to England. To the editor of the *Irish Republic*, the late Civil War was caused not only by southern secessionists but by "external tyrants." In his view, England hoped to use the destruction of the Union "to find a renewed lease of their unhallowed power." The journal also endorsed protective tariffs as a weapon against the English: "rest only when the last English merchant keel has ceased to trouble American waters, and the last rag of English manufacture has helped to swell a bonfire at the Battery in New York." Fenian leaders saw in the debate over the *Alabama* Claims an opportunity to fight the English. After the Civil War, American merchants sought compensation for damage suffered by their ships from Confederate raiders built in England. The *Irish Citizen* argued that "the losses were really great, and the sufferers should not be solicitous to keep down the amount." Fenians also sensed in the *Alabama* Claims controversy a chance to expose English hypocrisy about neutrality. If they allowed ships to be built in England for the Confederacy, how could they with any consistency ask the United States to stay neutral as to the Fenians? "Let our Government," pointed out the editor of the New York *Citizen*, "oppose the equipment and sailing of Fenian privateers with precisely the same alacrity and acrimony shown by England in preventing the fitting out and departure of the Alabama, Florida, Georgia."[44]

In their attempts at ethnic autonomy and political self-determination, southern whites, freedmen, and Fenians were forced to confront and work within the politics of Reconstruction. To a large extent, the main purpose of the Union Leagues and Ku Klux Klan was political. Each associated almost exclusively with one of the two political parties in the

43. Cleveland *Morning Leader*, October 3, 1866; October 6, 1866; Pittsburgh *Catholic*, April 6, 1867; *Irish Citizen*, February 22, 1868; Cleveland *Morning Leader*, October 19, 1866.

44. *Irish Republic*, May 11, 1867; *Irish Republic*, 487; *Irish Citizen*, March 2, 1868; New York *Citizen*, March 10, 1866. On the *Alabama* Claims, see Adrian Cook, *The Alabama Claims: American Politics and Anglo-American Relations, 1865–1872* (Ithaca: Cornell Univ. Press, 1975).

South. In terms of Reconstruction politics, the Fenians stand in greater isolation from the Leagues and the Klan. Partisan politics played a more minor role in their movement. But all three groups faced the powerful presence of Republican political hegemony during Reconstruction that helped define the limits of their own autonomy and power. Reconstruction politics served to direct their separatist inclinations along the lines of civic nationalism.

2
The Political Culture of Countersubversion

The Union Leagues, the Ku Klux Klan, and the Fenians were fraternal, paramilitary organizations that bonded their members in a brotherhood through elaborate and secret rituals. The roots of the Fenians lay of course in Ireland. In the eighteenth century, the Whiteboys initiated an Irish tradition of rural violence against landlords and their agents. The Society of Ribbonmen assumed the mantle of agrarian protest during the 1820s and 1830s, providing the groundwork for Fenianism during the 1860s. (The terms *whiteboys* and *ribbonmen* became synonymous with agrarian violence in Ireland throughout the 1800s). In the United States, the history of secret societies also extended back to the eighteenth century with the Masons. In the decade before the Civil War, the Know-Nothings were again quasi-secret societies that served as a vehicle for nativism. Copperhead dissent in the Civil War North provided even more precedents for secret societies during Reconstruction. One such group, the Sons of Liberty, divided states into military districts and initiated its members with impressive rituals. Another Copperhead society, the Knights of the Golden Circle, would later remind one Tennessee editor of Fenians in Ireland.[1]

1. Mary Ann Clawson, "Fraternal Orders and Class Formation in the Nineteenth-Century United States," *Comparative Studies in Society and History* 27 (October 1985): 672; Kevin Kenny, *Making Sense of the Molly Maguires* (New York: Oxford Univ. Press, 1998), 9 (Kenny provides a succinct survey of these movements in chapter 1); on Freemasonry, see Steven C. Bullock, *Revolutionary Brotherhood: Freemasonry and the Transformation of the American Social Order, 1730–1840* (Chapel Hill: Univ. of North Carolina Press, 1996); on the Know-Nothings, see Ray Allen Billington, *The Protestant Crusade, 1800–1860: A Study in the Origins of American Nativism* (1938; reprint, Chicago: Quadrangle Books, 1964), and Tyler Anbinder, *Nativism and Slavery: The Northern Know-Nothings and the Politics of the 1850s* (New York: Oxford Univ. Press, 1992); Frank L. Klement, *The Copperheads in the Middle West* (Chicago: Univ. of Chicago Press, 1960), 166; Chattanooga *Daily Gazette*, October 7, 1865.

Secret societies persisted in American life after the Civil War. One social commentator at the end of the century even noted a "remarkable increase in their number in this country" since 1865. There were clandestine labor organizations like the Knights of Labor, the Secret Order of the Knights of St. Crispin in Massachusetts, and the Ancient Order of Hibernians (a name often associated with the Molly Maguires) in the anthracite region of western Pennsylvania. Like the Ku Klux Klan, the Molly Maguires hid behind costumes of long white smocks, used members from other counties to carry out their killings, and were eventually undermined by arrests and convictions during the 1870s.[2]

As secret societies, the Fenians, the Union Leagues, and the Ku Klux Klan acquired their meaning in this context of postwar associationism. All three groups were perceived by their enemies as a potentially subversive force that operated outside the accepted boundaries of political contest. This was not totally an inaccurate perception. The Union Leagues and Ku Klux Klan had elaborate initiation rites and secret rituals. The Klan almost always operated at night, and the Leagues were often associated with mysterious nocturnal meetings. All three groups were strongly paramilitary in their organization and operations. Together, these factors created what might be called a political culture of countersubversion, a way of portraying and even demonizing political opposition as subversive of the established order. As perhaps the strongest unifying factor tying these three groups together, the theme of countersubversion is essential to understanding the emergence and nature of ethnic separatism and political self-determination in post-Civil War America.[3]

---

2. W. S. Harwood, "Secret Societies in America," *North American Review* 164 (May 1897): 617; David Montgomery, *Beyond Equality: Labor and the Radical Republicans, 1862–1872* (1967; reprint, Urbana: Univ. of Illinois Press, 1981), 141; John R. Commons et al., *History of Labour in the United States* (New York: Macmillan, 1921), 2:181–185; Kenny, *Making Sense of the Molly Maguires,* 11.

3. See the similar, though not exactly parallel, comments in David Brion Davis, "Some Themes of Countersubversion: An Analysis of Anti-Masonic, Anti-Catholic, and Anti-Mormon Literature," *Mississippi Valley Historical Review* 47 (September 1960): 205–224; and David Brion Davis, *The Slave Power Conspiracy and the Paranoid Style* (Baton Rouge: Louisiana State Univ. Press, 1969), 10.

In addition, the emphasis on countersubversion suggests how the political culture of Reconstruction was strongly shaped by the discourse of republicanism. This set of ideas on political liberty and independence inherited from the Revolutionary era was another factor that directed separatist impulses along the lines of civic nationalism and serves as a strong reminder of the continuities between the Ages of Jefferson, Jackson, and Lincoln.[4]

As a prelude to discussing the political culture of countersubversion shared by these secret societies during Reconstruction, it might be useful to trace the organizational histories of the Fenians, the Union Leagues, and the Ku Klux Klan. The roots of the Fenian movement and Irish American nationalism lay in the massive Irish immigration to the United States in the three decades before the Civil War. This period witnessed the greatest influx of foreign immigrants in proportion to the native population in American history. The devastation of the Great Famine in 1846 propelled Irish emigration to America. During the 1850s, the Irish constituted 49 percent of the total immigration to the United States. In the peak year of 1851, 221,253 Irish immigrants arrived in America. The Famine generation of Irish immigrants was primarily Catholic and poor, and hence more receptive to clerics and nationalist politicians who could offer satisfying explanations for the Great Famine.[5]

Irish immigrants flocked to cities such as Boston, Philadelphia, and New York. Everywhere they took low-paying jobs in construction and manufacturing and thus helped expand a growing antebellum urban working class. Irish immigrants were residentially segregated in urban slums plagued by filth, poverty, and crime. Yet these settlement patterns also encouraged group cohesiveness among Irish Americans. From 1845 to 1870, Irish immigrants set the institutional foundations for an Irish American community that helped assimilate them into modern in-

---

4. Mark Neely Jr. makes a similar point in *The Union Divided: Party Conflict in the Civil War North* (Cambridge, Mass.: Harvard Univ. Press, 2002), 171–172.

5. Richard B. Morris, ed., *Encyclopedia of American History,* Bicentennial Edition (New York: Harper and Row, 1976), 653; Kerby A. Miller, *Emigrants and Exiles: Ireland and the Irish Exodus to North America* (New York: Oxford Univ. Press, 1985), 295–298, 306.

dustrial life and protect them from Yankee Protestant nativism. They created fraternal associations, mutual aid societies, fire companies, and militias. Newspapers such as the New York *Irish American,* which began publication in 1849, became an important voice for Irish American communities.⁶

By the 1850s, politics had become the main avenue of assimilation for Irish American immigrants and the basis for group consciousness and conflict. The increasing rate of Irish immigration to the United States was expanding the number of Irish American voters. Between 1850 and 1855, Irish voters in Boston grew from 1,549 to 4,564. In 1855, 34 percent of all voters in New York city were Irish. Here Fernando Wood and the Tammany Democratic machine began to organize the Irish vote.⁷

Nativism was a major factor shaping the Irish American community. Protestantism had always been a powerful component of American cultural identity. The large influx of Irish immigrants in the antebellum era, coupled with the militant nature of the Catholic Church, created a wave of anti-Catholic and anti-Irish prejudice. The 1830s witnessed the burning of the Charlestown convent outside Boston and the rise of an anti-Catholic press. In New York, the establishment of the nativist New York Protestant Association in 1831 was followed by the American Democratic Association in 1835. In the 1840s, ethnic conflicts over public education spread into party politics pitting Whigs against Democrats. A fight over which Bible to use in public schools sparked an ugly riot in Philadelphia in 1844. Nativism increased during the 1850s, as the Know-Nothings (the American Party) and later the Republican Party benefited from state platforms that exploited anti-immigrant, anti-Catholic, and anti-Irish prejudices.⁸

---

6. Miller, *Emigrants and Exiles,* 315, 319; Robert Ernst, *Immigrant Life in New York City, 1825–1863* (1949; reprint, Syracuse, N.Y.: Syracuse Univ. Press, 1994), 46; Miller, *Emigrants and Exiles,* 328; Florence E. Gibson, *The Attitudes of the New York Irish Toward State and National Affairs, 1848–1892* (New York: Columbia Univ. Press, 1951), 28.

7. Oscar Handlin, *Boston's Immigrants, 1790–1880,* Fiftieth Anniversary Edition (Cambridge, Mass.: Belknap Press of Harvard Univ. Press, 1991), 191; Gibson, *Attitudes of the New York Irish,* 18, 91.

8. Gibson, *Attitudes of the New York Irish,* 70, 72, 74. The literature on antebellum nativism still begins with Billington, *The Protestant Crusade.* For a recent study of the public

Nativism persisted during the Civil War, encouraging the kind of group consciousness that nurtured nationalist movements like the Fenians. Upper-class Protestant New Yorkers were aghast at their city's Irish after events like the New York City Draft Riots, in which protestors from Irish working-class neighborhoods attacked the symbols of Republican rule and terrorized the black community of New York. Ethnic prejudice was somewhat abated by the substantial contribution Irish Americans made to the northern war effort. Roughly 145,000 Irishmen served in the Union armies in units like the famous "Irish Brigade" of the Army of the Potomac. These Irish American soldiers fought at the Second Battle of Bull Run, Fredricksburg, Chancellorsville, and Antietam, where they suffered close to 60 percent casualties.[9]

The Fenian movement of the 1860s also drew upon a long history of Irish nationalism dating back to the eighteenth century. Inspired by the American and French Revolutions, Irish nationalists like Wolfe Tone and his Society of United Irishmen led an abortive uprising against English domination in 1798. During the 1840s, Daniel O'Connell led a crusade to repeal the Act of Union of 1800. Though unsuccessful, the movement generated widespread support in the United States. In contrast, members of the Young Ireland movement that emerged in 1848 were more willing to use force to achieve their goals. Young Ireland received the support of Irish American workers who admired the nationalism and republicanism of the 1848 revolutions. For example, a group called the Friends of Ireland met in New York in June of 1848 to proffer their support. Despite a few attempted uprisings in some isolated locations, the revolt of these Romantic revolutionaries failed. Many of the

---

education question, see Martin L. Meenagh, "Archbishop John Hughes and the New York Schools Controversy of 1840–43," *American Nineteenth Century History* 5 (spring 2004): 34–65. On the Know-Nothings, see Anbinder, *Nativism and Slavery*. Studies of urban immigrant communities such as Handlin, *Boston's Immigrants,* and Ernst, *Immigrant Life in New York City,* also discuss nativism.

9. On the draft riots, see Adrian Cook, *The Armies of the Street: The New York City Draft Riots of 1863* (Lexington: Univ. Press of Kentucky, 1974), and Iver Bernstein, *The New York City Draft Riots: Their Significance for American Society and Politics in the Age of the Civil War* (New York: Oxford Univ. Press, 1990). Randall Miller, Harry S. Stout, and Charles Reagan Wilson, eds., *Religion and the American Civil War* (New York: Oxford Univ. Press, 1998), 261; Gibson, *Attitudes of the New York Irish*, 128, 162.

Irish political refugees from the failed revolution of 1848 fled to America. John Mitchel, who would later become an influential Irish American nationalist, settled in New York, where he began publishing the *Irish Citizen* in 1853.[10]

If the nineteenth-century Irish American community provided a setting for Irish American nationalism, Ireland supplied the original inspiration for Fenianism. In 1858, Irish nationalist James Stephens established the Irish Revolutionary Brotherhood in Dublin. He sought assistance across the Atlantic from the thousands of Irish emigrants in the United States. To direct the American crusade, Stephens chose John O'Mahoney, a veteran of the Irish uprising of 1848. In 1859, O'Mahoney founded the Fenian Brotherhood as the American branch of the Irish Revolutionary Brotherhood. The name of the organization derived from "Fianna Eirionn," an ancient Irish militia. The writer of an introductory manual for Fenian members explained that it was a standing army "employed only on home service for protecting the coasts from invasion." More recent historical precedents for Fenianism were revolutionary organizations such as the Carbonari in Italy that spread throughout Europe around the time of the Revolutions of 1848.[11]

Fenianism in the United States reached the height of its influence after the Civil War. By the time of Reconstruction, the Fenian movement had spread across the breadth of the United States. A Fenian treasurer's report for February 1869 listed circles in eighteen states and three territories (Idaho, Colorado, and New Mexico). Not surprisingly, Fenians were most visible and active in urban areas that contained high concentrations of Irish Americans. In 1865, Massachusetts had thirty-six circles. Manhattan itself had twenty. Fenians could also be found in southern cities, such as Louisville, Memphis, and New Orleans. There

---

10. Charles Callan Tansill, *America and the Fight for Irish Freedom, 1866–1922* (New York: Devin-Adair, 1957), 15–16; Mabel Gregory Walker, *The Fenian Movement* (Colorado Springs: Ralph Myles Publisher, 1969), 1–3; Ernst, *Immigrant Life in New York City*, 123; Gibson, *Attitudes of the New York Irish*, 20.

11. W. S. Neidhardt, *Fenianism in North America* (University Park: Pennsylvania State Univ. Press, 1975), 3–6, succinctly covers the origins of the movement; *The Fenian's Progress: A Vision* (New York: John Bradburn, 1865), 54; León Ó Broin, *Fenian Fever: An Anglo-American Dilemma* (New York: New York Univ. Press, 1971), 1–2.

also were Fenian circles in smaller manufacturing towns, such as Holyoke, Massachusetts. Even the West claimed its share of Fenians. The John Mitchel Circle in Beartown, Montana Territory, had 150 members. In the Idaho Territory, Irish miners formed the Fenian Emmet Circle. Fenians could be found in Oregon and Utah and were especially active in San Francisco. At its highest level of membership, according to one historian, the Fenian movement in the United States claimed forty-five thousand members.[12]

When it was founded in the late 1850s, the Fenians were organized as a series of secret cells reminiscent of revolutionary societies in Europe. The Fenian Brotherhood was directed by a Head Centre, who was assisted by a Central Council of ten. The Fenian organization in each state was headed by a State Centre, who controlled the local circles. At their national meeting in 1865, American Fenians changed their organizational structure to reflect their political surroundings. A president and General Congress made up of a Senate and House of Delegates replaced the Head Centre and Central Council. By the late 1860s, there were military branches of the Fenian Brotherhood, including a War Department and an Adjutant General's Office. The local unit of the Fenian organization was the circle, composed of a secretary, treasurer, and a committee of safety. The editor of the *Irish Republic* of Chicago spelled out how local Fenian circles were formed. "The process is very simple," he explained. "Call together say twelve men on whom you can rely. Talk the matter over thoroughly. See that no man is admitted among you who could have any desire to *use you* for personal or political purposes." Any candidate for the circle had to be proposed a week before initiation,

---

12. "Report of the Treasurer, of the Fenian Brotherhood, for the Month of February, 1869," Fenian Brotherhood Papers, Philadelphia Archdiocesan Historical Research Center, Philadelphia, Pennsylvania; *Proceedings of the Second National Congress of the Fenian Brotherhood, held in Cincinnati, Ohio, January, 1865* (Philadelphia: James Gibbons, 1865), 17–19; Dennis Clark, "Militants of the 1860s: The Philadelphia Fenians," *Pennsylvania Magazine of History and Biography* 95 (January 1971): 107; Constance M. Green, *Holyoke, Massachusetts: A Case History of the Industrial Revolution in America* (New Haven: Yale Univ. Press, 1939), 114; *Irish Republic*, July 14, 1867; July 13, 1867; Neidhardt, *Fenianism in North America*, 15; Thomas N. Brown, *Irish-American Nationalism, 1870–1890* (Philadelphia: J. B. Lippincott, 1966), 40.

for which the fee was one dollar. The size of local circles varied. There were twenty-six initial members of the Fenian circle in Cape Elizabeth, Maine. The Fenian circle in Danbury, Connecticut, had seventy-one members. Not unlike the campaign to spread the Union League in the South during 1867, Fenian leaders went around the country organizing Irish Americans. For example, Thomas Lavan, a senator of the Fenian Brotherhood, planned three lectures in Cleveland to be accompanied by "a Fair or Bazar [sic] to last for a Week."[13]

The Union League movement was born in the crucible of Civil War nationalism. It had been a bloody and sobering year for the Union in 1862. The Army of the Potomac suffered disastrous and demoralizing defeats in Virginia, and western armies could only claim a series of exasperating stalemates in Mississippi and Tennessee. Even "victories," like the September battle at Antietam, were costly. The Lincoln administration and the Republicans faced serious challenges on the political front as well. Republican ascendancy sustained a major challenge in the fall elections of 1862 when Democrats recaptured dozens of seats in Congress and received electoral majorities in Pennsylvania, New York, Ohio, Indiana, and Illinois. President Lincoln was beset by a cabinet crisis as his administration began to lose public confidence. Under these dire circumstances, some wealthy and influential citizens began a movement to boost northern morale and strengthen devotion to the Union cause. In late 1862, they founded the first Union League in Philadelphia. In the winter of 1863, New Yorkers established a Loyal Publication Society and the Philadelphia Union League created a Board of Publication to disseminate patriotic literature. Loyal Leagues, as they were often called, spread from the urban centers of the Northeast to the Midwest. The

13. Brown, *Irish-American Nationalism*, 38; *Proceedings of the Fenian Brotherhood* (1865), 35–36; Brown, *Irish-American Nationalism*, 39; see, for example, General Orders No. 4, May 1, 1869, and Circular Orders, Fenian Brotherhood Papers, 1857–1870, Philadelphia Archdiocesan Historical Research Center, Philadelphia, Pennsylvania; *Irish Republic*, May 4, 1867; *Proceedings of the Fenian Brotherhood* (1865), 38; *Irish Republic*, May 4, 1867; *Irish People*, April 20, 1867; Buffalo *Fenian Volunteer*, December 14, 1867; Thomas Lavan to Gallagher, October 26, 1867, Fenian Brotherhood Papers, Folder 12, Philadelphia Archdiocesan Historical Research Center, Philadelphia, Pennsylvania.

Union League forged close ties to the Republican administration and party. "Their best and most distinguished citizens," explained Union Leaguer Francis L. Cardozo of South Carolina, "animated by their devotion to the Union, assembled together to devise plans to strengthen and advance the loyal purposes of the Administration, and to destroy the rebellion." As a national organization closely connected to the Republican Party, the Union League became a means of spreading unionism and Republicanism to occupied areas of the Civil War South.[14]

Like the Fenians, the Union Leagues had a structured organization. There was a national council and one council for each state and territory. The extent of organization on the state level varied. For example, the League in Alabama was more highly structured and more centrally directed than it was in Mississippi. For most freedmen, the most meaningful unit of organization was the local chapter. Forming a Union League chapter required the presence of at least nine loyal men. The Deep River Union League in Guilford County, North Carolina, met every other week on Saturday evenings at 6 P.M. Dues were five cents per month. There were executive, financial, and "state of the Union" committees. The extant records of the Hamburg Lodge of the U.L.A. in South Carolina offers a closer look into the operations of a local League. Officers in this League, similar to others in the South, included a president, vice president, assistant vice president, treasurer, secretary, marshal, herald, sentinel, and chaplain. Prospective members would send in petitions to join; some were rejected for lack of suitable evidence of their loyalties. The Hamburg League averaged about twenty-five members at each meeting. Reflecting the racial composition of other Leagues during Radical Reconstruction, it initiated seven whites and forty-

---

14. Frank Freidel, ed., *Union Pamphlets of the Civil War, 1861–1865*, 2 vols. (Cambridge, Mass.: Belknap Press of Harvard Univ. Press, 1967), 1:5; F. L. Cardozo, *Address before the Grand Council of the Union Leagues at Their Annual Meeting, held July 27, 1870, by Hon. F. L. Cardozo, President* (Columbia, S.C.: John W. Denny, 1870), 4; Michael Fitzgerald, *The Union League Movement in the Deep South: Politics and Agricultural Change during Reconstruction* (Baton Rouge: Louisiana State Univ. Press, 1989), 10–13. For the origins and ideology of the Union Leagues, see also Melinda Lawson, "'A Profound National Devotion': The Civil War Union Leagues and the Construction of a New National Patriotism," *Civil War History* 48 (December 2002): 338–362.

seven blacks to membership at a meeting in June 1867. The number of members in local Leagues varied but seems to have been substantial. In the cotton regions of the Deep South, Leagues numbered between fifty and one hundred members. Freedman William V. Turner claimed there were over four hundred members of the Union League in Wetumpka, Alabama. A League organizer in Virginia reported that a local council in Lynchburg was "eleven hundred strong."[15]

The close similarities between the Union Leagues and the Ku Klux Klan form one of the striking paradoxes of Reconstruction. Both were semi-secret societies, structured organizations with initiation rites, paramilitary activities, and political goals. The origin of the term "Ku Klux Klan" was often unclear to contemporaries. The Memphis *Appeal* believed the name was "a Hebrew term," translated roughly as "Straw Club" since the Pharaoh had required Hebrew slaves to carry their own straw. "Others maintain," noted a Georgia editor, "that it is a corruption of 'click, click,'" the warning note of that terrible engine of destruction, the revolver." A Republican newspaper in North Carolina believed similarly that the name Ku Klux Klan "is taken from the 'click' in cocking a gun or pistol.—It means blood. It means that rebel desperadoes are organizing against the government." The name was also a descriptive noun that signified any kind of political terroristic violence. "The term Ku-Klux there," recalled a Maine Republican in Alabama, was understood "to cover all political outrages, all these political disorders. They are sort of called Ku-Klux whether men are in disguise or not." A North Carolinian believed similarly that the word was a com-

---

15. Walter L. Fleming, ed., *Documentary History of Reconstruction: Political, Military, Social, Religious, Educational, and Industrial, 1865–1906* (1907; reprint, New York: McGraw-Hill, 1966), 2:7; Fitzgerald, *Union League Movement in the Deep South*, 36; Steven Hahn, *A Nation under Our Feet: Black Political Struggles in the Rural South from Slavery to the Great Migration* (Cambridge, Mass.: Belknap Press of Harvard Univ. Press, 2003), 180; "Minute Book, 1868. Deep River Union League," Joel Romulus Welborn Papers, Perkins Library, Duke University, Durham, North Carolina; Minutes of the Hamburg Lodge of the U.L.A., page 1a, Brower Family Papers, Southern Historical Collection, University of North Carolina, Chapel Hill, North Carolina; ibid., pages 3, 16–18; Hahn, *A Nation under Our Feet*, 182; *Daily State Sentinel*, May 24, 1867; Dr. H. J. Brown to Thomas L. Tullock, July 23, 1867, Robert C. Schenck Papers (microfilm), Rutherford B. Hayes Memorial Library, Fremont, Ohio.

mon expression there for almost any kind of violence. To E. W. Seibels of South Carolina, "bushwhackers, Ku-Klux" were "all the same thing." Ku Klux was also used as a verb. James McCoy, a Georgia Unionist whose house was burned, explained that it was "a common word out there, if a man gets a little umbrage against another, to say, 'By God, I will Ku-Klux you.'" An African American woman testified before a congressional committee that she was "Ku-Kluxed" because she would not work for a neighboring white family. In a revealing linguistic subversion, a black man in Georgia was heard to say "he was going to ku-Klux the Ku-Klux."[16]

Like other ethnic nationalities, the Klan had its own myths of origin. A Georgia physician who wrote a fictional history of the Klan in the late nineteenth century thought that it was first organized in Iuka, Mississippi. A North Carolinian reported that former President Andrew Johnson was said to be the "Head Centre" in the United States. Historians today generally agree that the Ku Klux Klan of Reconstruction began as a social club of Confederate veterans in Pulaski, Tennessee, in 1866. The term was a corrupted version of a Greek word meaning circle or band. A white Mississippian, testifying before the congressional investigating committee of 1871, understood that the Klan originated in Tennessee; "that it was brought about by the odious political condition of the country as to the white people; that it was to protect the white people against outrages committed upon them by the opposite party." The Klan was transformed from a social club to a tool of white vigilantism because of the widespread opposition to the Republican rule of Governor William G. Brownlow. The first reputed Grand Wizard of the Ku Klux Klan was former slave trader and Confederate cavalry general Nathan Bedford Forrest. Many Klan members, such as John Taliaferro

---

16. Quoted in Charleston *Daily News*, April 7, 1868; *Central Georgian*, April 8, 1868; *North Carolina Standard*, quoted in Richmond *Daily New Nation*, March 31, 1868; KKK Hearings, Alabama, vol. 1, page 76; KKK Hearings, North Carolina, page 75; KKK Hearings, South Carolina, vol. 1, page 108; KKK Hearings, Georgia, vol. 1, page 396; KKK Hearings, South Carolina, vol. 1, page 589; KKK Hearings, Georgia, vol. 1, page 107. On the origins of the Klan, see also Stanley F. Horn, *Invisible Empire: The Story of the Ku Klux Klan, 1866–1871* (1939; reprint, Cos Cob, Conn.: John E. Edwards, 1969), 7–20.

of Noxubee County, Mississippi, understood "that General Forrest was the originator of it."[17]

The belief that the Ku Klux Klan was founded in response to the Union Leagues was common in the Reconstruction South. "The origin, as it is generally understood, the prime moving cause of the existence of the Ku-Klux," explained Governor Robert B. Lindsay of Alabama, "was the result of Union Leagues." George P. Burnett of Atlanta claimed that the "first object" of the Klan was "to cripple any effort that might be produced by Loyal Leagues." A Mississippi newspaper editor explained that the Union League had caused "counter organizations to spring up in many localities, such as ku-klux and vigilance committees, for home protection against the midnight incursion of oath-bound, unprincipled, unscrupulous, and Congress-chartered loyal leagues." A black woman in Meridian, Mississippi, heard afterward from the man who had raped her that he was after the Union Leagues. A North Carolina Republican attacked by the Klan was forced to recite the oath of the Union League, with which the Klan members were apparently familiar.[18]

The Ku Klux Klan was organized in a structure of layered authority not unlike the Fenians and the Union Leagues. The Klan's organiza-

17. Lyman W. Denton, M.D., "The Ku Klux Klan and the Days of Reconstruction, or In the Shadow of the Kennisaw," 17, typescript, Hargrett Rare Book and Manuscript Library, University of Georgia, Athens, Georgia; Ku Klux Klan Papers, Perkins Library, Duke University, Durham, North Carolina; KKK Hearings, Mississippi, vol. 1, page 126; Allen W. Trelease, *White Terror: The Ku Klux Klan Conspiracy and Southern Reconstruction* (Baton Rouge: Louisiana State Univ. Press, 1971), 49–50; KKK Hearings, Mississippi, vol. 1, page 236. See also David Schenck, "Diaries," vol. 6, page 5, David Schenck Papers, Southern Historical Collection, University of North Carolina, Chapel Hill, North Carolina.

18. KKK Hearings, Alabama, vol. 1, page 170; KKK Hearings, Georgia, vol. 1, page 68; *Weekly Panola Star,* August 8, 1868; KKK Hearings, Mississippi, vol. 1, page 38; KKK Hearings, North Carolina, page 119. Historian Michael Fitzgerald is thus correct in stating about the Klan that "counteracting the Union League was one of its major political goals" (*Union League Movement in the Deep South,* 200). For further evidence, see KKK Hearings, Georgia, vol. 1, page 308; KKK Hearings, Mississippi, vol. 1, page 262; "Autobiography," page 32, in James P. Brownlow Papers, Tennessee Historical Society, Nashville, Tennessee; and the excerpt from the New York *Herald* in the April 22, 1868, *Central Georgian.* See also George C. Rable, *But There Was No Peace: The Role of Violence in the Politics of Reconstruction* (Athens: Univ. of Georgia Press, 1984), 85–86.

tion was perfected at a meeting in Nashville in 1867. At the top of the hierarchy was the unit of the Empire, which consisted of all the southern states except Delaware. A Grand Wizard and a staff of ten Genii led the Empire. The next level was the Realm, a state unit directed by a Grand Dragon. A Dominion consisted of several counties overseen by a Grand Titan. A Grand Cyclops oversaw local dens. Each level of the organization had staff officers as well. The local organization of the Klan was the den. The cyclops of the den with four councillors comprised the council that would decide the necessary punishment for offenses by members. The names of local dens varied. One in Georgia went by the name of the "Keenesaw Ku Klux Klan, No. 1973." The Klan in Newton County, Mississippi, had three dens called Decatur, Hickory, and Newton.[19]

In several ways, the structure and form of these three societies influenced their search for ethnic autonomy and political self-determination. It is even possible for the Fenians and the Ku Klux Klan that their organizations served as a kind of proto-state, a model for envisioning a separate government based on race or ethnicity. The evidence is far from conclusive but nonetheless suggestive. Both groups were similar in creating a quasi-government with legislative, executive, and judicial functions. In 1865, the Fenian national meeting urged the formation of a "Provisional Government." It explained that the Fenian Congress "acts the part of a national assembly of an Irish Republic. Our organized friends in Ireland constitute its army." The Fenians even took on trappings of an international power, raising an army and issuing letters of marque and reprisal. Revealingly, a Fenian writing from New Orleans believed that a future Fenian army would need rules "for before we can hope for recognition as belligerents we must govern the army by[?] a code based upon public law and adopted by the legislature of the F.B." Essentially, the Fenians attempted to establish a government within a government. "Your organization," explained James Gibbons in an 1870 address to the Senate of the Fenian Brotherhood, "after years of toil and

---

19. Walter L. Fleming, *The Sequel of Appomattox: A Chronicle of the Reunion of the States* (Toronto: Glasgow, Brook, 1919), 248; KKK Hearings, North Carolina, page 231; Denton, "Ku Klux Klan," 30; Ruth Watkins, "Reconstruction in Newton County," *Publications of the Mississippi Historical Society* 11 (1910): 219–220.

care, has assumed a power hitherto unknown in revolutionary bodies, because partaking of all the elements of a Government . . . an Irish nation in America."[20]

The Fenian state in America would serve as a model for a future Irish republic. As John O'Neil explained to a national meeting in 1868, the Fenian organization "may be fittingly termed the first step of the Irish people toward free self-government." The present structure of the movement "is to-day the true type and representative of that nationality against which the power of England has been exerted in vain for seven hundred years." In particular, an Irish republic would reflect its origins in republican America, "a refuge and a rallying place, where her sons, in common with the persecuted of all nations, may come together, and by the exhibition of what freedom and the power of self-government have done for them." When the Fenians in America changed their organizational structure in 1865, they explained that "the organization would be reconstituted after the mold of the free institutions of this country—in a word, that the Fenians should make their own laws, elect and control their own officers as is meet that freeman should."[21]

There is little evidence for a similar phenomenon in the Ku Klux Klan, although there is some indication that the Klan might have been seen as an alternative political party. The extremism of the Klan reflected dissatisfaction with the centrist position of the Whig-dominated Conservative parties in southern states between 1868 and 1873. There are even hints of more democratic and less elitist politics, perhaps a precursor of Populism. For example, one Klan leader told an Alabama clergyman that "nothing can withstand the omnipotence of popular sentiment and public opinion." In an editorial entitled "The National

---

20. *Proceedings of the Second National Congress of the Fenian Brotherhood*, 14, 5; Brown, *Irish-American Nationalism*, 39; Edgeworth Dougherty to F. B. Gallagher, November 20. 1868, Fenian Brotherhood Papers, Folder 1, American Catholic Historical Society, Philadelphia, Pennsylvania; Ó Broin, *Fenian Fever*, 53; James Gibbons, *Address of the Executive Committee of the Senate, F.B. to the Officers and Members of the F.B.* (New York: n.p., 1870).

21. *Proceedings of the Senate and House of Representatives of the Fenian Brotherhood, in Joint Convention, at Philadelphia, PA, November 24, 25, 26, 27, 28 & 29, 1868* (New York: D. W. Lee, 1868), 5; ibid., 5; *Proceedings of the Second National Congress of the Fenian Brotherhood*, 6.

Disease," the editor of the newspaper *Ku-Klux* complained that America was "a country where the few get rich on the labor of the many."[22]

In an article entitled "Secret Societies in America" that appeared in the *North American Review* in 1897, W. S. Howard was impressed that there were still millions of men in oath-bound societies in the United States. What he found even more significant, however, was the "further fact that auxiliary to and a part of these orders are military branches... who are trained in military tactics... many of them thoroughly informed as to the history, the present needs, and the possibilities of military life." Although written at the end of the nineteenth century, Howard's observations apply well to the secret societies of Reconstruction. Military themes were a central component of the structure, values, and activities of the Union Leagues, the Fenians, and the Ku Klux Klan. "Paramilitary organization," suggests one historian, "had been fundamental to the social and political order of slavery; it remained fundamental to the social and political order of freedom." For all three groups, but to varying degrees, paramilitarism provided a basis for group cohesion, a means of conducting politics, and a possible foundation for a separate national identity.[23]

The paramilitary culture of American Fenians drew upon a strongly rooted tradition of local militia in antebellum Irish American communities. Although they were often mere fronts for social gatherings, military companies were part of the institutional networks of immigrant neighborhoods. During the 1850s, Irish Americans in Boston could join the Columbian Artillery, the Bay State Artillery, and the Sarsfield Guards. Milwaukee, like many other cities, boasted its own Emmet Guards. In New York City, several Irish military companies combined to form the Ninth Regiment of the New York State Militia, becoming the first Irish American regiment in the country. After the Civil War, the Fenians continued and strengthened the place of military organizations in Irish American communities. "Men meet for drill every night, by

---

22. KKK Hearings, Alabama, vol. 1, page 112; *Ku Klux*, December 14, 1871.

23. Harwood, "Secret Societies in America," 617; Hahn, *A Nation under Our Feet*, 266. See also Richard Zucek, "The Last Campaign of the Civil War: South Carolina and the Revolution of 1876," *Civil War History* 42 (March 1996): 18–31.

companies, at their rooms or in the fields adjoining the city," a reporter noted in Buffalo, New York. The Philadelphia *Public Ledger* indicated that Fenian circles in that city were reorganizing in 1866 and "a good many are joining the military organizations."[24]

Second, Fenian paramilitarism drew from the military experience of the Civil War. The Fenians had been highly successful in recruiting soldiers among Union regiments. According to one student of the New York Irish, "Fenian leaders worked actively in the ranks of the Union Army to enroll the Irish-American soldiers in the Nationalist organization." Military service in the Union army was seen as a useful training ground for future soldiers fighting for Irish independence. Brigadier General Thomas Smith was Head Centre of Fenians in the Army of the Potomac. In 1866, a Cleveland newspaper estimated that close to three-fourths of the Western Division of Fenians "had on some article of Federal uniform, and were unmistakably discharged soldiers." Nearly every man who engaged in a mock battle at a Fenian picnic in 1867 had served in the Civil War. Fenians marching in Cleveland on St. Patrick's Day wore blue trousers, green jackets, and "green fatigue caps, many of the latter having a jounty cut and ornamented with a tassel, a la Zouve." Fenian leaders saw military service during the war as an invaluable experience for soldiers who could later fight for Irish independence. The protagonist in the novel *The Fenian Chief* proclaims that a "Republic of Hibernia" would be created with the help of those "who have learned in the States what was impossible in their birthplace to gain for themselves—[they] are coming to expend blood and treasure to place their country on the list of nations!" For an observer of a St. Patrick's Day celebration in Cleveland, the military parade brought back memories of "the scenes, in camp and field, of years that have but just gone by."[25]

---

24. Handlin, *Boston's Immigrants*, 157; Bayrd Still, *Milwaukee: The History of a City* (Madison: State Historical Society of Wisconsin, 1965), 81; Ernst, *Immigrant Life in New York City*, 128; quoted in Philadelphia *Public Ledger*, November 29, 1866; Philadelphia *Public Ledger*, November 30, 1866.

25. Gibson, *Attitudes of the New York Irish*, 162, 174; Cleveland *Morning Leader*, May 31, 1866; *Irish Republic*, September 28, 1867; Cleveland *Morning Leader*, March 19, 1867; [Henry Llewellyn Williams], *The Fenian Chief; or, the Martyr of '65* (New York: Robert M. DeWitt, 1865), 93; Cleveland *Morning Leader*, March 19, 1867.

Military presentations became a large part of Fenian activity during Reconstruction. The staging of mock battles between Irish soldiers and British troops was a common part of Fenian picnics. On August 12, 1867, a sham fight took place at a day-long picnic in Troy, New York, that drew an estimated ten thousand Irish Americans. Military companies from nearby Albany were given the distinction of acting as the Fenian army. Those from Troy, "bearing the cross of St. George at their head," played the role of the English. Like the very real battles of the recent Civil War, this theatrical contest began with skirmishing. Perhaps to nobody's surprise, the Fenians proceeded to flank their enemy, "a regular Grant-like movement around Lee's army," and the performing English soldiers fled in disarray. At the end of the day, "the hated emblem of the oppressor was captured, the English laid down their arms, and victory perched upon the 'sunburst.'" At a mock battle staged by the Sheridan Circle of Manhattan, Fenian soldiers dressed in "green jackets and blue pantaloons" crossed a creek where they drove the British army "to the shelter of the woods." The ensuing capture of the English flag and the surrender of the English army "were hailed with joy by the multitude in the woods." An enthusiastic report from a Fenian picnic in Albany described the battle in similar terms: "Prodigies of valor were performed. The rifles cracked, the cannon bellowed and thundered, the bayonets glittered in the sun, sabers clashed, and the dead and wounded were strewn about the field. This is the usual result of all decisive battles, and on this occasion it was to be expected."[26]

The military character of Fenianism went beyond the ornamental or theatrical. It was instrumental in the creation of Irish American nationalism. Like Oliver Cromwell's soldiers in the English Civil War, Fenians believed that the army would be the harbinger of a new Irish republic. The author of *The Fenian's Progress* explained that the "leading axiom" of the movement was that "to effect an Irish revolution, a grand military preorganization is absolutely necessary; that a disciplined soldiery, led by experienced officers are a *sine qua non*; and that, in short, to destroy English dominion in Ireland, a desperate struggle must be encountered. Powder, shot and shell, rifles and cannon, are foremost in the Fenian lit-

26. *Irish Republic,* August 24, 1867; September 28, 1867; August 24, 1867.

any." The Fenian Congress emphatically made the same point in their national address of 1866: "Soldiers are now to supersede clubs; rifles will soon be substituted for pens; shelter tents, in the enemy's country, will take the place of rooms in New York; 'headquarters' will soon be in the field, and the Green Flag will change its place from the ballroom and the gay parade to the cloud and storm of battle." Fenian general John O'Neil argued that since Irishmen had already proved that they could fight for other people, their business now was to fight for themselves.[27]

Like the Fenians, the Ku Klux Klan also drew some of its paramilitary character from the experience of the Civil War. The link between the Ku Klux Klan and the Confederate army is especially compelling. A. P. Huggins of Aberdeen, Mississippi, stated that "many of them are confederate soldiers, and they served in the confederate army." In Florida, Klansman Thomas Barnes had been a sergeant in the Confederate army and still had the pack of dogs he had used to hunt down deserters. The Klan adopted a military organization similar to that of the Confederate army. A U.S. Army officer serving in Monroe City, Mississippi, testified that Klans were organized into military companies. John R. Taliaferro of Noxubee County, Mississippi, who had attended a Klan meeting, recalled that "they have what they call captains of bands, and first and second lieutenants, just as they have in a regular military company." In Rome, Georgia, each Klan had a captain. In Gwinnett County, the Klan was called the "Fourth Division."[28]

Slave patrols provided another precedent for the Ku Klux Klan and other such groups, suggesting the lines of continuity between the antebellum and postbellum South. Especially in the plantation districts of the Old South, neighboring whites would form police patrols to control

---

27. *The Fenian's Progress*, 48; *Proceedings of the Fourth National Congress of the Fenian Brotherhood, at Pittsburgh, Pa., February, 1866, with the Constitution of the F.B., and Addenda Thereto* (New York: J. Croft, 1866), 27; *Proceedings of the Senate and House of Representatives*, 14.

28. KKK Hearings, Mississippi, vol. 1, page 288; KKK Hearings, Florida, page 188; KKK Hearings, Mississippi, vol. 1, pages 467, 231; KKK Hearings, Georgia, vol. 1, pages 21, 351. According to Steven Hahn, the Klan attracted "young white men who had served in the Confederate army" (*A Nation under Our Feet*, 268). For similarities with the Union Leagues, see ibid., 178.

the activities of slaves. Possessing an unusual but potent combination of executive and judicial powers, patrols were feared by slaves. It was only the loose enforcement of the laws that lessened the potentially harmful impact of the patrols on the slave community. A recent student of slave patrols has called control of the nights "an exercise in power." The impulse behind slave patrols persisted in the South after emancipation. Vigilance committees, such as the Black Cavalry and Men of Justice in Alabama, arose in response to the Christmas 1865 insurrection scare. Like antebellum patrollers, Klansmen operated at night and on the local level. As a precursor of the Klan, the slave patrol should be seen, as one historian has stated, as "a potential organ for the reassertion of white control and domination."[29]

Military themes filled the practices of the Ku Klux Klan. "They gave their orders, marched, &c., all in military style," one South Carolinian explained: "They had evidently been soldiers, or had been trained." A Union officer stationed in Decatur, Georgia, told a congressional investigating committee that the Klan in his area "marched as soldiers do, and seemed to have some kind of drill and organization." In North Carolina, Georgia, and most other southern states, Klans were divided into companies and camps. According to the testimony of former members, the internal workings of a den or camp were also based on the military. One North Carolinian explained that he "was just as much under that chief as a soldier is under his officer."[30]

---

29. Sally E. Hadden, *Slave Patrols: Law and Violence in Virginia and the Carolinas* (Cambridge, Mass.: Harvard Univ. Press, 2001), 211; Lou Faulkner Williams, *The Great South Carolina Ku Klux Klan Trials, 1871–1872* (Athens: Univ. of Georgia Press, 1996), 27; William J. Cooper and Thomas E. Terrill, *The American South: A History* (New York: Knopf, 1990), 209–210; J. Michael Crane, "Controlling the Night: Perceptions of the Slave Patrol in Mississippi," *Journal of Mississippi History* 61 (summer 1999): 120; Hahn, *A Nation under Our Feet*, 151; Fleming, *The Sequel of Appomattox*, 245; Crane, "Controlling the Night," 136. Hadden, in *Slave Patrols*, 203–220, more fully and informatively discusses the connections between slave patrols and the Ku Klux Klan.

30. KKK Hearings, South Carolina, vol. 1, pages 281–282; KKK Hearings, Georgia, vol. 1, page 506; KKK Hearings, North Carolina, page 25; KKK Hearings, Georgia, vol. 1, page 395; Ku Klux Klan Papers, Perkins Library, Duke University, Durham, North Carolina; KKK Hearings, Georgia, vol. 1, page 25.

Like the Klan and the Fenians, the Union Leagues had their own military culture. According to one newspaper report, members of the League in Franklin, Tennessee, "gathered at one point, and formed in column for marching, displaying their banners conspicuously." In Columbus, Mississippi, Union Leagues paraded the streets armed with swords, rifles, and pistols. The Charleston *Daily News,* alarmed that secret military organizations were "spreading like a network over the State," condemned "this wretched juggle of flags and arms, of darkened rooms and deadly oaths, and flashing and smoking powder." The Union Leagues were following an emerging tradition of black politicization through paramilitary means. In Newton and Decatur, Mississippi, freedmen openly drilled on the streets during the day. Blacks in Lafayette Springs, Mississippi, had a military band. On drill days, freedmen lacking real guns and swords marched with long sticks. The close association between politics and paramilitarism in the postwar black community is illustrated in a resolution of a Republican meeting in Fort Valley, Georgia, which referred to Grant Clubs as "recruiting camps" for the upcoming election. Another military element of the Union Leagues was the use of drums for communication. In Meridian, Mississippi, freedmen marched around the streets beating their drums. In Georgia, a Freedmen's Bureau officer noted "Large crowds of freedmen parading the streets with Drum." Union Leagues in Mississippi beat drums to serenade the town or community after a meeting. Drumming had a long history in both African and slave communities, once again highlighting the continuities between slavery and freedom.[31]

31. Savannah *Daily News and Herald,* July 13, 1867; Edward Randolph Hopkins, "Some Reminiscences of Lowndes County History," 18, Ms.Z461f, Mississippi Department of Archives and History, Jackson, Mississippi; Charleston *Daily News,* September 17, 1868; Watkins, "Reconstruction in Newton County," 218; M. G. Abney, "Reconstruction in Pontotoc County," *Publications of the Mississippi Historical Society* 11 (1910): 238; Atlanta *National Era,* July 9, 1868; KKK Hearings, Mississippi, vol. 1, page 37; William A. Campbell, contrib., "A Freedmen's Bureau Diary by George Wagner," part 2, *Georgia Historical Quarterly* 48 (September 1964): 351; Hattie Magee, "Reconstruction in Lawrence and Jefferson Davis Counties," *Publications of the Mississippi Historical Society* 11 (1910): 192. The "militarization" of politics was part of a larger phenomenon of the Gilded Age. See Morton Keller, "The Politicos Reconsidered," *Perspectives in American History* 1 (1967): 401–408.

The Union Leagues and Ku Klux Klan, like other secret societies of nineteenth-century America, were distinguished by their use of elaborate and mysterious initiation rites and rituals. "There is perhaps no external tendency which so decisively and with such characteristic differences divides the secret from the open society," explained sociologist Georg Simmel, "as the valuation of usages, formulas, rites, and the peculiar preponderance and antithetic relation of all these to the body of purposes which the society represents." The Union Leagues, the Ku Klux Klan, and, to a lesser extent, the Fenians were no exception.[32]

Many commentators on the Union Leagues, in fact, impugned the organization by demeaningly suggesting that African Americans were somehow genetically susceptible to secret rites and rituals. "The league is said to have mysteries and penalties," noted the *Daily Press* of Augusta, Georgia, "—the one to allure, the other to frighten the colored people into joining it." As Reconstruction was ending in 1877, an author in the *Atlantic Monthly* wrote that all African Americans joined a League where they were "awed by their mystic rites." Historians critical of Reconstruction, often writing under the influence of William A. Dunning, belittled the Union Leagues by asserting that they catered to the superstitions of blacks. "Initiation into these secret societies," claims one such historian of Reconstruction in Florida, "was made sufficiently mysterious to favorably impress the black with their importance and satisfy his longing for some sort of hoodooism." Yet southern whites as well as African Americans were drawn to ritual fraternal orders. Joshua Marcus of Jackson, Mississippi, thought that "very frequently young men—boys and youth—are deluded into this thing by its novelty and mystery and secrecy; there is a sort of charm in this respect to young men, and they go into it frequently without realizing the extent of their wrongdoing." A resident of Macon, Mississippi, agreed: "Indiscreet young

32. Georg Simmel, "The Sociology of Secrecy and Secret Societies," *American Journal of Sociology* 11 (January 1906): 480, 485. Simmel also notes: "There is a peculiar fascination in the unreality of the initiation, an allurement about fine 'team' work, a charm of deep potency in the unrestricted, out-of-the-world atmosphere which surrounds the scenes where men are knit together by the closest ties, bound by the most solemn obligations to maintain secrecy as to the events which transpire within their walls" (621).

men in both races get into these societies, and become intoxicated, and do things that they would not do if they were not in there."[33]

The centrality of rituals to secret societies during Reconstruction is nowhere more evident than in their rites of initiation. For both the Union Leagues and the Ku Klux Klan, introduction into the organization was an elaborate event. The initiation rites of the Union Leagues, spelled out in a document that circulated throughout the South, were perhaps the most intricate and ornate. Candidates who wished to join a League came to a local meeting. They were first sent to a room adjoining the central place where the Council met. The assistant vice president entered this room, where he was to inform them of "the object of this League, and propound to them the necessary interrogations, as provided in the ritual." Then the marshal escorted the potential members into the Council room, marching arm in arm in double file, where they gathered around the altar. Now came the heart of the initiation ceremony. The altar contained several icons that depicted the ideology of the Union Leagues—an American flag with a copy of the Bible, the Declaration of Independence, and the Constitution of the United States. A sword was placed across the books. The altar also included a ballot box, a Censer of Incense, a Sickle, Anvil, "and other emblems of industry." The vice president then read a long address on the purpose of the League, reminding the initiates that the "legitimate fruits" of the Revolution were "yet to be secured in the complete ascendancy of the true principles of popular government; the establishment of equal liberty; the elevation and education of the toiling masses." The president, "in four raps, in couplets," then called upon the chaplain to deliver a prayer. Placing their left hand on the flag and raising their right hand, the initiates repeated their obligation and pledge. They were formally members of the Union League of America.[34]

---

33. Augusta *Daily Press*, April 5, 1867; *Atlantic Monthly* 39 (February 1877): 177; William Watson Davis, *The Civil War and Reconstruction in Florida* (New York: Columbia Univ. Press, 1913), 375; Fitzgerald, *Union League Movement in the Deep South*, 2–3; KKK Hearings, Mississippi, vol. 1, pages 323, 569.

34. The initiation ritual for the Union Leagues can be found in Walter L. Fleming, ed., *Union League Documents* (Morgantown, W.Va.: n.p., 1904), 17–25. All the quotes in this paragraph are from this document. In Mississippi, short passages relating to the

The initiation rites of the Ku Klux Klan were similar in several ways. There was also a table containing icons of the secret society, although according to one newspaper account a skull was placed on the table at Klan meetings. Candidates were asked a series of ten questions, such as whether they had fought in the Union army or were members in the Loyal League. Like the Union League initiates, they also took vows of secrecy. At the beginning, however, Klan initiations partook of the character of fraternal hazing. W. D. Mooney, recalling his youthful Klan activities in Pulaski, Tennessee, explained: "Part of the ceremony consisted in placing the blindfolded candidate, who had been decorated with Ass'es ears before a mirror and having him repeat that couplet of Robert Burns—'O wod some power the giftie give us / To see oursels as others see us.' Then the bandage was removed, and the assembled clansmen, all veiled and shrouded, yelled with Plutonian laughter." Strengthening the connection between the Klan, secret societies, and darkness, initiations often took place in the woods at night. J. J. Younger of North Carolina testified that he was initiated in the woods and that another meeting was held "in a pine thicket." In Georgia, people were admitted to the Klan in the woods over a coffin.[35]

Perhaps the most common denominator among the Fenians, the Union Leagues, and the Ku Klux Klan was their reputations as secret societies. *The Fenian Progress,* an introductory handbook for the movement, explained that the Irish Republican Brotherhood "was at first a semi-secret association; its meetings were secret, and though its chief officers were publicly known as such, the operations of the Brotherhood were hidden from the public view." The prescript of the Ku Klux Klan stated explicitly that the "most profound and rigid secrecy concerning any and everything that relates to the Order shall at all times be maintained." The

---

Exodus were read from the Bible at Union League meetings. W. H. Hardy, "Recollections of Reconstruction in East and Southeast Mississippi," *Publications of the Mississippi Historical Society* 4 (1901): 114.

35. Fleming, ed., *Documentary History of Reconstruction,* 2:348–349; W. D. Mooney, "Ku Klux Klan," Tennessee State Library and Archives, Nashville, Tennessee; Testimony of J. J. Younger, William W. Holden Governor's Papers, North Carolina Division of Archives and History, Raleigh, North Carolina; KKK Hearings, Georgia, vol. 1, page 416.

Union Leagues were also seen as secret societies. Southern Republicans sympathetic to the movement acknowledged the group's secret nature but sought to defend it. "Its secrecy may be objected to," argued a correspondent to the Charleston *Daily Republican*, "but even that has been essentially necessary to the existence of the nation and freedom itself, and is, therefore, under the circumstances, a desirable feature. Those who are weak-kneed in their devotion to the great principles of the Republican Party may hesitate to swear to that which they fully believe, but they can never object to those who are stronger in the faith and ready to seal their devotion by the most solemn and binding obligations."[36]

Some element of secrecy was clearly necessary for these organizations not only to pursue their goals but often to simply exist. Because their intention to invade Canada was well known, Fenian maneuvers in America were closely watched by authorities in both the United States and Great Britain. The assistant secretary for civil affairs in the Fenian Brotherhood asked one local leader to spread information to other Fenians "under the usual obligation of Secrecy." The foreign observer M. H. Vrignault recognized that the Fenians were "forced to work in secret."[37] For practical reasons, Union League secrecy meant safety. A writer to an Atlanta Republican newspaper agreed that the Union Leagues required secrecy not only to prevent their members from ostracism and personal violence but to facilitate the mobilization of Republican voters. This is why Union League meetings were often held at night. In Panola County, Mississippi, the Leagues were said to have gathered around sunset. The Leagues in Carroll County, Mississippi, assembled during the night, frustrating the efforts of their Democratic enemies to find them. The cover of darkness probably allowed freedpeople greater movement away from the suspicious eyes of white planters and employers. In addition, the night had traditionally been a time of greater autonomy for slaves, allowing them some measure of freedom to travel and worship among themselves. As a criminal conspiracy,

36. *The Fenian's Progress*, 43; *Revised and Amended Prescript of the Order of the * * * . . . .* (Pulaski, Tenn., 1868), 22–24; Charleston *Daily Republican*, August 24, 1870.

37. F. Remham to Francis B. Gallagher, October 17, 1868, Fenian Brotherhood Papers, 1857–1870, Folder 5, Philadelphia Archidocesan History Research Center, Philadelphia, Pennsylvania; Pittsburgh *Catholic,* April 6, 1867.

the Klan was forced underground to avoid detection and prosecution.³⁸ Klan violence against freedpeople and white Republicans therefore almost always occurred at night. "It is a peculiarity of the organization," testified a federal official in North Carolina, "that in their prowlings they go about the country on moon-light [sic] nights." A Klan member from Cub Lake, Mississippi, recalled that they made their raids "at mysterious hours of the night." A former solicitor general from western North Carolina remembered that nightly raids were so frequent in his area that people fled their houses and took refuge in nearby woods.³⁹

Moreover, it was as secret societies that these three groups were best known to contemporaries. This was particularly true in the postwar South. Conservative white opponents of Republican Reconstruction tended to paint the Union Leagues with the taint of secrecy. "It begins to be whispered about," a Georgia editor cautioned, "that, under the inspiration of cunning white leaders, a secret political society or league has been formed, the object of which is to coerce the whole negro vote." The Richmond *Enquirer and Examiner* maintained that *"emissaries, moving through the State as stealthily as burglars and house stealers, have organized oath-bound secret associations of negroes* in almost every county." In Mississippi, native white Republican Robert W. Flournoy opposed efforts to enlist the freedmen in Union Leagues. Responding to an attack published in the Jackson *Clarion,* Flournoy denied his membership in the Union League, explaining that he generally acts "open and above board."⁴⁰

---

38. Fred M. Witty, "Reconstruction in Carroll and Montgomery Counties," *Publication of the Mississippi Historical Society* 10 (1909): 123; John W. Kyle, "Reconstruction in Panola County," *Publications of the Mississippi Historical Society* 12 (1912): 51. Hahn, *A Nation under Our Feet,* 181.

39. KKK Hearings, North Carolina, pages 29, 103; Irby C. Nichols, "Reconstruction in DeSoto County," *Publications of the Mississippi Historical Society* 11 (1910): 311; Virgil S. Lusk File, page 2, North Carolina Division of Archives and History, Raleigh, North Carolina. See also KKK Hearings, Mississippi, vol. 1, page 83; David Schenck, "Diaries," vol. 6, page 4, Schenck Papers, Southern Historical Collection, University of North Carolina, Chapel Hill, North Carolina; *Proceedings in the Ku Klux Trials, at Columbia, S.C., in the United States Circuit Court, November Term, 1871* (Columbia: Republican Printing Company, 1872), 608.

40. Augusta *Daily Press,* April 5, 1867; Richmond *Enquirer and Examiner,* September 6, 1867; Harris, *Day of the Carpetbagger,* 100.

The Klan, too, was depicted as a secret society. Republicans hostile to the Ku Klux Klan used secrecy as a justification to stigmatize and delegitimize the group. Robert Douglas, addressing a mass meeting of Republicans in Smithfield, North Carolina, referred to the Klan as "a secret oath bound society." Secrecy connoted older republican fears of conspiracy and subversion. "Its movements and designs are still so mysterious," David Schenck of North Carolina confided to his diary, "that no one has a definite idea of its designs." The editor of the Knoxville *Whig* wrote in a similar vein: "As they burrow in darkness and skulls behind mysterious names and forms, they may think to escape detection, and even to elude suspicion." The emphasis on secrecy can be partly explained as a characteristic of any fraternal, oath-bound society.[41] Opponents of the Fenians often commented upon its secret nature. For example, a meeting of Irishmen in Massachusetts gathered to support Irish independence insisted that "no signs, grips or passwords shall be introduced into this Circle and that our meetings may be as public as may be consistent with the object we have in view."[42]

Secret societies, viewed from the perspective of countersubversion, tended to be associated with the night. Identifying the activities of secret societies with nighttime was a way to challenge their legitimacy and aims. The enemies of the Union Leagues seemed almost obsessed with their nighttime meetings. Ryland Randolph, editor of the rabidly racist Tuscaloosa *Independent Monitor*, spoke of the "dark-lantern councils of that glorious institution, the Loyal League." A Memphis editor concluded that a recent riot had been instigated in the "dark holes of the Loyal League." The meaning of night in Reconstruction political culture was vividly revealed in a speech by Anderson J. Peeler of Leon County, Florida, to a Conservative rally in 1867: "How did you join them? Was it at a meeting like this in broad, open daylight? No; it was when owls

---

41. Robert M. Douglas, *Speech of Col. Robert M. Douglas, of Washington, D.C., Delivered at a Republican Mass Meeting Held at Smithfield, N.C., July 12th, 1870* (Raleigh: "Standard" Steam Book and Job Press, 1870), 7; David Schenck, "Diaries," vol. 6, page 4, David Schenck Papers, Southern Historical Collection, University of North Carolina, Chapel Hill, North Carolina; Knoxville *Whig* quoted in Jonesboro (Tennessee) *Union Flag*, September 6, 1867. See also KKK Hearings, Florida, page 154.

42. *Irish Citizen*, March 21, 1868.

were hooting from the trees in the swamps and bats had left their holes, that away off in some obscure nook or corner, under lock and key, you were made to swear to a long riggamarole of stuff that you did not understand, and then, after swearing to it, you were told that you would be guilty of false swearing if you did not keep your oath."[43]

Sharing the political culture of countersubversion, the Klan was similarly identified with the night. Republicans chose to denounce the Klan by associating them with the night. "The Ku-Klux," explained the Tallahassee *Sentinel,* "are very particular to accomplish their hellish purposes under the cover of darkness or in isolated localities." References to the Klan in Reconstruction sources are filled with night imagery. The Forest *Register* of Scott County, Mississippi, carried this notice (obviously with encoded messages): "K.K.K.s. You are ordered to assemble at the Dark Valley on the night of the first mortal month at the hour of Silence. Come prepared. Work to do. Lamps to extinguish. Darkness to follow." The conservative *Southern Standard* of Arkadelphia, Arkansas, used nocturnal allusions to oppose a Ku Klux bill pending before the state Senate. "Whenever left in the dark by themselves," noted the editor about the bill's proponents, "they imagine they can see the weird and ghostly forms of the terrible Ku Klux hovering around them like avenging spirits to punish them for the many wrongs and miseries they have inflicted upon the people and country." Revealingly, George Campbell of Mississippi received a letter from the Klan accusing him of being "a white man in day-time and a dam [sic] negro at night."[44]

For both the Union Leagues and the Ku Klux Klan, night became the temporal arena for subversive activities. Behind this rhetoric lurked the fear that a racial order was being turned upside down. It is not surprising, then, that night could insinuate perhaps more familiar biblical dangers of darkness. William A. Moore of North Carolina insisted that

---

43. Tuscaloosa *Independent Monitor,* October 9, 1867; Memphis *Daily Avalanche,* May 16, 1867; Davis, *The Civil War and Reconstruction in Florida,* 484. See also KKK Hearings, Georgia, vol. 1, page 183; *Weekly Panola Star,* July 18, 1868.

44. Tallahassee *Sentinel,* June 17, 1871; KKK Hearings, Mississippi, vol. 1, page 37; *Southern Standard,* March 13, 1869; KKK Hearings, Mississippi, vol. 1, page 580. See also Forrest Cooper, "Reconstruction in Scott County," *Publications of the Mississippi Historical Society* 13 (1913): 128.

the Klan had "the determination of Satan not to yield" and spoke of its members as the "Arch Enemy" of mankind.[45] At one level, the emphasis contemporaries placed upon secrecy seems curiously misplaced. It was mostly the Ku Klux Klan that qualified as a secret society, and even here Klan members were often lax in keeping their signs and tactics undisclosed. In some ways, the Union Leagues and the Fenian movement were as much public and open as they were private and secret. Both organizations held national conventions and local mass meetings, published newspapers, and made the names of their officers easily accessible. The extent to which their enemies considered them secret societies is thus puzzling. Why did Americans in the post-Civil War era tend to see the Fenians, Union Leagues, and Ku Klux Klan in this way?

Part of the explanation lies in the association between secrecy and countersubversion. Before Reconstruction, Americans had regarded secret societies as dangerous enclaves of aristocratic privilege or unrepublican behavior. During the Civil War, Democrats in Jackson County, Indiana, declared their opposition to Know-Nothings, the Knights of the Golden Circle, and other secret political organizations, considering them to be "anti-Democratic in their tendencies, and nurseries and hotbeds of treason." The editor of the Democratic *Illinois State Register* explained that in contrast to concealment and deceit, true democracy "works in the light of day." These attitudes persisted into Reconstruction. Thurlow Weed, the venerable Whig editor from New York, likened the Union Leagues and other secret societies to "pestilential diseases." The editor of the Pittsburgh *Catholic* considered the possibility of permanent secret societies to be "the worst of all." With a long history of opposition to secret societies, the Roman Catholic Church in 1870 called for the excommunication of anyone who joined the Fenians.[46]

The preoccupation with secrecy and night suggests that the theme of countersubversion, which had a long history in America dating back to the Revolution, remained a potent element in the political culture of

45. William A. Moore, *Law and Order v. Kuklux Violence: Speech of Col. Wm. A. Moore, of Chowan, Delivered in the House of Representatives, January 19, 1870* (n.p., n.d.), 5.
46. Frank L. Klement, *The Copperheads of the Middle West* (Chicago: Univ. of Chicago Press, 1960), 163, 167; *Alabama Beacon*, May 25, 1867; Pittsburgh *Catholic*, April 6, 1867; Gibson, *Attitudes of the New York Irish*, 202.

Reconstruction. In this context, republicanism remains a helpful conceptual framework for understanding the discourse surrounding the Klan, the Leagues, and the Fenians.[47]

Americans typically considered secret societies inimical to the standards of republican government. "We hold it to be a manifest truth," proclaimed the conservative Constitutional Club of Mobile, "that secret, oath-bound, political societies are in direct antagonism to the principles and policy of a free government and a free people." The Raleigh *Standard* warned that in a country governed by secret societies, "there is always danger to life, liberty, and property." A Charleston newspaper considered them "of necessity at variance with a real self-government, and with Republican as distinguished from Monarchial institutions. . . . The reign in a Republic should be one of intelligence and honest opinion, and not of force, whether through secret organizations or through publicly displayed bayonets." The comments of an Alabama editor reveal seemingly paradoxical themes in republicanism, a hostility to aristocracy and a distrust of democracy: "Secret political societies," stated the Montgomery *Advertiser*, "form no part of the machinery of reconstruction as contemplated by the law; and is only a scheme gotten up to entrap those who are thought to be ignorant; and to promote the few at the expense of the many."[48]

Secret societies were harmful to a republican form of government because they threatened the independence of voters. "When men join a secret political society," explained the *Federal Union* of Georgia, "they give up their own judgment, their freedom of thought, and action, their conscience, and often their soul, into the keeping of others." The editor believed that the purpose of the Union Leagues was to control the

---

47. On countersubversion, see especially David Brion Davis, *Slave Power Conspiracy* and his edited collection of essays *The Fear of Conspiracy: Images of Un-American Subversion from the Revolution to the Present* (Ithaca: Cornell Univ. Press, 1971). Attention should still be paid to Richard Hofstader, *The Paranoid Style in American Politics and Other Essays* (New York: Knopf, 1966).

48. Mobile *Daily Advertiser and Register*, February 1, 1868; Newspaper Clippings, Ellison Summerfield Keitt Papers, South Caroliniana Library, University of South Carolina, Columbia, South Carolina; Montgomery *Advertiser*, quoted in Jacksonville *Republican*, May 11, 1867.

votes of freedmen. The imagery of slavery, so common in republican political discourse, also crept into the writing of southern white conservatives. One Alabama editor referred to Union Leagues as "slave pens." The attorney general of Virginia, speaking to a mass meeting in Richmond, warned of secret societies that would coerce blacks to vote a certain way. The freedman, he claimed, "has exchanged slavery of body for the more degrading slavery of mind." North Carolina Klan leader Randolph A. Shotwell believed that blacks were forced to join the Leagues "whereby they could be kept in subjection to their new masters." The Laurensville *Herald* explained similarly that blacks formed the "habit of screening one another" during slavery, a penchant that was only intensified "under the worse slavery of their Union Leagues." These comments reflect a conservative strain of republicanism which feared that a dependent population could be easily swayed by demagogues.[49]

In his influential essay on the sociology of secret societies, Georg Simmel argued that "structures, which place themselves in opposition to and detachment from larger structures in which they are actually contained, nevertheless repeat in themselves the forms of the greater structure." Simmel's insight allows us to look into the ways in which the organizational patterns of the Union Leagues, the Ku Klux Klan, and the

49. *Federal Union*, quoted in Natchez *Democrat*, May 2, 1867; Mobile *Daily Advertiser and Register*, September 3, 1868; Richmond *Whig and Public Advertiser*, April 16, 1867; J. G. de Roulhac Hamilton, ed., *The Papers of Randolph Abbott Shotwell* (Raleigh: North Carolina Historical Commission, 1929–1936), 2:263; Laurensville *Herald*, January 13, 1871.

The belief in conspiracy was a large part of the discourse of countersubversion in the early nineteenth century. In addition, sociologist Georg Simmel suggests that the emergence of secret societies "appears dangerously related to conspiracies against existing powers" (Simmel, "Sociology of Secrecy and Secret Societies," 498). Fenian leader W. R. Roberts, however, did present the enemy England as "an unscrupulous and unprincipled foe, skilled in all the arts of hypocrisy and deceit, and who resorted to every expedient which selfish and depraved minds could invent, to deceive a people who were obedient, trusting, and truthful" (*Lecture by W. R. Roberts, Delivered Before the Fenian Brotherhood of New York, at Cooper Institute, on Wednesday, Sept. 27th, 1865* [New York: J. Croft, 1865], 8). Gordon Wood has suggested that a belief in conspiracy rested on a view of causality that began losing force in the early nineteenth century. See "Conspiracy and the Paranoid Style: Causality and Deceit in the Eighteenth Century," *William and Mary Quarterly* 39 (1982): 401–441.

Fenians reflected the institutional forms and values of Reconstruction America. For example, the Fenians in 1865 patterned their national organization along the structural lines of the American government. Secret societies, with their regimented organizational patterns, ritualistic bonds, and use of disguises, also suggest what Simmel refers to as "a leveling of individuality." The precedence of the collective over the individual might have reflected the general reorientation in American thought during the Civil War era from individualism to organicism.[50]

In contrast, the Fenians, the Union Leagues, and the Ku Klux Klan might be viewed as "counter-institutions." Their mere existence testifies to needs of African Americans, Irish Americans, and southern whites that were not being met by the existing political order. As we have seen, their opponents presented them as subversive of American republican institutions. The discourse of countersubversion that runs through the literature about all three groups might indeed suggest a certain anxiety over fluidity and status that persisted in American culture since the Jacksonian era. Indeed, it is tempting to see the response to the Leagues and Klan as part of a paranoid style of American politics delineated by historian Richard Hofstader. Yet in several crucial ways, these groups did not fit what David Brion Davis termed "the typologies of American enemies." Unlike the Slave Power, Monster Bank, Masonry, or the Catholic Church, secret societies were not seen as privileged aristocratic oligarchies that would gain control of the federal government through surreptitious means. It is possible that Reconstruction witnessed a kind of reversal of this typology, demonizing groups at the margins who were claiming a place in the mainstream of American politics.[51]

---

50. Simmel, "Sociology of Secrecy and Secret Societies," 482; Clawson, "Fraternal Orders and Class Formation," 674. This shift in American culture is most convincingly presented in George M. Fredrickson, *The Inner Civil War: Northern Intellectuals and the Crisis of the Union* (New York: Harper and Row, 1965), and John Higham, *From Boundlessness to Consolidation* (Ann Arbor, Mich.: Clements Library, 1969).

51. Simmel sees secret societies as a response to the centralization of power ("Sociology of Secrecy and Secret Societies," 497). See also Davis, *Slavery Power Conspiracy*, 1, and Richard Hofstader, *The Paranoid Style in American Politics*.

Cover for the novel *The Fenian Chief, or The Martyr of '65*
Courtesy American Antiquarian Society

Union League insignia reproduced in the *South Carolina Leader*, March 31, 1866

Union League insignia reproduced in *The Great Republic*, September 27, 1866

"Ho! For Salt River!"
Reproduced with permission from the Gilder Lehrman Collection

"K.K.K. Shadowy Forms Awake!"
Broadside, Sanders Family Papers, Filson Historical Society, Louisville, Kentucky

3
NATIONALITY AND CLASS
The Land Question

Class relations provided one of the arenas in which Fenians, freedpeople, and southern whites fought for self-determination and a separate identity during Reconstruction. From W. E. B. Du Bois in the 1930s through Eric Foner in the 1980s, historians have shown that relations between labor and capital were essential in shaping the politics of the 1860s and 1870s. Various studies have documented how the conflicting material interests of planters and freedpeople influenced the transition from slave to free labor. Class has also become fundamental to understanding Reconstruction in the North. Historians now acknowledge that the growing class divisions in northern society helped set the parameters of Radical Reconstruction for the nation. Class conflict, David Montgomery suggested in his seminal study of the labor movement during Reconstruction, "was the submerged shoal on which Radical dreams foundered." The discovery of class in the mid-nineteenth-century North has helped rescue the Fenians from historiographical oblivion. Urban and working-class historians have seen in Irish American nationalism a manifestation of immigrant working-class discontent and the hardening of class lines in late-nineteenth-century American cities. These historiographical trends make class an essential element in any study of Reconstruction.[1]

---

1. Michael Fitzgerald, *The Union League Movement in the Deep South: Politics and Agricultural Change during Reconstruction* (Baton Rouge: Louisiana State Univ. Press, 1989), 4; Eric Foner, *Reconstruction: America's Unfinished Revolution, 1863–1877* (New York: Harper and Row, 1988), 428; David Montgomery, *Beyond Equality: Labor and the Radical Republicans, 1862–1872* (1967; reprint, Urbana: Univ. of Illinois Press, 1981), x. Class relations in the North are central to Foner's *Reconstruction,* especially chapters 10 and 11. On the importance of class in the transition from slave to wage labor, see the important statements by Armstead L. Robinson, "Beyond the Realm of Social Consensus: New Meanings of Reconstruction for American History," *Journal of American History* 68 (September

The relationship between class and nationalism merits investigation, although few guides for such an inquiry exist. The debate over Zionism in the early twentieth century led some Marxist thinkers to explore nationalism in class terms. Rosa Luxemburg believed that "the nationality question is, like all other social and political questions, primarily *a question of class interests.*"[2] Students of nineteenth-century labor history have tended to look at ethnicity in terms of class relations. Some have suggested that the significance of Irish American nationalism lay in its ideological contributions to working-class movements of the Gilded Age. Eric Foner argues that the Irish Land League pioneered in the articulation of a producerist, anti-monopoly ideology that influenced such labor organizations as the Knights of Labor. The Land League's critique of land ownership in Ireland was transformed in the United States into an attack on industrial monopolies.[3] There is indeed evidence to associate the Fenians with working-class formation and the labor movement of the 1860s. The Irish were prominent among the first leaders of labor organizations in Massachusetts after the Civil War. La-

---

1981): 276–297; Julie Saville, *The Work of Reconstruction: From Slave to Wage Laborer in South Carolina, 1860–1870* (New York: Cambridge Univ. Press, 1994); and Joseph P. Reidy, *From Slavery to Agrarian Capitalism in the Cotton Plantation South: Central Georgia, 1800–1880* (Chapel Hill: Univ. of North Carolina Press, 1992). For discussions of Fenianism in labor history, see Richard Schneirov, *Labor and Urban Politics: Class Conflict and the Origins of Modern Liberalism in Chicago, 1864–97* (Urbana: Univ. of Illinois Press, 1998), and John B. Jentz and Richard Schneirov, "Chicago's Fenian Fair of 1864: A Window into the Civil War as a Popular Political Awakening," *Labor's Heritage* 6 (winter 1995): 4–19.

2. Walker Connor, *The National Question in Marxist-Leninist Theory and Strategy* (Princeton: Princeton Univ. Press, 1984), 5; Mitchell Cohen, *Zion and State: Nation, Class, and the Shaping of Modern Israel* (New York: Columbia Univ. Press, 1992), 33.

3. See Eric Foner, "Class, Ethnicity, and Radicalism in the Gilded Age: The Land League in Irish-America," in *Politics and Ideology in the Age of the Civil War* (New York: Oxford Univ. Press, 1980), 150–200; Victor Walsh, "A Fanatic Heart: The Cause of Irish-American Nationalism in Pittsburgh during the Gilded Age," *Journal of Social History* 15 (winter 1981): 187–204; David Brundage, "Irish Land and American Workers: Class and Ethnicity in Denver, Colorado," in *"Struggle a Hard Battle": Essays on Working-Class Immigrants,* ed. Dirk Hoerder, 46–67 (DeKalb: Northern Illinois Univ. Press, 1986); Schneirov, *Labor and Urban Politics;* and Michael A. Gordon, *The Orange Riots: Irish Political Violence in New York City, 1870 and 1871* (Ithaca: Cornell Univ. Press, 1993).

bor newspapers of the period followed Fenian developments. The conventional wisdom among both labor and immigration historians is that Irish American nationalism was most pervasive among working-class immigrants.[4]

Yet a class interpretation of Fenianism goes only so far. In terms of chronology, most histories that connect Irish American nationalism to class conflict focus on the 1880s. The Irish Land League was most active in the early years of this decade, and the American labor movement was more organized and mature then than it had been shortly after the Civil War. In contrast, the height of Fenianism was reached in the 1860s. Ideologically, Fenian leaders tended to think of freedom in national rather than class terms. Their ideas are actually more akin to those of the workingmen parties of the 1830s, who saw labor struggles through the lens of republicanism, than to those of the labor leaders of the Gilded Age. Michael Scanlon, for example, in an editorial in the *Irish Republic* of Chicago, framed the conflict between labor and capital in terms of "the fight that has existed from time immemorial between Liberty and Tyranny." Reflecting antebellum labor protest, Scanlon then likened contemporary capitalists to southern slave drivers. John Mitchel, editor of the *Irish Citizen,* argued similarly that the solution to class warfare in a democracy was to be sought through politics. Since Mitchel had been pro-secessionist and continued his hostility to the Republicans through Reconstruction, he believed labor's grievances would be best redressed under the Democrats.[5]

Nonetheless, the role of class in the nationalist aspirations of Irish Americans, African Americans, and southern whites during Recon-

---

4. Montgomery, *Beyond Equality,* 126, 133; Kerby A. Miller, *Emigrants and Exiles: Ireland and the Irish Exodus to North America* (New York: Oxford Univ. Press, 1985), 342. Montgomery claims that the "great strength of Fenians was among industrial workers" (*Beyond Equality,* 127).

5. Even Montgomery acknowledged that the movement showed "scarcely a trace of awareness of 'labor issues'" (*Beyond Equality,* 127). The best discussion of Jacksonian labor ideology is Sean Wilentz, *Chants Democratic: New York City and the Rise of the American Working Class, 1788–1850* (New York: Oxford Univ. Press, 1984); *Irish Republic,* May 11, 1867; June 1, 1867; *Irish Citizen,* August 29, 1868.

struction deserves examination. One accessible way to explore this question is through land, an issue central to the struggles of all three groups. For the Fenians, land was a pillar of Irish nationalism. In 1867, a correspondent to the New York *Irish People* insisted that "the despotism of an alien landed proprietary is the main and radical grievance of Ireland."[6] Meanwhile, the land question became the locus of bitter economic and political struggles for freedpeople and southern whites in the post–Civil War South. It was a frequent point of contention between the Union Leagues and the Ku Klux Klan. When Republican Albion Tourgée organized Leagues in Caswell County, North Carolina, he apparently told the freedmen that he was sent by the government to see that they got forty acres of land. Indeed, other League meetings in North Carolina during 1867 and 1868 announced the policy of "forty acres in real estate for each negro." One former slave in South Carolina recalled hearing from a Union League leader that the freedmen would get land.[7] The efforts of blacks to acquire land often met with violent resistance from the Ku Klux Klan. William Coleman of Winston County, Mississippi, was beaten because he owned his own land. Charles H. Pearce, a minister in the Methodist Episcopal Church in Florida, testified before a congressional investigating committee that blacks were attacked on the land they owned. According to one Florida freedman, Klan members beat him while asking, "[D]idn't I know they didn't allow damned niggers to live on land of their own?" Land appears often enough in the sources for all three groups to merit a closer look.[8]

Historians have long noted the importance of land in Reconstruction. Marxist scholars writing in the 1930s maintained that the failure of land confiscation doomed the democratic potentials of Reconstruction. W. E. B. Du Bois, in his classic *Black Reconstruction in America*,

6. "W.M.C.," in *Irish People*, March 9, 1867.

7. Fitzgerald, *The Union League Movement in the Deep South*, 176; "Testimony of John G. Lea," page 1, Reconstruction Files, North Carolina Division of Archives and History, Raleigh, North Carolina; KKK Hearings, North Carolina, page 312; KKK Hearings, South Carolina, vol. 1, page 445. See also the testimony of John B. Gordon in KKK Hearings, Georgia, vol. 1, pages 306–307.

8. KKK Hearings, Mississippi, vol. 1, page 484; KKK Hearings, Florida, pages 167, 238; KKK Hearings, Florida, page 279. See also KKK Hearings, Georgia, vol. 1, page 213.

1860–1880, argued: "The Negroes were willing to work and did work, but they wanted land to work, and they wanted to see and own the results of their toil. It was here and in the west that a new vista opened. Here was a chance to establish an agrarian democracy in the South: peasant holders of small properties, eager to work and raise crops, amenable to suggestion and general direction."[9] Following the lead of Du Bois, Post-Revisionist historians writing in the past few decades have also emphasized the centrality of land to Reconstruction in the South. Viewing the freedmen as an incipient class as well as an emancipated race, they have seen in conflicts over land class struggles over the ownership of productive resources. For example, an historian of the Union Leagues in Alabama and Mississippi argues that the League "took on the character of an agrarian movement—indeed, it generated rural strife almost unequaled in southern history." Another historian discovered traditional patterns of agrarian protest in the efforts of South Carolina Sea Island freedpeople to hold on to the land promised them in the "Sherman Reserve." For these and other historians, emancipated slaves in the Reconstruction South behaved like proto-peasants in other emancipation societies who challenged the values of the marketplace. This chapter will approach the land question during Reconstruction from the perspective of movements for self-determination and ethnic autonomy. What meanings did the Fenians, African Americans, and southern whites attach to land? How was land incorporated into the construction of a collective identity?[10]

For the Fenians, land was a means of dramatizing English oppression of Ireland. In the Reconstruction South, land became a terrain on which freedpeople and southern white planters struggled to define the meaning and limits of freedom. Thus, land was instrumental in creat-

---

9. W. E. B. Du Bois, *Black Reconstruction in America, 1860–1880* (1935; reprint, New York: Atheneum, 1975), 67. Another Marxist historian, James Allen, claimed that "the landless Negro peasantry clung tenaciously to the idea that the land belonged to them." (James S. Allen, *Reconstruction: The Battle for Democracy, 1865–1876* [New York: International Publishers, 1937], 65).

10. Fitzgerald, *The Union League Movement in the Deep South*, 176. See also Julie Saville, "Rites and Power: Reflections on Slavery, Freedom and Political Ritual," *Slavery and Abolition* 20 (April 1999): 81–102.

ing a focal point for debating questions of identity and self-determination. Yet it fell short of becoming the sole basis for a separate nationality, for all three groups were firmly rooted in the political culture of republicanism and thus tended to see land ownership in individualistic rather than collective terms.[11]

Fenians frequently used the land question in their plea for Irish independence. At their meeting in Wappingers Falls, New York, in May 1868, the local Fenian circle declared that the Irish people "have been groaning under the unmerciful tyrant's heel of oppression for the past seven centuries." Another Fenian leader speaking to a circle in Houston stated similarly that "the sad recollections of the past cruelties of our oppressors" should "excite the indignation of the world." American Fenians knew their Irish history well. For centuries, Ireland had suffered as a result of English conquest and domination. The confiscation of Irish land and the oppression of the Irish peasantry accompanied Protestant persecution of Irish Catholics. After Oliver Cromwell wiped out the last vestiges of Catholic resistance in Ireland in 1658, Catholics were left with only 20 percent of Irish land. By 1700, that figure had dropped to 14 percent. It is estimated that by the 1870s fewer than sixty-five hundred English proprietors held more than 90 percent of Irish land. This concentration of land was a major reason for the emergence of the Fenian movement in Ireland in 1858. According to one historian, Fenianism was "an anti-landlord movement" with broad appeal among the rural working classes. Part of their attraction to the Irish peasantry was the promise of the restoration of ancient lands. In the Fenian rebellion of 1867, the provisional government declared that "The soil of Ireland belongs to . . . the Irish people, and to us it must be restored." James

---

11. See, for example, Reeve Huston, *Land and Freedom: Rural Society, Popular Protest, and Party Politics in Antebellum New York* (New York: Oxford Univ. Press, 2000), and Charles W. McCurdy, *The Anti-Rent Era in New York Law and Politics, 1839–1865* (Chapel Hill: Univ. of North Carolina Press, 2001). Good, basic studies of land policy in nineteenth-century America remain Benjamin Horace Hibbard, *A History of the Public Land Policies* (New York: Macmillian, 1924), and Roy Robbins, *Our Landed Heritage: The Public Domain, 1776–1936* (Princeton: Princeton Univ. Press, 1942).

Stephens, one of the founders of the Fenian movement and the editor of a Fenian newspaper in Dublin, insisted that in an independent republic Irish peasants would own their own land.[12]

Irish American Fenians regularly attacked the Irish land system. "The present system of land-tenure in Ireland is doomed to speedy destruction," explained the *Irish Citizen* of New York; "it is based upon the feudal system, to which Ireland was a stranger; and further embittered by repeated confiscation for 'rebellion.'" Another New York Fenian paper argued similarly that the first obstacle to Irish independence was "the aristocratic feudalism which is maintained by England in Ireland." The root of the problem was landlordism, a "hell-born system of robbery and tyranny." A mass meeting of Fenians in Troy, New York, complained that Irish farmers were abused by inhuman landlords. To the *Irish People* of New York, landlords were the "land Shylocks" who were "guilty before God and humanity." Fenian leaders maintained that English landlords were sustained by a sympathetic governing and legal system. "There are innumerable laws enacted for the protection and benefit of the landlords," insisted one correspondent to the *Irish People*, "and there is not one for the protection of the tenants." The same Fenian enthusiast insisted that "the landlord has made the laws of England for centuries and he has selfishly endowed his own class with unjust privileges." Tenants had few rights in a structure that favored English landlords over customary Irish practices of land tenure. For example, land proprietors in Ireland were given increasing powers in the early nineteenth century to evict tenants, restrict the subdivision of land, and limit joint tenancies. Evictions rose as the Great Famine approached. One estimate posits close to 150,000 evictions between 1839 and 1843. In

---

12. *Irish Citizen*, May 23, 1868; *Irish People*, March 9, 1867; Miller, *Emigrants and Exiles*, 21; E. D. Steele, *Irish Land and British Politics: Tenant-Right and Nationality, 1865–1870* (Cambridge: Cambridge Univ. Press, 1974), 3; Kerby A. Miller, "Class, Culture, and Immigrant Group Identity in the United States: The Case of Irish-American Ethnicity," in *Immigration Reconsidered: History, Sociology, and Politics*, ed. Virginia Yans-McLaughlin (New York: Oxford Univ. Press, 1990), 100; Paul Bew, *Land and the National Question in Ireland, 1858–82* (Dublin: Gill and Macmillan, 1978), 38–39; Steele, *Irish Land and British Politics*, 31; Bew, *Land and the National Question in Ireland*, 40. See also *Irish Republic*, July 20, 1867.

1867, the *Irish Republic* informed its readers that evictions were still of "daily occurrence."[13]

The role of land in the construction of Fenian Irish American nationalism is illustrated in a speech delivered by John Mitchel in 1868. Mitchel was a Unitarian from County Down in Ireland who had been active in the Repeal Movement of the 1840s. Inspired by the ferment of the European revolutions of 1848, he established the *United Irishmen,* which openly advocated revolution and Irish independence. He was found guilty of sedition by an English court and sentenced to imprisonment. Though he was not as active in the later Fenian crusade, Mitchel did take the Fenian oath and continued to support armed rebellion against England. Mitchel began his 1868 address with a comparative survey of land systems in Ireland and Europe. "Ireland is a bye-word, a proverb, an astonishment to them all," he insisted. The condition of the Irish tenant, Mitchel explained, would be "utterly unintelligible to most civilized Europeans." The tenant had no recourse to the law and could arbitrarily be driven from his land. In contrast, other nations in Europe possessed land systems Mitchel believed more compatible with republican ideology: "the land, divided into small properties, is in the absolute ownership of the peasantry; and that in other countries, custom, strong as law, and the universal recognition of man's title to live by independent industry on the soil that gave him birth, protect the rights of labor."

The resolution to the land problem, Mitchel insisted, was indispensable to the future of Irish nationalism: "Whether Ireland is to become a free nation or no, depends upon the way in which our garrison of farmers acquit themselves, and stand upon the rights of property." As Thomas Jefferson had done a generation before, Mitchel envisioned a republic that linked freehold tenure to national existence. "In vain shall we try to raise national spirit," he concluded, "if the very men who make the nation sink into paupers before our face. Paupers have

13. *Irish Citizen,* February 1, 1868; *Irish People,* March 3, 1867; *Irish Republic,* August 31, 1867; *Irish People,* March 23, 1867; January 26, 1867; Miller, *Emigrants and Exiles,* 41; *Irish People,* March 9, 1867; June 15, 1867; Miller, *Emigrants and Exiles,* 46, 213; *Irish Republic,* October 19, 1867. See also the comments of "W.M.C.," in *Irish People,* May 18, 1867.

no country, no rights, no duties." If Irish farmers were to be reduced to pauperism, Mitchel concluded, "there is an end of Ireland."[14]

The importance of land in Fenian ideology can also be seen in *The Fenian Chief, or The Martyr of '65*, a novel written by Henry Llewellyn Williams and published in New York in 1865. The hero of the story, a young Irishman named Maurice O'Connell, unintentionally murders a magistrate while protesting injustices faced by Irish farmers. O'Connell's primary antagonist in the novel is an English landlord named Beechcroft, the "rich landholder" who owned "acres and acres of well-cultivated ground: hills and dales, wood and water." The plight of the Irish is depicted by Maurice's grandmother, who tells him: "The child of an O'Connell, the widow of an O'Connell, the mother of an O'Connell has no land. They have taken and spoilt them." In his struggle for justice and eventual martyrdom, Maurice spells out the importance of land:

> Ours is a war with England and against those bastards of the soil who deny us *the bit of land*—the bit of land to be our own without dread of slaving for another—*the bit of land* which the poor man can cultivate when may be he has worked his twelve hours for his landlord, or that his wife and children can manage when he is absent. We may not have as our own a portion of the soil which was ALL our fathers; not as a gift, but as a reward of labour, the crown of industry; but, by all the winds in heaven, will have it, or the lives of those who keep their feet upon our necks and yet tell us that we are free![15]

For Fenian spokesmen, the issue of land was a powerful way to dramatize British despotism in Ireland and justify calls for a separate Irish nation. It would have undoubtedly brought back bitter memories to the immigrants of the Great Famine generation. Yet the land question was not a dominant theme in the writings of American Fenians in the

---

14. Stephen Gwynn, *History of Ireland* (New York: Macmillan, 1923), 445, 456, 468. Mitchel's speech appears in the *Irish Citizen*, February 1, 1868.

15. [Henry Llewelyn Williams], *The Fenian Chief; or, the Martyr of '65* (New York: Robert M. DeWitt, 1865), 28, 15, 54. This was a volume in DeWitt's Twenty Five Cent Novel series.

late 1860s. It would become far more central to the Irish National Land League, which appeared with significant force in the United States in 1880 and 1881.[16] The relative lack of attention to land in Fenian literature can be explained in several ways. Unlike southern whites and blacks, Irish Americans in the mid-nineteenth century had no immediate economic interest in land. Driven by the agricultural devastations of the Great Famine, Irish Americans settled primarily in urban areas, where the ownership of land was no longer a relevant nor feasible economic goal. Rather, Fenians in the United States placed more emphasis on political self-determination and national liberty.

The land question proved to be even more important in the struggles between former slaves and slaveholders. The African American desire for land during Reconstruction is well known. In a January 1865 meeting with Secretary of War Edwin M. Stanton and General William T. Sherman, the black minister Garrison Frazier contended that the "way we can best take care of ourselves is to have land, and turn it and till it by our own labor." To freedpeople and their Republican allies, black land ownership was essential to the success of Reconstruction. "If they [freedmen] would become independent," the Republican Charleston *Advocate* explained, "they must become their own employers. This can be done by directing all their efforts and means in the purchase of land. They should get farms of their own, and go to cultivating the soil." The New York *Tribune* affirmed the importance of proprietorship for ex-slaves: "Nothing else—not even education—is so urgent as this."[17]

The black desire for land created its own legends during Reconstruction. One of the most common was the idea that the freedmen were

---

16. On the Land League, see Norman D. Palmer, *The Irish Land League Crisis* (1940; reprint, New York: Octagon Books, 1978), and the very suggestive essay by Eric Foner, "Class, Ethnicity, and Radicalism in the Gilded Age." For a contemporary document, see *First Annual Convention of the Irish National Land League held at Buffalo, New York, January 12th and 13th, 1881* (Richmond: P. Keenan, 1881).

17. Ira Berlin, Joseph P. Reidy, and Leslie S. Rowland, eds., *Freedom's Soldiers: The Black Military Experience in the Civil War* (Cambridge: Cambridge Univ. Press, 1998), 148–149; Charleston *Advocate*, October 17, 1868; Du Bois, *Black Reconstruction*, 72; New York *Tribune*, quoted in Charleston *Daily Republican*, October 1, 1869.

given stakes to mark off their territories. In Panola County, Mississippi, freedmen planted stakes with small flags to mark off their desired land. Ambrose Wright, editor of the Augusta *Chronicle and Sentinel,* told a congressional investigating committee that northern carpetbaggers "would go down there and sell painted stakes to the negroes, and tell them that all they had to do was put down the stakes on their owners' farms, and forty acres of land would be theirs after the election." A New York physician living in postwar Georgia also recalled that red stakes were sold to the freedmen in the belief that it entitled them to forty acres of land. It led to the proverb: "De red stake am cold comfo't fo' de poo' mo'nah." These stakes "were all numbered and painted," recalled E. W. Seibels, secretary and treasurer of the Union Reform Party in South Carolina, "and the negroes were told that if they bought those stakes they could after this year go anywhere in the State, and wherever they found forty acres of land they wanted, all they had to do was drive down one of those stakes, and that would secure it to them." There were also stories that phony deeds were being sold with the promise of land ownership. The *Daily Newbern Commercial* warned its readers of a person "going through South Carolina collecting money from persons of color, and giving them in return certificates for land, which he says will be taken from the white people in about fifteen days and delivered to them." It should be noted that most of these stories are from sources typically hostile to the freedmen. Their veracity is thus questionable, though the stories themselves suggest the deep concerns raised by talk of black land ownership.[18]

Freedpeople in the Reconstruction South were perhaps the most insistent on land as the material basis of independence and security. Their determination for land was rooted in their experience as slaves, a republican tradition of yeoman proprietorship, and the free soil ideology of the Republican Party. Many historians have argued convincingly that the reluctance of Republicans both North and South to secure lands for

18. John W. Kyle, "Reconstruction in Panola County," *Publications of the Mississippi Historical Society* 12 (1912): 74; KKK Hearings, Georgia, vol. 1, page 272; Lyman W. Denton, M.D., "The Ku Klux Klan and the Days of Reconstruction, or In the Shadow of the Keenesaw," 5–6, typescript, Hargrett Rare Book and Manuscript Library, University of Georgia, Athens, Georgia; *Daily Newbern Commercial,* May 2, 1867.

the freedmen was one of the great failures of Reconstruction. Still, the hegemonic power of Republican ideas on land and southern Republican land policies led southern blacks toward an individualistic view of landholding and away from a collectivist one.

The desire for land in the Reconstruction South had varied sources. In some areas of the South, like the lowcountry of South Carolina and Georgia, slaves working under the task system earned time to cultivate small gardens and grow crops for both subsistence and the market. These provision gardens engendered a sense of proprietorship among freedpeople. Republican leader Carl Schurz, traveling through the South, observed that in some localities in South Carolina, "the idea has got into the heads of the negroes that the land belongs all to them." Discussing worker unrest on the rice plantations of the Georgia lowcountry, the Savannah *Herald* noted that the ex-slaves "thought they had a life estate in it."[19] In addition, the black experience under slavery could be interpreted from a labor theory of value to justify land confiscation. Since they had worked the land, they had acquired the rights to property. "The property which they hold was nearly all earned by the sweat of our brows—not theirs," announced an African American convention to the people of Alabama. As traitors, white landowners should be subject to confiscation. The black soldier Melton R. Linton explained similarly that "we raised them, and sent them to school, and bought their land, and now it is as little as they can do to give us some of their land—

---

19. Foner, *Reconstruction*, 104–105; Savannah *Herald*, quoted in Laurensville *Herald*, February 1, 1867; Foner, *Reconstruction*, 290. On the social and political implications of slave provision grounds, the seminal essay is Sidney W. Mintz and Douglas Hall, "The Origins of the Jamaican Internal Marketing System," *Yale University Publications in Anthropology* 57 (1960): 1–26. See also Ira Berlin and Philip D. Morgan, eds., *Cultivation and Culture: Labor and the Shaping of Slave Life in the Americas* (Charlottesville: Univ. of Virginia Press, 1993), part 3, and Dylan Penningroth, "Slavery, Freedom, and Social Claims to Property among African Americans in Liberty County, Georgia, 1850–1880," *Journal of American History* 84 (September 1997): 405–435.

It should be at least noted here that the idea of confiscating planter land also surfaced among southern whites. See, for example, William T. Auman and David S. Scarboro, "The Heroes of America in Civil War North Carolina," *North Carolina Historical Review* 58 (autumn 1981): 345, and Wayne Durrill, *War of Another Kind: A Southern Community in the Great Rebellion* (New York: Oxford Univ. Press, 1990).

be it little or much." One freedman in Alabama asked his African American audience if they did not "clear the white folks' land." Answering in the affirmative, voices in the crowd insisted as well that "we have a right to it!"[20]

The goal of independent proprietorship evident during slavery was consonant with and reinforced by Republican Party ideology. To attract both whites and blacks to their fledgling party, southern Republicans embraced a Jeffersonian yeoman vision for the reconstructed South. "The love of the soil," declared the Opelika, Alabama, *Era and Whig*, "is the most common passions of humanity." A system of small farms, explained the *South Carolina Republican*, "is worth more to this State than all the Northern capital we are straining after and begging for.... Small farms underline the daily growing riches, the civilization, and the enterprise of the Eastern and Middle States." The Wilmington *Daily Post*, one of the leading Republican newspapers in North Carolina, argued that land and home ownership accounted for the prosperity of New England since "a native pauper is scarcely seen in that section." African American leaders urged black landownership in these yeoman terms. "An intelligent farming population," reasoned the Mobile *Nationalist*, "is what is most wanted to secure the colored people their rights." The editor of this black newspaper explained that with farm ownership, "he can thereafter be independent, and accumulate rapidly, for he will get all the profit on what he raises." Free soil ideology exerted a powerful influence over the ways southern blacks approached the land question.[21]

Land was part of a larger Republican middle-class identity geared for an upwardly mobile society. In their attempt to "northernize" the South during Reconstruction, Republicans linked the ownership of land to a domestic ideal of the family farm. Lyman Trumbull, a key architect of Reconstruction legislation, said that "a homestead is worth more to these people than almost anything else: and if you will make the Negro an independent man, he must have a home." Southern Republicans

---

20. Montgomery *Daily State Sentinel*, May 21, 1867; *South Carolina Leader*, March 31, 1866; Foner, *Reconstruction*, 290.

21. Opelika (Alabama) *Era and Whig*, February 10, 1871; *South Carolina Republican*, December 19, 1868; Wilmington *Daily Post*, September 18, 1867; Mobile *Nationalist*, June 21, 1866. See also the *Weekly Mississippi Pilot*, December 4, 1869.

similarly associated land with the home and family. George Cox, speaking to his fellow freedmen in Tuscaloosa, Alabama, in 1867, argued that the Republican Party intended that "every man shall own a home for his family, where they may by industry surround themselves with all the comforts of life and be happy." However unrealistic, the Republican Houston *Union* urged every freedman to get a house: "Move your family into it, and begin to live as one who is responsible to God, and who is determined to show that slavery has not robbed him of all his manhood." Republicans spoke of land ownership in terms of middle-class values. The *Tri-Weekly Austin Republican* lauded Republican homestead plans so that every man "may live in peace, under his own vine and fig tree, and where he may lie down master and get up master of the soil necessary for the support of himself and his family." One South Carolinian optimistically told freedmen that they "will be the honored heads of happy families, in homes of your own, rearing your children in virtue and respectability."[22]

Some Republicans believed that the realization of a yeoman republic would require the division of large landholdings into smaller farms. "The owners of large estates," explained the Wilmington *Daily Post*, "should divide and subdivide their lands and sell them at reasonable rates to those who need them and can improve them." The Norfolk *Journal* concurred that "our system of cultivation must change from large farms to small." An editorial entitled "Land and Land-Holders in Alabama" that appeared in the Montgomery *Daily State Sentinel* in May 1867 illustrated the way in which these calls for land divisions reflected Republican political economy. "The system . . . which involved the feasibility of large plantations and numerous hands on each plantation is now impracticable," began the editor. Instead, large plantations should be divided into small farms of not more than one hundred acres that would be open for sale to both blacks and whites. The free soil vision was thus revised along biracial lines: "Now cut up these broad

---

22. William S. McFeely, *Yankee Stepfather: General O.O. Howard and the Freedmen* (New Haven: Yale Univ. Press, 1968), 213; *Daily State Sentinel*, June 24, 1867; Houston *Union*, January 6, 1869; *Tri-Weekly Austin Republican*, November 19, 1867; Charleston *Daily Republican*, August 31, 1869. See also the *Daily State Sentinel*, June 14, 1867.

acres; offer the colored man, as well as the white, an equal chance for success in life; let him know that his labor will redound to the benefit of himself and his children; that he can secure a home for those as dear to him as are the children of the white man to him; let him, in a word, see that he has a man's chance, and he will prove himself a man."[23]

The Republican-controlled federal government made several efforts at land reform for the freedmen, though most failed to achieve any significant redistribution of property. In 1865, the Freedmen's Bureau controlled almost a million acres of southern land that it leased to freedmen. General William T. Sherman, in his famous Special Field Order No. 15, reserved land along the coastal areas of South Carolina and Georgia for freed slaves. These lands, however, were restored to their plantation owners by President Andrew Johnson. In June 1866, Congress passed the Southern Homestead Act that set aside 44 million acres of land in the South for freedmen and white Unionists. Homestead laws were also popular in the southern states under Radical Reconstruction. In 1870, the Texas legislature passed a homestead act that allowed 160 acres of public domain land to every head of a family not already residing on a homestead. South Carolina established a Land Commission to facilitate the transfer to freedmen of land forfeited for nonpayment of property taxes. Union League leader Francis L. Cardozo praised the homestead measure as "a mark of advanced civilization." The Charleston *Daily Republican* explained that under the Land Commission, "every industrious man now in the State, or who will hereafter come with us, will be able to get a home of his own, a farm to cultivate, and reap the full benefits of his own industry." To further encourage land ownership among freedmen, Republican legislatures in South Carolina, Georgia, Texas, and Virginia passed homestead exemption laws that protected land from the claims of creditors.[24]

23. Wilmington *Daily Post*, August 25, 1867; Norfolk *Journal*, quoted in Vicksburg *Republican*, January 14, 1868; *Daily State Sentinel*, May 18, 1867. See also Dan T. Carter, *When the War Was Over: The Failure of Self-Reconstruction in the South, 1865–1867* (Baton Rouge: Louisiana State Univ. Press, 1985), 114–115.

24. James M. McPherson, *Ordeal by Fire: The Civil War and Reconstruction* (New York: Knopf, 1982), 506–507; Foner, *Reconstruction*, 162–169; McPherson, *Ordeal by Fire*, 58; Jerrell H. Shofner, *Nor Is It Over Yet: Florida in the Era of Reconstruction, 1863–1877*

White planters strongly resisted these efforts at creating a black yeomanry. Emmanuel Fortune, an African American carpenter from Jackson County, Florida, believed that the white refusal to sell small quantities of land was "the great obstacle in the way of colored people getting land." Charles H. Pearce, a minister in Florida, complained similarly that large landowners were refusing to sell their lands. The registrar at the U.S. land office in Jefferson County explained that not only would whites generally not sell land to blacks but that they set the price so high as virtually to exclude blacks from purchasing land. Sadly, the dream of an independent black yeomanry never materialized in the post–Civil War South. Of 23,609 successful applicants for homesteads in the South under Reconstruction, only 4,000 were freedman families.[25]

The most ambitious attempt to make the freedmen independent yeoman farmers involved the leasing and selling of confiscated lands in the former slaveholding South. In their efforts to become landowners, ex-slaves found allies among Radical Republicans like George W. Julian of Indiana and Thaddeus Stevens of Pennsylvania. Throughout Reconstruction, Stevens and Julian were determined advocates of confiscating

---

(Gainesville: Univ. Presses of Florida, 1974), 134–135; W. C. Nunn, *Texas under the Carpetbaggers* (Austin: Univ. of Texas Press, 1962), 38; F. L. Cardozo, *Address before the Grand Council of the Union Leagues at Their Annual Meeting, held July 27, 1870, by Hon. F. L. Cardozo, President* (Columbia, S.C.: John W. Denny, 1870), 11; Charleston *Daily Republican,* September 6, 1869. For the homestead exemption laws, see Francis Butler Simkins and Robert Woody, *South Carolina during Reconstruction* (1932; reprint, Gloucester, Mass.: Peter Smith, 1966), 100; Elizabeth Studley Nathans, *Losing the Peace: Georgia Republicans and Reconstruction, 1865–1871* (Baton Rouge: Louisiana State Univ. Press, 1968), 64; Nunn, *Texas under the Carpetbaggers,* 38; and Richard Lowe, *Republicans and Reconstruction in Virginia, 1856–70* (Charlottesville: Univ. Press of Virginia, 1991), 139. On the Southern Homestead Act, see also Warren Hoffnagle, "The Southern Homestead Act: Its Origin and Operation," *Historian* 32 (August 1970): 612–629, and Michael L. Lanza, *Agrarianism and Reconstruction Politics: The Southern Homestead Act* (Baton Rouge: Louisiana State Univ. Press, 1990). For background on the constitutional conventions, see Jack B. Scroggs, "Carpetbagger Constitutional Reform in the South Atlantic States, 1867–1868," *Journal of Southern History* 27 (November 1961): 475–493, and Eric Foner, "Politics and Ideology in the Shaping of Reconstruction: The Constitutional Conventions of 1867–1869," in *The Evolution of Southern Culture,* ed. Numan V. Bartley (Athens: Univ. of Georgia Press, 1988).

25. KKK Hearings, Florida, pages 97, 168, 101; McFeely, *Yankee Stepfather,* 215.

the land of ex-slaveholders and distributing them in forty-acre plots to the freedmen. Thaddeus Stevens's speech on confiscation remained quite popular among blacks in the Reconstruction South. Stevens himself was said to be the leading presidential choice of Republican freedmen.[26]

Planters and other conservative whites throughout the South shuddered at the mention of confiscation. "Even the *impression*," observed the New Bern *Republican* in 1867, "that the lands and property of thousands of leading participants in the late rebellion may yet be liable to confiscation, has caused, and still causes deep suspense and anxiety." The idea of confiscation, noted the Shelbyville *Republican* in 1866, "may shock us here as a very great outrage upon our *constitutional* rights." The *Alabama Beacon* likened confiscation to highway robbery. "If there is one thing that the former slaveholders of this State dislike more than another," F. L. Cardozo told a South Carolina audience, "it is to see their former slaves become the owners of land, and thereby independent." The Austin *Daily State Gazette* warned: "The negroes are without land, and with little or no personal property; they will legislate to get both." Jonathan Worth of North Carolina feared that with black suffrage, African Americans and poor white farmers would cooperate to appropriate plantation lands. Benjamin F. Perry of South Carolina worried that laws staying the collection of personal debts and repudiation of the state debt would lead to a division of lands and a democratization of property ownership. White landowners in the South sought to retain control of their property. Merchants in upcountry Georgia and Democrats throughout the state, for instance, condemned the homestead exemption provision in the Georgia constitution.[27]

---

26. See, for example, Montgomery *Daily State Sentinel,* June 19, 1867, and Natchez *Democrat,* September 11, 1867. Confiscation is discussed in most studies of the Reconstruction South. See, for example, Foner, *Reconstruction,* 235–236, 309–311, and Claude F. Oubre, *Forty Acres and a Mule: The Freedmen's Bureau and Black Land Ownership* (Baton Rouge: Louisiana State Univ. Press, 1978).

27. New Bern *Republican,* May 4, 1867; Shelbyville (Tennessee) *Republican,* October 10, 1866; *Alabama Beacon,* May 25, 1867; Cardozo, *Address before the Grand Council of the Union Leagues,* 11; Austin *Daily State Gazette,* November 6, 1867; J. G. de Roulhac Hamilton, ed., *The Correspondence of Jonathan Worth,* 2 vols. (Raleigh: Edwards and

Southern conservatives worried that the confiscation of land portended a more general leveling process. "Agrarianism in its worst shape, will soon rear its hideous form among us," warned the Montgomery *Mail*. Discussing an order to put labor liens upon crops, the conservative Tuscaloosa *Independent Monitor* argued that the measure was "designed to deprive the landowners at the South of more privileges than were the Agrarian laws of Rome adopted to equalize the patricians and plebeians." Benjamin F. Perry feared that "agrarianism at home" would result in "a bloody contest of extermination to one race or the other." A North Carolina state senator was alarmed at the prospect of being "overwhelmed by the combination of Southern radicalism and free negroism."[28]

The question of confiscation forced some Republicans to confront the internal contradictions of their ideology. The possible expropriation of land challenged their beliefs in the sanctity of private property and the dictates of the Constitution. On the other hand, denying land to the freedmen might be difficult to justify considering the large land grants Republicans had been giving to railroads. Nonetheless, southern Republican leaders seeking white support were understandably reluctant to push confiscation. Most Republican spokesmen in the South in the late 1860s did not favor it. Henry McNeill Turner told a mass meeting in Macon, Georgia, that he was opposed to confiscation and did not want the whites to lose their property, which he believed were "the views of the majority of colored men." A judge addressing a freedmen's meeting in Edgefield, South Carolina, insisted that confiscation was "a myth" that "had no real, tangible, visible existence."[29]

These comments exposed the assumptions underpinning Republican free soil ideology. Like any farmer in an open and mobile society, the

---

Broughton Print Company, 1909), 2:1048; *Southern Watchman*, May 15, 1867; Steven Hahn, *The Roots of Southern Populism: Yeoman Farmers and the Transformation of the Georgia Upcountry, 1850–1890* (New York: Oxford Univ. Press, 1983), chapter 5; Nathans, *Losing the Peace*, 86. See also Carter, *When the War Was Over*, 103.

28. Tuscaloosa *Independent Monitor*, October 9, 1867; November, 20, 1867; Perry quoted in *Southern Watchman*, May 15, 1867; Raleigh *Daily Standard*, March 6, 1867.

29. Macon *Daily Telegraph*, August 28, 1867, Newspaper Clippings, Henry P. Farrow Papers, Hargrett Rare Book and Manuscript Library, University of Georgia, Athens, Georgia; Edgefield (South Carolina) *Advertiser*, July 17, 1867.

freedmen would have to earn their lands. Freedpeople who gathered for a meeting in Edgefield District, South Carolina, were told not to expect land division or confiscation. If the freedmen wanted land, "they must assuredly do so by hard work, and with their own money." Similarly, Colonel David Heaton of New Bern, North Carolina, warned freedmen not to listen to "idle stories about confiscation and free gifts of property." The primacy Republicans attached to property rights also worked against confiscation. As explained by Alabama Union League organizer John C. Keffer, it "would be directly contrary to its principles to take away property from one set of men and give it to another set of men." Conservative southern whites were obviously relieved by the Republican hesitation to press for confiscation. When the northern black leader John Langston advised freedmen to work for their land, the Natchez *Democrat* considered his comments "particularly sensible and explicit." But the negative response of freedmen testified to their continuing desire for land. When Union League organizer Henry Farrow told a group of freedmen "to look for no confiscation—that by the sweat of their brows they must obtain property," they were clearly disappointed. At a Republican meeting in Pratville, Alabama, in 1868, a speaker warned the assembled freedmen not to expect land after the election. "Many of the negroes," reported the local newspaper, "looked much crestfallen after this announcement, and seemed as if they did not care to hear anymore."[30]

The freedmen's desire for land, phrased in individualistic terms that reflected the powerful influence of Republican thinking, inhibited a class vision of land. At the same time, there is suggestive—if limited—evidence that freedpeople in some parts of the Reconstruction South glimpsed the possibility of land as a means of collective self-determination. A correspondent for the New York *Herald*, following an inspection tour

30. Edgefield (South Carolina) *Advertiser*, July 17, 1867; New Bern *Republican*, June 18, 1867; *Daily State Sentinel*, May 23, 1867; Natchez *Democrat*, July 6, 1867; Cartersville (Georgia) *Express*, August 23, 1867; Newspaper Clippings, Farrow Papers, Hargrett Rare Book and Manuscript Library, University of Georgia, Athens, Georgia; Cherokee *Georgian*, August 23, 1867, Newspaper Clippings, Farrow Papers; Mobile *Daily Advertiser and Register*, February 1, 1868; *Daily Chronicle* (Augusta, Georgia), May 11, 1867, in Newspaper Clippings, Farrow Papers.

by Generals John Steedman and James Scott Fullerton in the Georgia Sea Islands in 1866, reported that "the territorial aspirations of the negroes received their richest development and culminated in the virtual establishment of a NIGGER EMPIRE. . . ." The land question was particularly acute in the lowcountry of South Carolina and Georgia, a region set apart from other slaveholding areas by distinctive demographic, environmental, and economic characteristics. These rich coastal lands of the Deep South had supported the cultivation of rice and Sea Island cotton. Slave labor on lowcountry plantations was completed by the task system, which allowed slaves time to cultivate small garden patches and grow crops for subsistence and even for sale in the market. This pattern continued after the war, when freed men and women were able to cultivate their provision gardens, sell their produce, and even acquire property. "Each family has a certain patch of ground for itself," Carl Schurz observed while visiting a plantation near Beaufort, South Carolina, "on which vegetables and sometimes cotton are raised." These conditions led to an unusually strong attachment to land in the lowcountry, intensified by the use of land set aside by General Sherman. The expropriation of land from the freedmen and the economic difficulties that plagued rice planting after the Civil War created the conditions for conflict. Labor strife was particularly acute in the lowcountry. In January 1867, black workers on one plantation along the Back River near Savannah refused to sign contracts for the coming year in hopes of gaining land.[31]

31. Edwin D. Hoffman, "From Slavery to Self-Reliance: The Record of Achievement of the Freedmen of the Sea Island Region," *Journal of Negro History* 41 (January 1956), 29; William J. Cooper Jr. and Thomas E. Terrill, *The American South: A History* (New York: Knopf, 1990), 186–187; Joseph H. Mahaffey, ed., "Carl Schurz's Letters from the South," *Georgia Historical Quarterly* 35 (September 1951): 230, 241; Foner, *Reconstruction*, 51; Hoffman, "From Slavery to Self-Reliance," 32. On the Combahee strikes for higher wages in 1876, see Eric Foner, *Nothing but Freedom: Emancipation and Its Legacy* (Baton Rouge: Louisiana State Univ. Press, 1983), chapter 3. Further background sources on the lowcountry include Philip D. Morgan, *Slave Counterpoint: Black Culture in the Eighteenth-Century Chesapeake and Lowcountry* (Chapel Hill: Published for the Omohundro Institute of Early American History and Culture, Williamsburg, Va., by the Univ. of North Carolina Press, 1998); Peter A. Coclanis, *The Shadow of a Dream: Economic Life and Death in the South Carolina Low Country, 1670–1920* (New York: Oxford Univ. Press, 1989); and Charles W. Joyner, *Down by the Riverside: A South Carolina Slave Community* (Urbana: Univ. of Illinois Press, 1984).

The peculiar history of the lowcountry helps explain the tenacity with which the freedmen in that region insisted on their right to the land. As early as July 1865, a prominent rice planter in South Carolina complained that on the Cooper River plantations the freedpeople were "carrying on things with a high hand—claiming every thing as belonging to them." Two years later, a group of concerned planters wrote military authorities in Savannah that the freedmen were "impressed with the belief that the lands are to be divided among them." The Savannah *Daily News and Herald* reported similarly that ex-slaves on one plantation "said the lands belonged to them; they had paid taxes to the Government, and that they would not leave."[32]

South Carolina blacks fought aggressively to retain the Sea Island grant. In an editorial entitled "The Island Lands" written in October 1865, the editor of the black newspaper *South Carolina Leader* argued: "An experiment is being tried here in reference to the employment of free labor, and the ability of the colored race to take care of themselves. Sufficient time has not been given to demonstrate the feasibility of the former, or establish the fact of the latter, to the minds of all men; and we say let the experiment go on." He maintained that ex-slaves accepted these lands "with the understanding that they were to be kept in possession of them." Because of the strong commitment to the Sherman grant by Freedmen's Bureau officials O. O. Howard and Rufus Saxton, lowcountry planters began to appeal directly to President Andrew Johnson for the restoration of their lands. By November 1865, Sea Island planters were pushing hard to get their lands restored.[33]

The way in which land could support the separatist aspirations of freedmen can be glimpsed in the violence that broke out on several rice plantations along the Ogeechee River in coastal Georgia in late 1868 and

---

32. Elias Horry Deas to his daughter, July 15, 1865, Deas Papers, South Caroliniana Library, University of South Carolina, Columbia, South Carolina; *South Carolina Leader*, October 21, 1865; Savannah *Daily News and Herald*, November 16, 1867; January 21, 1869.

33. *South Carolina Leader*, October 21, 1856; William Whaley to [J.J.?], July 18, 1865, Jenkins Papers, South Caroliniana Library, University of South Carolina, Columbia, South Carolina; McFeely, *Yankee Stepfather*, 220. On the restitution process, see the Jenkins Papers at the South Carolinaina Library and the Joseph Frederick Waring Papers, Georgia Historical Society, Savannah, Georgia.

early 1869. The incident was triggered by the arrest of the black president of a local Union League who was actively organizing blacks in the plantation districts around Savannah. In seeking an explanation for the violence, the Savannah *Republican* maintained that "the class of negroes who have been tampered with and brought under the influence of the organizers of what are called the loyal leagues, were passing over the river, with arms in their hands, to join the robbers residing on this side of the river." The Ogeechee uprising took the form of a general strike. "They will not work," complained the Savannah *Daily News and Herald*, "and by threats and violence prevent those who are willing to labor, from serving their employers, their object being to prevent the rice crop from being secured by day that they may steal it at night." Rice was in fact taken from plantations. Homes were sacked and the large Middleton and Tucker plantations were targeted for more violence. Over one hundred people were arrested for assault, robbery, and other crimes, including what one Augusta newspaper called "insurrection and rebellion."

Land was foremost in the minds of the Ogeechee rebels. According to one planter in the area, the freedmen on the Middleton plantation "became dissatisfied with anyone having possession of those places, they having had them pretty much to themselves. I heard them say that they had a right to the lands." The Savannah *Morning News* reported that black leaders in Washington had assured the insurrectionists that once they had "captured and held the country" they would be supported in their claims.[34]

34. Edmund L. Drago, *Black Politicians and Reconstruction in Georgia: A Splendid Failure* (Baton Rouge: Louisiana State Univ. Press, 1982), 78; Savannah *Republican*, January 5, 1869; E. Merton Coulter, *Negro Legislators in Georgia during the Reconstruction Period* (Athens: Georgia Historical Quarterly, 1968), 79; Drago, *Black Politicians and Reconstruction in Georgia*, 123–124. The unrest can be followed in the January 5–7, 1869, Charleston *Daily Republican*. The disturbances were noted by other newspapers in the South, for example the Tallahassee *Weekly Floridian*, January 5, 1869. For some economic background of the Ogeechee disturbances, see James M. Clifton, "Twilight Comes to the Rice Kingdom: Postbellum Rice Culture on the South Atlantic Coast," *Georgia Historical Quarterly* 62 (summer 1978): 146–154, and Thomas F. Armstrong, "From Task Labor to Free Labor: The Transition Along Georgia's Rice Coast, 1820–1880," *Georgia Historical Quarterly* 64 (winter 1980): 432–447. African American women were often quite active in these events. See

These lowcountry insurgents seem to have been seeking territory for self-determination. The Savannah *Morning News,* for example, worried that the rice workers "seem determined to take forcible possessions of the lands and substance of the whites and drive them from the country." One overseer on a plantation reported that between two and three hundred blacks threatened to kill him while they proclaimed that *"no white man should live between the two Ogeechees."* George Baxley, a white storeowner on the Ogeechee road, was beaten by a group of African American insurgents. While lying in a ditch, Baxley overheard a group of freedpeople say "that no white man should ever live on the Ogeechee neck again."[35]

The Reconstruction South furnishes other examples of land as a basis for black collective self-determination. On St. Simon's Island in the Georgia lowcountry, Union League leader Tunis Campbell organized farmers into the Belle Ville Farmers Association and negotiated with the owner for land. Campbell settled about 127 people on a colony called Belle Ville Hundred with the idea of "securing to themselves and their children good and comfortable homes." Davis Bend in Mississippi was a better-known experiment. In 1863, the U.S. government leased land near Vicksburg formerly owned by Jefferson Davis and his brother, Joseph, to a group of freedmen. Under the leadership of Benjamin Montgomery, the Davis Bend community became economically viable and politically self-sufficient. It had its own system of government and earned a profit of $160,000 by 1865.[36]

Land was as important to southern whites during Reconstruction as it was to freedpeople. As the basic economic resource in the predominantly

---

Leslie A. Schwalm, "'Sweet Dreams of Freedom': Freedwomen's Reconstruction of Life and Labor in Lowcountry South Carolina," *Journal of Women's History* 9 (spring 1997): 9–38.

35. Savannah *Morning News,* December 31, 1868; January 1, 1869. See also the similar statement of a white storeowner on the Ogeechee road reported in the Savannah *Morning News,* January 4, 1869. I want to be careful here not to confuse nationalism with community self-determination. In other parts of the Reconstruction South, African Americans made similar attempts at collective land ownership. For coastal Georgia, see Russell Duncan, *Freedom's Shore: Tunis Campbell and the Georgia Freedmen* (Athens: Univ. of Georgia Press, 1986), especially 38–41.

36. On Campbell, see Duncan, *Freedom's Shore;* and Foner, *Reconstruction,* 58–60.

agricultural South, it was the main avenue to economic security and social and political power. But land was also a way for elite whites to construct an identity in the postwar South. Like their former slaves, southern planters and white farmers spoke of land in individualistic terms. They, too, had imbibed the Jeffersonian ideal of an independent citizenry based on the ownership of land. The resistance of southern planters to the economic aspirations of the freedmen is well known. Looked at from the perspective of separatism and ethnic nationalism, what merits another look is the role of land in the construction of a collective racial identity.

A strong sense of anxiety runs through the writings by and about southern white landowners after the Civil War. At first glance, it is tempting to dismiss these fears as unfounded. After all, by the end of the 1870s planters had generally retained control of land and labor and had successfully weathered assaults from African Americans, Independents, and Greenbackers. Yet from the vantage point of early Reconstruction, their feelings of insecurity were not without foundation. The economic problems they faced significantly influenced the meaning southern planters attached to land.

The basic outlines of postwar economic change are now well known. The demise of slavery led to fundamental changes in the labor system of the former slaveholding states. Gang labor gave way to experiments in wage labor that were ultimately replaced by tenant farming and sharecropping. Land ownership in the Reconstruction South remained concentrated in a few hands. James Chesnut testified before a congressional committee investigating the Ku Klux Klan that land in South Carolina was held in generally large tracts of between three thousand and six thousand acres primarily by those who held it before the war. Large plantations in the cotton- and sugar-growing areas of the South survived the Civil War. Between 1860 and 1880, the number of plantations in Louisiana actually increased by 287 percent.[37]

---

37. KKK Hearings, South Carolina, vol. 1, page 470; Cardozo, *Address before the Grand Council of the Union Leagues*, 13; Bernard Bailyn, et al., *The Great Republic: A History of the American People*, 4th ed. (Lexington, Mass: D. C. Heath, 1992), 2:18. On the economic transformation of the South, the best place to begin is Roger L. Ransom and Richard Sutch, *One Kind of Freedom: The Economic Consequences of Emancipation* (Cambridge: Cambridge Univ. Press, 1977). A valuable guide to the literature is Harold Woodman, "Sequel

Nonetheless, southern planters faced a number of challenges. One of the most persistent was the declining value of land. In Morgan County, Georgia, for instance, land was being sold for three-eighths of its assessed value. Land assessed at $2 per acre was selling for 75 cents per acre. A planter in Chattooga County, Georgia, was offered $30,000 for his land in 1866. By the next year, he was complaining that "the same lands will not bring more than one third that value." The values of livestock and farm implements dropped similarly.[38] The declining price of cotton only worsened matters. The Augusta *Chronicle and Sentinel* lamented that the price of upland cotton had fallen below the cost of production. A Texas correspondent to the Columbus (Georgia) *Sun* warned in July 1866 that the prospect for cotton was "anything but flattering." Anticipating the ideas of the Grange and the Populists, cotton planters in Bullock County, Alabama, met in September 1868 to discuss plans for storing cotton and hence keeping it off a declining market.[39]

Planters also faced pressure from southern whites other than Republicans to end the antebellum system of large landholdings. "The South must divide to prosper!" proclaimed the Charleston *Mercury* in 1867: "Wherever practicable, plantations must be divided into farms of small area, so that every acre of the soil may be cultivated." The Mobile *Tribune* also urged landholders to "sub-divide your lands into small farms, and give encouragement to white labor, and you will soon see your land all well-cultivated and yourselves handsomely benefited by the operation." The call for the division of large plantations was echoed by upcountry farmers, perhaps resentful of the monopoly and power exercised by

---

to Slavery: The New History Views the Postbellum South," *Journal of Southern History* 43 (November 1977): 523–554. Roger W. Shugg, "Survival of the Plantation System in Louisiana," *Journal of Southern History* 3 (August 1937): 311–325, and Jonathan Wiener, *Social Origins of the New South: Alabama, 1860–1885* (Baton Rouge: Louisiana State Univ. Press, 1978), provide evidence for the continued concentration of land ownership.

38. John Durdin to Benjamin Conley, March 3, 1868, Conley Papers, Georgia Department of Archives and History, Atlanta, Georgia; John Kincaid to E. K. Anderson, January 5, 1867, Kincaid-Anderson Family Papers, South Caroliniana Library, University of South Carolina, Columbia, South Carolina.

39. *Central Georgian*, January 22, 1868; Macon *Daily Telegraph*, July 6, 1866; Cecil E. McNair, "Reconstruction in Bullock County," *Alabama Historical Quarterly* 15 (spring 1953), 107.

large planters, especially in the lowcountry. The Yorkville *Enquirer* of South Carolina believed that "we would be a happier people if we would abandon all our notions about large farms and cultivate small patches." Farming on a large scale, the editor claimed, was no longer economically feasible. The division of lands was the theme of several editorials by Colonel D. H. Jacques, one of the coeditors of the *Rural Carolinian* and a future leader of the Granger movement in South Carolina. "Our great farms must be subdivided," Jacques wrote, "and the smaller area cultivated made more productive and valuable by drainage, deepculture, manuring and other improvements." An "UP COUNTRY FARMER" complained in the same journal that the best lands of the state were "locked up in the hands of a few men that were once 'big planters'" and therefore no longer contributing to the prosperity of South Carolina.[40]

Because of the importance of land in an agricultural slaveholding society, southern planters rested much of their identity on its independent ownership. After the Civil War, they clung to both their land and to Jeffersonian ideals. In an agrarian society, land was a source of virtue. A farmer from Union Springs, Alabama, called farming "the most delightful and pleasant occupation . . . in which a person can be engaged." It provided the basis for that essential republican virtue of autonomy: "Each planter feels and knows his entire independence; this is certainly a source of the most supreme satisfaction." An aggrieved landowner from Williamstown, South Carolina, writing Governor Robert K. Scott to stop proceedings against his farm, connected his ownership of land to his independence before the war. The farming journal *Southern Field and Factory* called farmers "more powerful conservators of liberty than frowning battlements or bristling bayonets."[41]

The meaning of land to the southern planter class is not easily recoverable. Critics of former slaveholders noted how land was the founda-

---

40. Charleston *Mercury*, quoted in *Gadsden Times*, February 22, 1867; Mobile *Tribune*, quoted in *Alabama Beacon*, March 2, 1867; Yorkville (South Carolina) *Enquirer*, November 2, 1870; *Rural Carolinian* 1 (November 1869): 113; (May 1870): 521.

41. *Messenger and Advertiser* (Troy, Alabama), May 11, 1869; Rev. C. P. Dean to Robert K. Scott, July 29, 1868, Robert K. Scott Papers, South Carolina Department of Archives and History, Columbia, South Carolina; *Southern Field and Factory* 1 (June 1871): 1. See also the Mobile *Tribune*, quoted in the *Alabama Beacon*, March 2, 1867.

tion of status in what they believed had been a hierarchical society. The *Southern Republican* explained that the "true Southern planter hates to part with his lands. They are all that is left to him of his former greatness, and he hangs on to them with the same tenacity that he holds on to life, and would rather forego many comforts of life than sell." The agricultural journal *Turf, Field, and Farm* sarcastically acknowledged that land division would hurt "the honorable pride of the holder to alienate even a portion of his ancestral acres." The meaning of land to former slaveowning planters is further revealed in a petition sent by a group of South Carolina lowcountry planters to President Andrew Johnson in September of 1865 to recover lands in Edisto, St. John's, and Wadmalaw Island, South Carolina, that had been part of the Sherman Reserve. Land connoted domesticity, they claimed—a belief similar to the Republican notions held by freedmen. The petition referred to "their *lands* of those Islands which are now doubly dear to them, from their having lived there all their lives." Land was given meaning through personal history. The Sea Islands, the petitioners maintained, were "the places of their birth, the scenes of their childhood & subsequent maturity & (with many of them) of their old age." These lands also included family graveyards "in which are deposited the last remains of those whom they tenderly loved when alive, & whose memory they reverently & affectionately cherish, now dead."[42]

The significance of land to former planters during Reconstruction is also illustrated in an address delivered by Willoughby Newton before the Virginia State Agricultural Society in November 1866. Newton, who fancied himself an agricultural reformer before the Civil War, was the president of the State Agricultural Society. In the 1840s, he had served as a Whig congressman from Westmoreland County, Virginia. His strong states' rights views had led him in the late 1850s to support secession. Newton shared the worldview of the antebellum planter aristocracy of Tidewater Virginia. In his opposition to the breakup of large planta-

---

42. *Southern Republican,* March 24, 1869; *Southern Field and Factory* 1 (February 1871): 58; "Petition to Andrew Johnson from Sea Island Planters, 23 September, 1865," Edward M. Stoeber Papers, South Caroliniana Library, University of South Carolina, Columbia, South Carolina.

tions into small farms, he revealed how land had been the material base for an elite class. Division would mean that "the halls of ancient hospitality must be abandoned; the elegance and refinement of manners that heretofore distinguished the families of the country must retire to the cities and towns, and the race of country gentlemen become extinct." The plantation meant "ample space for the development of the individual man." It had given rise to a social type, "the race of country gentlemen," which had made the name of Virginia immortal. Since land had made a landowning class possible, Newton urged his fellow planters to "preserve our lands, and with them our ancient manners and social institutions which came to us from our British ancestors." Newton's elitism was filled with the imagery of the Jeffersonian yeoman. Ironically for Newton, any land conveyed to its owner a certain status. "Whether their possessions be great or small, if endowed with virtue and intelligence, they are already Nature's noblemen, and they will be so regarded by all ages and countries." Newton also stated the connection between land, family, and perpetuity: "Whether it be the humble cottage or the stately mansion that has sheltered you and your fathers, let it continue to shelter your children and your children's children. Teach the rising generation to preserve the landmarks, to venerate the 'patrimonial oaks,' and have each shrub and tree planted by their fathers as if it were a sentient being. You will thus cherish a sentiment stronger than law, by which your homes will be preserved to your posterity."[43]

The relationship between land, collective self-determination, and identity for southern whites can also be seen in the efforts during Reconstruction to encourage immigration to the South. While southern Republicans advocated immigration (especially from the North) for economic development, planters were interested in immigration as a solution to what they saw as their labor problem. "The labor question," explained the *Southern Argus* of Selma, Alabama, "is discussed on

---

43. Craig D. Simpson, *A Good Southerner: The Life of Henry A. Wise of Virginia* (Chapel Hill: Univ. of North Carolina Press, 1985), 154; Henry T. Shanks, *The Secession Movement in Virginia, 1847–1861* (1934; reprint, New York: AMS Press, 1971), 34; *Southern Planter*, New Series, 1 (February 1867): 24–29.

the stump, through the press, wherever two or three are gathered together." The constant refrain was that freedmen were not good workers. The New Hanover Agricultural Society in North Carolina lamented that the present labor system in the South was "utterly disorganized and demoralized."[44]

Southern planters and their Conservative/Democratic spokesmen believed that immigration could solve their labor problem. "The inauguration of a successful system of immigration," argued the conservative Wilmington *Journal*, "is, beyond doubt, the only certain solution of these troubles." The *Rural Carolinian* agreed that "the almost universal verdict" was that the labor problem would be erased "by the introduction of laborers from abroad." In an editorial entitled "Emigration," the Keowee *Courier* of South Carolina argued that incoming white labor, "by competition, will induce the blacks to work." The Savannah *Daily News and Herald* observed that people throughout the South were "arousing to the sense of the importance of substituting white labor for that of the blacks who have shown themselves so deadly hostile to those who have heretofore employed them."[45]

White planters and landowners, especially in the plantation areas, organized to advocate immigration from abroad. As early as 1865, a Virginia and North Carolina Land, Immigration, and Colonization Society was meeting in Norfolk. In 1866, Texas planters helped charter the Waverly Emigration Society. Planters of the lower Arkansas Valley organized the Arkansas River Valley Immigration Company in 1869. In Florida, plantation owners could subscribe for a particular number of workers at the Leon County Industrial and Immigration Association.[46]

---

44. *Southern Argus*, June 23, 1869; Wilmington (North Carolina) *Journal*, June 14, 1868. See also *Rural Carolinian* 1 (October 1869): 43, and the *Hansboro Democrat*, quoted in *Southern Field and Factory* 1 (August 1871): 304.

45. Wilmington (North Carolina) *Journal*, June 12, 1868; *Rural Carolinian* 1 (October 1869): 43; Keowee (South Carolina) *Courier*, January 13, 1866; Savannah *Daily News and Herald*,, November 13, 1867.

46. Robert H. Woody, "The Labor and Immigration Problem of South Carolina during Reconstruction," *Mississippi Valley Historical Review* 18 (September 1931): 202; Norfolk *Virginian*, November 22, 1865; Robert A. Calvert, ed., "The Freedmen and Agricultural

For conservative southern whites, immigration was also a means of race control. The Mobile *Tribune* explained that the South wanted "a wall between the two races; and this can only be effected by inviting the foreigner to make his home among us." The *Wilcox County News* of Alabama explained that the "white man has established himself on this continent as the rightful controller of its destinies. While his power continues he cannot admit a divided authority, especially with the African." The Montgomery *Advertiser* promised that beyond the material and commercial advantages of white immigration would be "a speedy and final cure, for negro domination." The removal of blacks from the southern landscape would have political benefits as well. One Georgia editor suggested that properly managed Chinese laborers "be made a set-off against the negro and the carpetbagger, enabling the people again to assume control of the political affairs of the country." The conservative Tuscaloosa *Independent Monitor* agreed that immigration would provide "security against Negro domination and Radical persecution." These comments suggest the growing strength of white racial identity in the Reconstruction South.[47]

African Americans, who constituted the bulk of the labor force in the plantation areas of the South, opposed any plan of immigration. The Rev. James Lynch, addressing the Tennessee Colored Convention in

---

Prosperity," *Southwestern Historical Quarterly* 76 (April 1973): 461–471; Thomas S. Staples, *Reconstruction in Arkansas, 1862–1874* (New York: Columbia Univ. Press, 1923), 341; Tallahassee *Sentinel*, February 11, 1871. For other organizations, see the Valdosta (Georgia) *Times*, quoted in the Savannah *Daily News and Herald*, September 16, 1867.

On the immigration crusade in the Reconstruction South, see Roland Berthoff, "Southern Attitudes Toward Immigration, 1865–1914," *Journal of Southern History* 17 (August 1951): 328–360; C. G. Belissary, "Tennessee and Immigration, 1865–1880," *Tennessee Historical Quarterly* 7 (1948): 229–248; and Robert F. Futrell, "Efforts of Mississippians to Encourage Immigration, 1865–1880," *Journal of Mississippi History* 20 (April 1958): 59–76.

47. Mobile *Tribune*, quoted in Tuscaloosa *Independent Monitor*, December 4, 1867; *Wilcox County News*, September 20, 1867; *Montgomery Advertiser*, quoted in *Messenger and Advertiser* (Troy, Alabama), June 14, 1869; Savannah *Morning News*, July 7, 1869; Tuscaloosa *Independent Monitor*, December 4, 1867. During Reconstruction, southern planters gave considerable thought to bringing in Chinese immigrants to replace black plantation labor. For some contemporary comments on this issue, see the *Weekly Mississippi Pilot*, January 22, 1870, and the Little Rock *Daily Republican*, quoted in the *Arkansas Freeman*, October 5, 1869.

1865, considered the idea of replacing black with foreign labor as "absurd." The Charleston *Advocate* regarded it as "folly to talk of bringing white labor to compete with and drive out the colored." The African American *Arkansas Freeman* admonished its readers to shun the Little Rock *Republican* because it was in favor of importing Chinese labor. The Charleston *Advocate* seemed to capture the white logic behind immigration schemes. "It has puzzled the North," the editor began, "to find out why a call for labor should be made, where it was then, and is yet, more abundant than capital." He suspected that the answer lay "in the social and political proclivities of the men who passed it." Clearly, that the immigration crusade was "an inimical blow at the freedmen, no one can doubt." Immigration meetings, the editor of the Charleston Republican paper concluded, were "for the sole purpose of supplanting the freedmen, and thus compelling them to seek homes and work elsewhere."[48]

In a similar vein, most African American leaders rejected ideas of black emigration from the South. "It is not our purpose to emigrate or colonize," explained an African American from Raleigh, "and we do not want to be driven away." The reasons given by black spokesmen indicate a strong identification with their native soil. "No land can be fairer in our eyes," insisted the *Colored Tennessean*, "than the sunny one beneath whose skies we have lived. We were born here. Most of us will die here. We are Americans, and prouder of the fact than ever." A convention of freedmen in Georgia expressed similar sentiments: "This is your country, but it is ours too; you were born here, so were we; your fathers fought for it but our fathers fed them. Therefore we know of no country but this." The opposition of southern blacks to emigration bespeaks a powerful civil identification with the United States, a factor that would limit the potential for black nationalism.[49]

    48. *Colored Tennessean*, August 12, 1865; Charleston *Advocate*, November 7, 1868; *Arkansas Freeman*, October 5, 1869. Charleston *Advocate*, March 2, 1867. It should be noted that at least one black newspaper, the Fort Smith (Arkansas) *New Era*, did endorse immigration. See the quotation in *Journal of Freedom*, October 14, 1865.
    49. *Journal of Freedom*, October 21, 1865; *Colored Tennessean*, August 12, 1865; *Proceedings of the Freedmen's Convention of Georgia, Assembled at Augusta, January 10th, 1866* (Augusta: Loyal Georgian Office, 1866), 19. See also the speech of the Reverend J. V. Hood printed in the *Journal of Freedom*, October 7, 1865. For an interesting example of freedmen wanting

Land was closely linked to the separatist proclivities of southern whites, African Americans, and Irish Americans. For the Fenians, it served the symbolic function of depicting British despotism and rallying support for the restoration of an Irish nationality in Ireland. For freedpeople and white planters in the agricultural South, the land question was a more vital material concern. Yet even here land was instrumental in the formation of class and collective racial identities in the fluid postwar environment of the late 1860s.

Could land have served as a foundation for a nationalism based on race or ethnicity? First, the philosophical incompatibility between Marxist class theory and nationalism should be noted. As political scientist Walker Connor explains: "Nationalism is predicated upon the assumption that the most fundamental divisions of humankind are the many vertical cleavages that divide people into ethnonational groups. Marxism, by contrast, rests upon the conviction that the most fundamental human divisions are horizontal class distinctions that cut across national groupings." How class identity might well subsume national loyalties is suggested by a statement in the *Irish Republic* in 1867: "Labor is the coming goddess, whose mission will be the dethronement of national hatred, and the establishment of a bond of brotherhood between her children. Labor is our fruitful mother; then we of all nations and languages are brothers."[50]

Republican ideas were the major factor that counteracted nationalist aspirations based on land or class. The political economy of southern and northern Republicans, which stressed individual land proprietorship and the protection of private property, might have mitigated the impulse toward land as a basis for a collective national identity. In addition, the African American drive for citizenship led to an embrace of American nationalism, which might have undercut the drive for eth-

---

to immigrate to Liberia, see the petition brought by blacks near Halifax, North Carolina, to Republican congressman E. B. Washburne (James Padgett, ed., "Reconstruction Letters from North Carolina, Part III, Letters to Elihu B. Washburne," *North Carolina Historical Review* 18 (October 1941): 395).

50. Connor, *The National Question in Marxist-Leninist Theory and Strategy*, 5; *Irish Republic*, June 1, 1867. Mitchell Cohen also criticizes Marxists for not "adequately" understanding nationalism (*Zion and State*, 27).

nic separatism. A racial nationalism among southern whites was theoretically possible without land. They, too, wanted to restore their power within the American political nation state. The Fenians spoke more in terms of creating an Irish republic. Whatever the basis of a potential nationalism would be during Reconstruction, it would not rest on land.[51]

51. The basic works here are Eric Foner, *Free Soil, Free Labor, Free Men: The Ideology of the Republican Party Before the Civil War* (New York: Oxford Univ. Press, 1970); Heather Cox Richardson, *The Greatest Nation of the Earth: Republican Economic Policies during the Civil War* (Cambridge, Mass.: Harvard Univ. Press, 1997); and David Montgomery, *Beyond Equality: Labor and the Radical Republicans, 1862–1872* (1967; reprint, Urbana: Univ. of Illinois Press, 1981).

4
Ethnic and Racial Nationalism

Race and ethnicity were another key framework in which southern whites, freedpeople, and Irish Americans sought a collective identity and struggled for political self-determination. The race question—the place of newly emancipated black men and women in American civic and social life—lay at the heart of Reconstruction. It provided the main rationale for the emergence of the Union Leagues and Ku Klux Klan in the South. Ethnicity also became an increasing concern in the period after the Civil War. The enormous influx of foreign immigrants during the antebellum period continued in the Civil War years as the Irish came to the eastern seaboard and Chinese immigrants streamed into California. If the Civil War provided visible evidence of the commitment of Irish immigrants to the Union cause, events like the New York City Draft Riots of 1863 raised serious questions in the minds of some white Americans about the integration of Irish Americans into the political life of the nation. The Chinese immigrants who came to California during the Gold Rush continued to be welcomed as railroad laborers, yet by 1870 became the targets of an ultimately successful exclusionary movement backed by white organized labor. The salience of race and ethnicity in American life after the Civil War is also evident with Native Americans. In the rapidly expanding West, hostilities between white settlers and Plains Indians increasingly occupied the attention of a government and an army already burdened with the process of Reconstruction in the South. Race and ethnicity even surfaced in postwar foreign affairs. Expansion into the Caribbean and Pacific were raising questions about the assimilation of nonwhites into American society.[1]

---

1. David Herbert Donald does a nice job of fitting the Chinese exclusionary movement into the context of Reconstruction. *Liberty and Union* (Lexington, Mass.: D. C. Heath, 1978), 201–202. See also Alexander Saxton, *The Indispensable Enemy: Labor and the Anti-*

Fenians, southern whites, and African Americans in the South clearly saw themselves in ethnic or racial terms. Fenian leader John O'Neil believed there were "nationalities with marked and ineffaceable characteristics, distinguishing them from those by which they were surrounded." The *Irish Nationalist* maintained that "the Irish race, after centuries of foreign rule, is still a distinct people." A black newspaper editor in Georgia spoke of the "Anglo-African," while another in New Orleans described his people as "a race so ancient, so well connected, and so intimately associated with the leading events in universal history." Southern whites spoke naturally about a biracial South. For these reasons, it might be reasonable to look for manifestations of ethnic nationalism among southern whites, freedpeople, and Irish American Fenians. According to social scientists, ethnic nationalism is often manifested by an awareness of the separate origins and distinctive characteristics of a given people. The construction of a functional history, similar to what historian Eric Hobsbawm has termed the "invention of tradition," also helps in the creation of nationalist identity based in ethnic terms. These criteria provide useful points of entry for studying these three groups.[2]

Chinese Movement in California (Berkeley: Univ. of California Press, 1971), and Frederick Randolph, "Chinamen in Yankeedom: Anti-Unionism in Massachusetts in 1870," *American Historical Review* 53 (October 1947): 1–29. On the acquisition of Cuba, see Allan Nevins, *Hamilton Fish: An Inner History of the Grant Administration* (New York: Dodd, Mead, 1936), chapter 9. In an essay that should be better known to historians, C. Vann Woodward suggests the value of looking at Native Americans in the context of the Reconstruction South (see *New York Review of Books*, May 12, 1988, 24).

2. *Proceedings of the Senate and House of Representatives of the Fenian Brotherhood, in Joint Convention, at Philadelphia, PA, November 24, 25, 26, 27, 28 & 29, 1868* (New York: D. W. Lee, 1868), 12; *Irish Nationalist*, January, 23, 1873; *Colored American*, September 19, 1868; *Free South*, February 15, 1868. See also *Irish Citizen*, October 19, 1867. For some examples of southern white thinking on race, to be explored in much greater detail in the rest of this chapter, see the *Arkansas State Gazette*, November 25, 1865, and the Raleigh *Sentinel*, March 27, 1867. According to one student of nationalism, "The faithful must be given a history; they must be endowed with a foundation charter; their identity and destiny must be fixed; and their decline from past grandeur and present fortunes must be explained" (Anthony D. Smith, "The Crisis of Dual Legitimation," in *Nationalism*, ed. John Hutchinson and Anthony D. Smith, [Oxford: Oxford Univ. Press, 1994], 117).

As with any social science concept, the idea of ethnic nationalism must be used with some caution. There is the danger of forcing evidence into a preconceived typology. Such

Indications of ethnic nationalism were not uniformly evident among southern whites, freedpeople, and the Fenians. The least overt expression of an ethnic or racial basis for nationalism probably belongs to African Americans, who tended to see themselves more in civic terms as American citizens. Yet appearances of racial identity do surface in the speeches and writings of black Reconstruction spokesmen. A more overt demonstration of ethnic nationalism can be found among Irish Americans. In Fenian thinking, the goal of freedom from English rule and the creation of an independent Irish republic would mark the restoration of the Irish race to a nationality. Southern white conservatives actually came closest to meeting the criteria of ethnic nationalism. The confrontation with emancipated slaves created a strong sense of racial identity, which, coupled with a deep resistance to Radical Reconstruction, could express itself in terms of racial nationalism.

Yet what is striking in all three groups is the relative weakness of ethnic nationalism. The predominance of Reconstruction politics for all three groups mitigated against a national identity based on race or ethnicity. It might be more accurate for the Reconstruction era to speak in terms of a kind of "proto-ethnic nationalism," where ingredients of racial or ethnic nationalism may exist though this consciousness of commonalities never coalesce into a national identity. Equally important, the language of race and ethnicity provided a basis for a collective identity that could mask divisions among their ranks and hence serve as a unifying force.[3]

The case for ethnic nationalism among southern African Americans is somewhat ambivalent. On the one hand, Pan-African immigration schemes—perhaps the foremost expression of black nationalism during the antebellum era—made little headway among freedmen during Re-

---

concepts are often static and tend to diminish the crucial dynamic of change in history. I hope I have kept these warnings in mind.

3. The concept of proto-nationalism is a slippery one, although it has potential for historians. For short discussions of the subject, see Walker Connor, *Ethnonationalism: The Quest for Understanding* (Princeton: Princeton Univ. Press, 1994), 114, and Wilson Jeremiah Jones, ed., *Classical Black Nationalism: From the American Revolution to Marcus Garvey* (New York: New York Univ. Press, 1996), 6–8.

construction. It was after Reconstruction, in the late 1870s, when the Exoduster movement to Kansas and renewed colonization efforts to Liberia emerged. Black leaders during Reconstruction occasionally acknowledged distinctly racial traits. "It is true that God did not make us all alike," stated Henry McNeill Turner: "This difference is even perceptible in the works of nature—no two leaves are exactly similar." The editor of the Raleigh, North Carolina, black newspaper *Journal of Freedom* also noted that the love of home and localities was "one of the most prominent features of the character of the colored man."[4] But potential elements of proto-nationalism were checked by powerful countercurrents. Blacks recognized that their best chances for civil equality and economic security lay with a powerful American state rather than a separate black nation. In addition, their struggle for equality was framed within a mid-nineteenth-century universalist outlook. The attempt to form a black racial identity then illustrates both the promises and limitations of ethnicity as a basis for a separate nationality during Reconstruction.[5]

One characteristic of ethnic nationalism, the belief in a separate past of greatness, can be found in the writings of African American Reconstruction leaders. Henry M. Turner constructed a version of black history appealing to those yearning for racial pride. He told one audience

---

4. Newspaper Clippings, Henry P. Farrow Papers, Hargrett Rare Book and Manuscript Library, University of Georgia, Athens, Georgia; *Journal of Freedom*, September 30, 1865.

5. This ambivalence toward ethnic nationalism was perhaps a heritage of slavery itself, the condition out of which a majority of freedmen emerged. Historian Eugene D. Genovese has argued eloquently for "an embryonic national religion in the consciousness of the slave class," but one beset by contradictions (*Roll, Jordan, Roll: The World the Slaves Made* [New York: Pantheon, 1974], 281). See also Sterling Stuckey, *Slave Culture: Nationalist Theory and the Foundations of Black America* (New York: Oxford Univ. Press, 1987). Recently, historians have begun to stress the importance of slavery in understanding the ideology of freedmen. See, for example, Steven Hahn, *A Nation under Our Feet: Black Political Struggles in the Rural South from Slavery to the Great Migration* (Cambridge, Mass.: Belknap Press of Harvard Univ. Press, 2003); Julie Saville, "Rites and Power: Reflections on Slavery, Freedom and Political Ritual," *Slavery and Abolition* 20 (April 1999): 81–102; and Dylan Penningroth, "Slavery, Freedom, and Social Claims to Property among African Americans in Liberty County, Georgia, 1850–1880," *Journal of American History* 84 (September 1997): 405–435.

that Ham and his descendants "were the first great men of the world. They founded the first cities and formed the first empires; they were the greatest generals, and the greatest mechanics; they carried the alphabet first to proud Greece, and the mathematical problems of Euclid still puzzle the world; besides, we count three hundred black bishops in the Primitive Church." On another occasion, Turner claimed that the Bible and history showed that Classical Greece and Rome were indebted to blacks for learning and civilization. Martin Delany of South Carolina, another important black leader of Reconstruction, also credited ancient African civilization with impressive achievements: "The Greeks when visited by the Africans were pitiable barbarians, generally naked, a few covered with skins for clothing, like the Indians of America when first discovered by Columbus." Both Turner and Delany were subsequently active in the African emigration movement of the late 1870s, suggesting perhaps that the seeds of a nascent ethnic separatism had been planted during Reconstruction.[6]

In the hands of black leaders, more recent history could also become a tool in forging a sense of black nationalism. The experience of slavery fashioned a distinctive racial character and collective identity. According to a report in the Alexandria (Virginia) *Gazette,* a meeting of freedmen in Richmond argued that whites were unfit to represent them. Instead, the blacks wanted "men who have endured the pangs of slavery, and the ignominy of caste." Similar to the belief in an Irish diaspora, blacks saw themselves as a people who had made a journey from slavery to freedom. Wilson Cook, a freedman who represented Greenville County in the South Carolina constitutional convention of 1868, told his constituents: "Once we were slaves—now we are freedmen." Black leaders recognized the damage that enslavement had inflicted on their people. "The system of slavery which generated in them qualities

6. *Colored American,* January 13, 1866; Newspaper Clippings, Farrow Papers, Hargrett Rare Book and Manuscript Library, University of Georgia, Athens, Georgia; Charleston *Daily Courier,* September 2, 1871; Eric Foner, *Freedom's Lawmakers: A Directory of Black Officeholders during Reconstruction,* rev. ed. (Baton Rouge: Louisiana State Univ. Press, 1996), 60, 216. A freedmen's convention in Raleigh, North Carolina, in September 1865 hailed the recognition of the independence of Haiti and Liberia by the United States (*Journal of Freedom,* October 7, 1865).

of patience, peacefulness, and hope," explained the editor of a North Carolina black newspaper, "also deprived them to a certain extent of the spirit of manhood. How could a slave respect himself—the property of another?" With revealing language, the Hilton Head correspondent to the black *South Carolina Leader* told his readers that it was not expected "that a people so lately out of the house of bondage should exhibit the highest phase of social life. . . . No nation on earth would have shown such a transformation as that."[7]

Southern whites also perceived the legacies of slavery during Reconstruction, another sign of the continuities across the watershed of the Civil War. In the opinion of an Augusta, Georgia, man testifying before a congressional investigating committee, former slaves "look upon the white man as having cheated them all their lives." In reporting on a black political rally in 1867, the Natchez *Democrat* heard "strong appeals to the passion of revenge" based on the belief in "all the supposed wrongs, injuries and cruelties which the Southern masters are said to have visited upon their slaves before and during the war." While the anxiety southern whites felt about emancipation and Reconstruction undoubtedly colored their interpretation of African American words and behavior, their insights can still be revealing signs of a black racial identity.[8]

Partly to ease this anxiety, African American leaders maintained that under slavery blacks conducted themselves with admirable qualities of restraint. "No race," insisted a writer to an Augusta black newspaper, "ever served a people more faithfully than we have served them who were our masters. When they were carrying on a war, the object of which was, to rivet our bonds still more firmly, and to make slavery perpetual, we at home conducted ourselves peaceably." According to the Raleigh, North Carolina, *Journal of Freedom*, slaves had "preserved their reputation as a quiet, unobtrusive people" during the Civil War. The editor believed that they had conducted themselves in a manner which earned for them "the name of peace-loving and submissive people."

---

7. Quoted in *Wilcox County News*, August 23, 1867; Charleston *Advocate*, April 20, 1867; *Journal of Freedom*, September 30, 1865; *South Carolina Leader*, December 24, 1865.

8. KKK Hearings, Georgia, vol. 1, page 291; Natchez *Democrat*, April 18, 1867.

General Davis Tillson, commander of the Freedmen's Bureau in Georgia, applauded an audience of freedmen for abstaining from violence during slavery: "In this respect you have a history, and a record, unsurpassed in the annals of the human race."[9]

Religion was another component in the construction of a black racial identity. Here the legacy of slavery remained particularly strong. Historian Eugene D. Genovese once suggested that slave religion provided "the roots of an embryonic national religion in the consciousness of the slave class." During Reconstruction, religion and the church were at the foundation of black communities. African American ministers often played key roles in Reconstruction politics. From his perspective, one North Carolina public official concluded that the black preachers were inciting their people to wage race war. A "gentleman of color" from Georgia announced that he was in favor of making the Bible his political platform. Freedpeople identified with the Old Testament account of the exodus of the Jews from slavery to freedom. "The slaves were familiar with the story," recalled a white physician from Georgia, "and it was easy for the yankees to make them believe that all the property in the South rightfully belonged to them."[10]

Black racial consciousness was expressed in ways more ominous to whites than history and religion. The danger of a race war instigated by former slaves against southern whites runs throughout Reconstruction sources. These comments must be used with caution, for it is often difficult to separate the apprehensions of whites from the beliefs of African Americans. Yet these fears appear with enough frequency to merit notice. One speaker to a black rally in Gaston, North Carolina, reputedly told his audience that "he thinks it necessary & important to make

---

9. *Colored American*, January 6, 1866; *Journal of Freedom*, September 30, 1865; *Proceedings of the Freedmen's Convention of Georgia, Assembled at Augusta, January 10th, 1866* (Augusta: Loyal Georgian Office, 1866), 7.

10. On Genovese, see note 5 to this chapter. C. C. Emerson, 1865 "Notice," in William W. Holden Governor's Papers, North Carolina Division of Archives and History, Raleigh, North Carolina; Newspaper Clippings, Henry P. Farrow Papers, Hargrett Rare Book and Manuscript Library, University of Georgia, Athens, Georgia; Lyman W. Denton, M.D., "The Ku Klux Klan and the Days of Reconstruction, or In the Shadow of the Kennesaw," Hargrett Rare Book and Manuscript Library.

a clear wipe-out of the entire *white race.*" A banner at an African American parade in Baton Rouge, Louisiana, read "White man, your time is played out; our time now." A former Klansman from Mississippi recollected that the freedpeople in his area had "a vague idea that they would ultimately exterminate the whites." The steward of the Citizen's Hospital in North Carolina wrote the governor that a black patient had told him of a conspiracy "among the colored race, to murder the white race, the old Slave owners, to get their lands and Houses."[11]

Some black leaders denounced the idea of a race war against the whites, undoubtedly in part to reassure anxious whites and hence protect themselves from retribution. "We deny emphatically that there is any possibility of a race war," proclaimed the editor of the *Colored Tennessean*, "unless it be commenced by the whites, and shall be fanned into flame by demagogues who care not what suffering may come, so long as they ride in the tempest, and think they control the whirlwind." The black *South Carolina Leader* wondered: "Whence comes this quaking fear, this mortal dread of a rising of the freedmen to indiscriminate slaughter of the whites? It flows to us from the fountain of slavery a legitimate stream whose waters are turbid with treason." The Mobile *Nationalist* claimed similarly that the threat of a race war was coming only from those who opposed Republican Reconstruction and hence not a legitimate fear.[12]

The contribution of the Union Leagues to a racial proto-nationalism among southern blacks shows similar ambivalence. Although many Leagues throughout the South included former white Unionists, they became more identified with black politics after 1867. Southern whites

---

11. J. A. Mason to William W. Holden, October 28, 1868, William W. Holden Governor's Papers, North Carolina Division of History and Archives, Raleigh, North Carolina; New York *Citizen*, October 14, 1867; Julia C. Brown, "Reconstruction in Yalobusha and Grenada Counties," *Publications of the Mississippi Historical Society* 12 (1912): 234; C. C. Emerson, 1865 "Notice," in Holden Governor's Papers. See also John Dawson to William W. Holden, July 12, 1865, Holden Governor's Papers; and W. R. Robertson to A. B. Springs, Springs Family Papers, Southern Historical Collection, University of North Carolina, Chapel Hill, North Carolina.

12. *Colored Tennessean*, August 12, 1865; *South Carolina Leader*, December 24, 1865; Mobile *Nationalist*, quoted in *Daily State Sentinel*, May 24, 1867.

who opposed Radical Reconstruction often conflated efforts at self-determination with racial hostility. One Nashville resident complained in 1867 that the Leagues had already instigated a race war in the South. In Alabama's Black Belt, whites were told that the only whites admitted to the Union Leagues were those "willing to swear enmity to their race." According to testimony given before the Ku Klux Klan hearings, a black porter accused of instigating the Union League of Tuscumbia, Alabama, to set fire to a female academy told the black members of the League "that they were at war with the white race and should use the torch on them."[13]

The ambivalence of African American nationalism in the Reconstruction South becomes clear in the debate over black emigration. During the 1850s, an incipient black nationalism appeared in movements for blacks to leave the United States and migrate to Africa or the Caribbean. Perhaps the greatest antebellum spokesman for colonization was Martin Delany, whose *The Condition, Elevation, Emigration and Destiny of the Colored People of the United States* (1852) advocated emigration as a means of racial uplift. "Our race is to be redeemed," Delany wrote, "and it is a great and glorious work, and we are the instrumentalities by which it is to be done. But we must go from among our oppressors; it never can be done by staying among them." There was renewed discussion of black migration to Liberia during Reconstruction. In the spring of 1868, the Savannah *Daily News and Herald* reported increasing interest of blacks in migration to Liberia. After General John Pope was re-

---

13. *Wilcox County News*, August 16, 1867; Dallas County Political Scrapbook, Alabama Department of Archives and History, Montgomery, Alabama; KKK Hearings, Alabama, vol. 1, page 179. The depiction of Union Leagues as fomenters of racial strife reappeared in histories of Reconstruction written under the guidance of William A. Dunning. According to a student of Reconstruction in Panola County, Mississippi, the goal of League organizers was "to keep aglow in all of them the fires of racial hostility." A similar study of Mississippi claimed that the Leagues were "thoroughly indoctrinated with the hatred of their former masters, who were their best friends." John W. Kyle, "Reconstruction in Panola County," *Publications of the Mississippi Historical Society* 12 (1912): 50; Forrest Cooper, "Reconstruction in Scott County," *Publications of the Mississippi Historical Society* 13 (1913), 122. According to Cooper, a former black member of the Union League in Scott County, Mississippi, claimed that "it arrays the races in hostility to each other" (Cooper, "Reconstruction in Scott County," 123).

moved as the commanding general of their military district, a disillusioned black leader told a group of freedmen in Alabama that "all we can do is leave for Liberia." The *Colored American*, noting that Liberia had passed an act granting lands to families, assured its readers that the African colony was flourishing. A group of North Carolina blacks, in a petition to Illinois congressman Elihu B. Washburne, offered some reasons why freedpeople might want to immigrate to Liberia: "We are of the religious portion of the colord [sic] people & wish to get home to our forefathers land . . . we have no desire for any thing in this country . . . we donot [sic] want this land because it is poluted [sic] with our blood." Significantly, these North Carolina freedpeople also complained that they were unable to get land from the whites.[14]

Most black Reconstruction leaders, however, rejected emigration, insisting that the South was a biracial society in which blacks and whites must live together. "We of the South have to be one," insisted a black carpenter from Columbus, Georgia; "what is the white man's interest must and will be the colored man's. All have been born on Southern soil—same masters and same slaves." The *Freeman's Standard* of Savannah rejected the "pernicious idea that white and black men could not live in this country unless the one should be enlightened and dominant while the other should remain ignorant and servile." Perhaps more importantly, emigration was rejected out of a belief in a universal brotherhood inclusive of all races. "We are bone of one bone, blood of one blood," explained the Nashville *Colored Tennessean;* "we are part of this race, though our skins have darker hue." Francis L. Cardozo, president of the Union League of South Carolina, saw "almost a divine purpose running through the history of this country, pointing to the great future destiny of a people composed of all the nations of the earth, liv-

---

14. Eric Foner, *Reconstruction: America's Unfinished Revolution, 1863–1877* (New York: Harper and Row, 1988), 26–27; Vincent Harding, *There Is a River: The Black Struggle for Freedom in America* (New York: Harcourt Brace, 1981), 176; Savannah *Daily News and Herald,* May 15, 1868; *Central Georgian,* January 8, 1868; *Colored American,* March 2, 1867; James A. Padgett, ed., "Reconstruction Letters from North Carolina, Part III, Letters to Elihu B. Washburne," *North Carolina Historical Review* 18 (October 1941): 395–396. See also Howard H. Bell, "The Negro Emigration Movement, 1849–1854: A Phase of Negro Nationalism," *Phylon* 9 (summer 1959): 132–142.

ing under the great Christian principle of brotherhood to all men. God in his infinite wisdom has chosen the African as one of the component elements of this great people." These beliefs in a kind of racial universalism would militate against the formation of an identity based on ethnic distinctiveness.[15]

The absence of an overt racial nationalism among southern blacks might be explained by the contours of Reconstruction. In their struggle for citizenship and equal rights, freedmen tied their political aspirations to the Republican Party. Indeed, the African American push for citizenship led to an embrace of American nationalism, which might have undercut the drive for ethnic separatism.[16]

There are several parallels between African American and Irish American attempts to forge an ethnic national identity during Reconstruction. Both made claims to a past of greatness; both feared genocide from their enemies. Racial and ethnic prejudice hovered over each community. At first glance the potential for ethnic nationalism seems to have been greater among the Fenians. Their main goal was the independence of Ireland from English rule rather than acceptance as equals into a British Commonwealth system. While it was stronger than the efforts of African Americans, the Fenian construction of an ethnic nationalism also remained ambivalent and unfulfilled.

Like some black leaders during Reconstruction, Fenian spokesmen assumed that nationalities had "marked and ineffaceable characteris-

---

15. Savannah *Daily News and Herald*, August 31, 1867; *Freeman's Standard*, February 15, 1868; *Colored Tennessean*, August 12, 1865; Charleston *Daily Republican*, August 25, 1870.

16. The basic works here are Eric Foner, *Free Soil, Free Labor, Free Men: The Ideology of the Republican Party Before the Civil War* (New York: Oxford Univ. Press, 1970), Heather Cox Richardson, *The Greatest Nation of the Earth: Republican Economic Policies during the Civil War* (Cambridge, Mass.: Harvard Univ. Press, 1997); and David Montgomery, *Beyond Equality: Labor and the Radical Republicans, 1862–1872* (1967; reprint, Urbana: Univ. of Illinois Press, 1981). A good example of American nationalism among freedmen can be found in a speech by Burrell Hatcher reprinted in the Montgomery *State Sentinel*, June 6, 1867. For a brief but suggestive discussion of post-Civil War nationalism, see Donald, *Liberty and Union*, 214–224.

tics." In particular, they argued that the Irish possessed an inherent national character that had persisted throughout history. As late as 1873, the *Irish Nationalist* insisted that the "Irish race, after centuries of foreign rule, is still a distinct people." Fenians in Pennsylvania claimed that the Irish national character was indestructible. In commenting upon the legal code of ancient Ireland, the New York *Citizen* noted that "the great delineation of ancient Irish nationality remain in their purity and retain their primitive originality." Irish nationality cast its eyes toward Ireland. "Irishmen in all lands," explained the *Irish Citizen,* "turn a longing gaze to the cradle of their race, as Mohammedans turn toward Mecca."[17]

Fenian leaders argued that the Irish race was different from the English. "Her people are a distinct race," insisted the *Irish Republic,* "separated by blood and history, by likes and dislikes, from the English people." In their 1867 Declaration of Principles, the Fenian Brotherhood in the United States asserted that the "God of nature" had placed between the Irish and English "the distinctions marked by differences of national character." Labeling the English as "our natural enemies," the vociferous editor of the *Irish Citizen* reminded his readers that the English "people is not our people, neither is their God our God." John Mitchel most dramatically drove the wedge between the two people when he said simply that the Irish and English were "oil and water."[18]

According to the Fenians, an inborn impulse toward national freedom was a distinctive characteristic of the Irish race. Fenian leader William R. Roberts claimed that the Irish people "from their earliest history, worshipped freedom and independence." The editor of the New York *Irish People* spoke similarly of the "vitality of the Irish national spirit and the fraternal feeling which makes all true Irishmen sensitive to the wrongs of their country." In a circular of 1869, the chairman of

17. *Proceedings of the Senate and House of Representatives of the Fenian Brotherhood,* 12; *Irish Nationalist,* January 26, 1873; New York *Citizen,* March 10, 1866; *Irish Citizen,* October 19, 1867.

18. *Irish Republic,* June 29, 1867; see also the issue of September 7, 1867; *Declaration of Principles, By the Representatives of the Fenian Brotherhood, in Congress Assembled* (Cleveland: n.p., 1867), 20–21; *Irish Citizen,* November 16, 1867.

the Executive Committee of the Fenian Brotherhood insisted that it was "the wild yearning of the Irish heart to deliver Ireland from her bondage, and lead her forth to liberty."[19]

Similar to African American leaders like Delany and Turner, Fenian spokesmen created a usable history. The editor of the *Irish People* of New York insisted that the old Celts of Britain "were not altogether the rude and naked savages that the modern English historians have loved to depict them." Rather, the Irish had played a distinguished role in the progress of western civilization. William R. Roberts described the Irish as "the descendants of the old Celtic race, whose genius blazes on every page of history." Some Fenian claims were perhaps a bit overstated. The *Irish Citizen* insisted that the Irish were a people of "maritime strength and adventure" who were the first to discover America.[20]

The construction of a usable past, one characteristic of ethnic nationalism, was more evident in the emphasis Fenians gave to the Celtic language. Even their name harkened back to Gaelic's legendary heroes. The *Irish Citizen* believed that "a language as ancient as the Irish must necessarily be one of the most valuable remnants of antiquity." Irish Americans were indeed proud of their linguistic ancestry. "No nations of modern Europe," claimed a Fenian from Quincy, Illinois, "had books or histories written in their own language earlier than the Irish." William Grace of Iowa boasted that Ireland possessed a national literary renown "when Britain was a land of painted savages." Ever alert to English wrongdoings against the Irish, Fenians saw the oppressive hand of English cultural imperialism behind the slight to Celtic culture. To the editor of *Irish Citizen,* "the neglect of the Celtic languages and of the antiquities of Ireland, discernable in pagan worship, legend, history and literature, only shows the very great stupidity of the British philologists and men of learning." He called on the Irish in America to "liberate themselves from the prejudices of English literature, and

---

19. W. R. Roberts, *Lecture by W. R. Roberts, Delivered Before the Fenian Brotherhood of New York, at Cooper Institute, on Wednesday, Sept. 27th, 1865* (New York: J. Croft, 1865), 7; *Irish People,* April 6, 1867; Fenian Brotherhood Papers, RG10, Folder 10, Philadelphia Archdiocesan Historical Research Center, Philadelphia, Pennsylvania.

20. *Irish People,* February 2, 1867; Roberts, *Lecture by W. R. Roberts,* 24; *Irish Citizen,* November 2, 1867.

the modes of English thought" and give Celtic languages a prominent place in school curricula. Fenian spokesmen saw nationalist potentials in language. "To-day, National literature is as potent as in the days gone before," argued a writer to the *Irish Republic* of Chicago: "It alone can bind the Irish people to their holy cause; it alone can cheer them to the struggle." The New York *Citizen* believed similarly in the translation of Celtic texts, "of those exciting reminiscences of a glorious past which ever stimulate the enthusiasm of a nation, and increase its strength in the presence of social and political difficulties." In this spirit, a Celtic Literary Club was established in Buffalo, New York.[21]

Yet not all Fenians shared the enthusiasm for Irish cultural history as a basis for Irish American nationalism. Editor Michael Scanlon, a frequent adversary of John Mitchel, urged his readers to think less of the past and more about the present. Even after reprinting an article on the Ancient Irish, Scanlon wished that all his correspondents "would deal with the living present, [rather] than be eternally rummaging among the dust of the remote past." Calling tradition a "'Will-o'-the-wisp' that rises from our fathers' graves and leads us to prisons and poorhouses," he urged Fenians to turn their backs on Irish history. Instead, according to Scanlon, the first duty of the Irish was to create "a great independent nation" to make "our present history worthy of the past."[22]

Another sign of Irish American ethnic nationalism can be found in the claim that the Irish were victims of racial genocide. In 1866, the annual national meeting of the Fenian Brotherhood warned that "in a very few years our race and nationality will cease to exist." Fenians in San Francisco felt that mobilizing Irish Americans for the regeneration of Ireland would prevent "the total extinction of our race."[23] This

---

21. Kerby A. Miller, *Emigrants and Exiles: Ireland and the Irish Exodus to North America* (New York: Oxford Univ. Press, 1985), 336; *Irish Citizen*, October 26, 1867; *Irish Republic*, May 11, 1867; August 31, 1867; *Irish Citizen*, October 26, 1867; *Irish Republic*, May 25, 1867; New York *Citizen*, March 10, 1866; Fenian Brotherhood Papers, Philadelphia Archdiocesan Historical Research Center, Philadelphia, Pennsylvania.

22. *Irish Republic*, 486; *Irish Republic*, May 11, 1867.

23. *Proceedings of the Fourth National Congress of the Fenian Brotherhood, at Pittsburgh, Pa., February 1866, with the Constitution of the F.B., and Addenda Thereto* (New York: J. Croft, 1866), 46; *Proceedings of the First General Convention of the Fenian Brotherhood of*

conception of Irish nationalism rested on the argument that the English were systematically attempting to destroy Ireland. The editor of the *Irish Republic* claimed that England had "deliberately purposed, and carefully computed, the extinction of our race." The English strategy of national genocide was partly economic. She was draining the wealth of Ireland, trying to keep the vassal nation locked in an agricultural economy. The Great Famine confirmed Irish fears that there existed a pattern of efforts that revealed a systematic plan to exterminate the Irish people.[24]

Another English strategy was cultural, evident in the many assaults on the Celtic cultural past. A writer to the *Irish People* of New York summarized well the logic of Fenian nationalism:

> The denationalization of Ireland long ago, like that of Poland in the present day, has been systematically carried out by the suppression of the language, laws, customs and symbols which tend to preserve us as a distinct people. So far as we are able we must undo the work of the usurper and renationalize our people. We must bring forth our long buried history, revive the study of our much-neglected language, rebuild our shattered national monuments, and rear again those ancient emblems around which so many glorious recollections and such sacred significance cling.

As late as 1873, the *Irish Nationalist* claimed that the policy of England "has been to destroy us as a nation if she could not utterly exterminate us." Even the Great Migration itself would spell the end of Ireland. San Francisco Fenians argued that emigration "has been steadily depopulating our native land, and which, together with other causes, will, if not soon counteracted, lead to the total extinction of our race." Ireland was becoming a wilderness, worried the editor of the *Irish Republic*, and Irish immigrants to the United States were "getting every day absorbed in the great American notion of humanity."[25]

---

the Pacific Coast, Held in San Francisco, California, September 1864 (San Francisco: George W. Stevens and Company, 1864), 11.

24. *Irish Republic*, May 4, 1867; Miller, *Emigrants and Exiles*, 307.

25. *Irish People*, April 6, 1867; *Irish Nationalist*, January 26, 1873; *Proceedings of the First General Convention of the Fenian Brotherhood of the Pacific Coast*, 11; *Irish Republic*, August 24, 1867.

These factors of ethnic proto-nationalism—the assumption of national racial characteristics, the construction of a great but buried Irish cultural history, and a fear of Irish genocide at the hands of the English—could go a long way in creating a nationalist identity among the Fenians. Yet like the case of African Americans in the South, other forces worked against ethnic nationalism. Some Fenian leaders acknowledged a subtle distinction between race and nationality. "We have abandoned all the old rigmarole about Celt and Saxon," claimed a writer to the *Irish People* of New York: "Our contest is not that of Ireland against England, but of Ireland against the present government of Ireland."[26]

Perhaps the strongest force working against ethnic nationalism among the Fenians was their tendency to think in universalist terms. Throughout the 1860s, American Fenians consistently maintained that the fight for Irish independence was part of a larger worldwide struggle for liberty. "Our fight is not for Ireland alone," insisted the Fourth National Fenian Congress, "—it is for freedom, for humanity at large. All the oppressed peoples of the earth are interested in the spread of human liberty." The editor of the *Irish Republic* explained that Fenianism was "but another name for universal liberty and eternal justice. It demands freedom for the Irishman and not for him only, but for every other man whom the God of freedom has created, be his country, or race, or color what it may." This belief in the universality of the Fenian cause was enshrined in their "Declaration of Principles," published in 1867: "It is not alone the cause of a nation striving for its own independence: it is the effort of enslaved humanity to emancipate itself from the thraldom and debasement of feudal tyranny." An Irishman writing to the Omaha *Republican* insisted that liberty knew no boundaries of space or ethnicity: "We want it all over God's creation, wherever a human being is known to exist."[27]

Fenian leaders often drew parallels between their crusade and other battles for national independence. A speaker at a Fenian gathering in Chicago expressed his hopes for an Irish republic, Polish inde-

---

26. *Irish People*, April 20, 1867.

27. *Proceedings of the Fourth National Congress*, 28; *Irish Republic*, June 8, 1867; *Declaration of Principles*, 23; *Irish Republic*, September 14, 1867.

pendence, and Hungarian freedom. The Second National Congress of Fenians similarly applauded "the noble and almost desperate struggle, which the gallant sons and faithful daughters of Poland are at present maintaining against the giant despotism of Russia." For both the Fenians and African Americans, the powerful belief in the universal nature of their struggles for liberty dissuaded nationalist impulses along the lines of ethnicity.[28]

The role of religion in the construction of Fenian Irish American nationalism was both more potent and more ambivalent than it was for African Americans. The Catholicism of Irish immigrants of the Great Famine generation was perhaps their most manifest trait to nineteenth-century Americans. Despite the growing political strength of Irish Americans in post–Civil War urban politics, nativism remained a factor in the formation of Irish American nationalism.[29] The relationship between Fenianism and Catholicism in the United States was primarily an adversarial one. The traditional, authoritarian, and conservative nature of the institutional Church was intrinsically hostile to the reform movements of the mid-nineteenth century. The powerful Bishop John Hughes of New York, for example, opposed both the Young Irelanders of 1848 and the Fenians. One Irish bishop in Ireland is reputed to have said that hell was not hot enough nor eternity long enough to punish the Fenians. In turn, Irish American nationalists were highly critical of the Catholic Church. John Mitchel and other Young Ireland veterans blamed priests for failing to support their cause. This attitude persisted among American Fenians. "We never appealed to the Pope for his approval," explained W. R. Roberts; "we do not consider the liberation of Ireland a matter that in any way calls for his action or interference, unless we thought that his influence could aid us in achieving it." Some historians have suggested that the Fenian movement received

---

28. *Irish Republic,* August 10, 1867; *Proceedings of the Second National Congress of the Fenian Brotherhood, held in Cincinnati, Ohio, January, 1865* (Philadelphia: James Gibbons, 1865), 56.

29. Florence E. Gibson, *The Attitudes of the New York Irish Toward State and National Affairs, 1848–1892* (New York: Columbia Univ. Press, 1951), 70–74; Miller, *Emigrants and Exiles,* 323–324. For some examples of negative ethnic stereotypes, see the Cleveland *Morning Leader,* February 5, 1866; June 8, 1866.

support from those working-class immigrants untouched by the Catholic Church. Yet the powerful presence of Catholicism in Irish immigrant urban communities must have created among some Fenians a real conflict of loyalties between religion and nationalism.[30]

Religion, however, does appear in Fenian appeals to Irish Americans. Thomas Lavan, addressing a Fenian celebration of St. Patrick's Day in Cleveland in 1866, told his listeners that Fenians preached a "gospel" of independence, liberty, and self-government that was older than Christianity. Like freedpeople recently out of bondage, some Fenians made a comparison between the Irish search for freedom and the biblical exodus. The address of the Fenian Brotherhood in 1865 contained a parallel between Ireland and ancient Israel. J. P. Hadnett optimistically predicted that "the day is not distant when upon the hills of Ireland the great monitors of freedom and twin-sisters, the Star Spangled Banner and Green Flag, may be seen kissing the mountain sides and heralding the joyous tidings of liberty and everlasting happiness to the poor children of Israel." On the other hand, the universalist nature of Fenian nationalism weakened the importance of religion. A Fenian from Milwaukee insisted that "Ireland was as much persecuted by England when the latter was Catholic, as she has been under any Protestant form of government." True to revolutionary republicanism, the *Irish Republic* called for freedom of religion.[31]

Southern whites came the closest to achieving some semblance of ethnic nationalism during Reconstruction. The foundation of this identity was white supremacy. Southern white opponents of Reconstruction drew upon two centuries of racial oppression of blacks. What was new in Reconstruction was the use of racism to defend white hegemony against political challenges from African Americans and to efface class

30. Gibson, *Attitudes of the New York Irish*, 28, 162; David Montgomery, *Beyond Equality*, 129; Miller, *Emigrants and Exiles*, 334–335; Roberts, *Lecture of W. R. Roberts*, 15; Miller, *Emigrants and Exiles*, 342. On the role of the Catholic church in Irish immigrant communities, see Jay P. Dolan, *The Immigrant Church: New York's Irish and German Catholics, 1815–1865* (Baltimore: Johns Hopkins Univ. Press, 1975).

31. Cleveland *Morning Leader*, March 19, 1866; *Proceedings of the Second National Congress*, 47; *Irish Republic*, July 21, 1867; August 3, 1867; September 7, 1867.

divisions among whites. A belief in white supremacy fills the writings of southern white conservatives during Reconstruction. "We are inflexibly wedded to a belief in the superiority of the Anglo-Saxon race," proclaimed the Wilmington *Herald* in 1865. That same year, the Nashville *Gazette* asserted "that there is a radical difference in the mental constitution—the brain—of the negro and that of the white man." Sentiments like these appear in private writings as well. "I utterly loathe the negro and all my sympathies and hopes are with the white race," one North Carolinian confided to his diary. To white southerners, Reconstruction had starkly drawn the lines of racial warfare. Former provisional governor of Alabama Lewis Parsons told the Constitutional Club of Mobile that resistance to Reconstruction was a means of racial protection. The *Southern Argus* argued similarly that "the law of self-preservation indicate[s] the first duty of the whites is to themselves." Ku Klux Klan members printed a public notice stating "By the Patriotic Soul, Save our Race and Land."[32]

In the crucible of Reconstruction, many southerners maintained that whites and blacks could not coexist in the same land. "I am sufficiently conversant with the habits of both races," one North Carolinian wrote in 1866, "to know that they cannot live together in harmony." The *Arkansas State Gazette* considered a biracial society impossible. North Carolina lawyer David Schenck worried that with the present state of racial animosity, "the first spark will kindle a flame not easily extinguished." Schenck later elaborated on his fear in his diary: "It is the Beginning of the End—The inauguration of the *second* 'Irrepressible Conflict'—and which must sooner or later end in the extinction of the negro race.—Civilization and Barbarism cannot exist together—The Anglo-Saxon and the African can never be equals in government—One or the other must fall." One southerner explained that the elevation of freedmen to

---

32. Wilmington *Herald*, July 27, 1865; Nashville *Gazette*, October 26, 1865; David Schenck, "Diaries," vol. 6, page 3, Southern Historical Collection, University of North Carolina, Chapel Hill, North Carolina; Mobile *Daily Advertiser and Register*, February 1, 1868; *Southern Argus*, August 18, 1869; Ku Klux Klan File, MS 582, University of Georgia Library, Athens, Georgia. Forrest G. Wood, *Black Scare: The Racist Response to Emancipation and Reconstruction* (Berkeley: Univ. of California Press, 1970), remains a valuable discussion of postwar racial attitudes in both the North and South.

political equality will "exasperate these people against the white races, and in the end lead to a new war of races which will deluge the country in blood." A race war, the Richmond *Enquirer and Examiner* predicted, would end in the extermination of blacks.[33]

Even without a racial war, southern whites expected the demise of the black race after emancipation. "The negro population of Georgia," noted the Macon *Georgia Journal and Messenger,* "is traveling with giant strides towards total extinction." Thinking in ethnic terms, southern whites predicted that African Americans would repeat the fate of Native Indians. "I think the negro will follow the Indian, and that Speedily," predicted a Virginia lawyer in 1865. A writer to the Selma *Southern Argus* concurred "that the time is not far distant when the black face and wooly head of the African will be as great a curiosity in Alabama as a wandering Creek or Choctow Indian now is." If a race war did come, agreed the *Wilcox County News,* "the negroes may read their fate in that of the Indians. They will be exterminated or driven out of the country." One black newspaper editor, however, challenged the comparison between the Indian and African American. "The idea that the colored man of America will share the fate of the Indian," insisted the *Colored American,* "is without any sanction in philosophy or history."[34]

Southern whites viewed Reconstruction as the beginnings of racial despotism. "Ignorant negroes have been enfranchised," a correspondent to the *Independent Monitor* angrily lamented in 1867, "whilst the intelligent white man has been robbed of the proudest right of a free-

33. James A. Padgett, ed., "Reconstruction Letters from North Carolina, Part I, Letters to Thaddeus Stevens," *North Carolina Historical Review* 18 (April 1941): 182; *Arkansas State Gazette,* November 25, 1865; David Schenck, "Diaries," vol. 6, pages 22, 57, Southern Historical Collection, University of North Carolina, Chapel Hill, North Carolina; A. C. Garlington to A. B. Springs, February 17, 1866, Springs Family Papers, Southern Historical Collection; Richmond *Enquirer and Examiner,* July 25, 1868.

34. Quoted in *Weekly Panola Star,* June 13, 1868; John Lyon to A. B. Springs, September 22, 1865, Springs Family Papers, Southern Historical Collection, University of North Carolina, Chapel Hill, North Carolina; Selma *Southern Argus,* July 7, 1869; *Wilcox County News,* August 23, 1867; *Colored American,* June 1, 1867; March 2, 1867; September 19, 1868. See also the comment of the *Floridian* in the Fernandina (Florida) *Courier,* October 24, 1867; Wood, *Black Scare,* 29; and Dan T. Carter, *When the War Was Over: The Failure of Self-Reconstruction in the South, 1865–1867* (Baton Rouge: Louisiana State Univ. Press, 1985), 166–167.

man." The *Weekly Panola Star* looked at the proposed Republican constitution for Mississippi in a similar light: "Depriving our people of the privileges most dear to Anglo-Saxons, and placing the white race under the dominion of the black race; enforcing a system of amalgamation so hideous that all nature cries out against it, the proposed constitution is the very embodiment of discord." Black suffrage in particular augured the subjugation of whites. Robert B. Lindsay, the Democratic governor of Alabama from 1871 to 1872, saw in congressional plans for black suffrage a design to degrade southern whites. Lewis Parsons of Alabama explained that he opposed black suffrage "not for the purpose of crushing them, but to prevent them from crushing us."[35]

According to southern whites, black suffrage would lead inexorably to social equality. "They will say, perhaps, that negro suffrage does not involve social equality," noted the Austin *Daily State Gazette;* "but we answer that it inevitably will and does already.... It cannot be avoided. How long will the negro magistrate or judge, upon whom his white neighbor depends for security in his property or person, be excluded from his table. Will not the negro and white members of the legislature sit together, side by side? Political equality involves social equality where the numbers of each race are so equal, and the Northern abolitionists knew this well when they attempted to force negro suffrage upon us." The *Independent Monitor* of Tuscaloosa claimed that rather than agreeing to social equality, "we would either abandon the land, or force the negro to leave."[36]

---

35. Tuscaloosa *Independent Monitor*, November 20, 1867; *Weekly Panola Star*, June 6, 1868; see also Mobile *Daily Advertiser and Register*, February 1, 1868; KKK Hearings, Alabama, vol. 1, pages 191, 89. The Richmond *Dispatch* cited the economic ruin and political chaos of Haiti as an example of the "sort of self-government which the negro has proved himself capable of after the fairest test which was ever afforded a community." It warned that in the United States, Republicans were seeking "to bring a similar fate upon ten Southern States of the Union by making the negro the ruling class of society" (quoted in *Central Georgian*, May 6, 1868). The Savannah *Daily News and Herald* claimed similarly that Haiti presented a spectacle of "continuous succession of revolutions—discord, imbecility, poverty and semi-barbarism" (Savannah *Daily News and Herald*, December 24, 1867).

36. Austin *Daily State Gazette*, November 12, 1867; Tuscaloosa *Independent Monitor*, December 4, 1867. See also the Austin *Daily State Gazette*, November 6, 1867.

The racial ideas of southern whites culminated in the notion of a white republic. "We have always contended that this is a *White Man's Government,*" an Alabama editor proclaimed, "and should be alone controlled and governed by white men." The Richmond *Dispatch* was explicit: "The Caucasian race must rule here." The legitimacy of a white republic was supported by history. "The government of the United States," explained a Mississippi editor, "was invented by the white statesmen of the thirteen original states for white men and their posterity forever. Any attempt to make an inferior race, politically, or socially, the equal of the superior, is a wanton violation of our political and social rights, and an insult to God himself, for it is at war with those eternal laws of racial distinction which will reassert their power in spite of the puny efforts of wicked men." The Wilmington *Journal* inquired further: "Why should not this country be ruled by white men? They formed it. They civilized it. They have governed it in the past, and they are bound to, they must, and shall rule it in the future."[37]

The link between racial supremacy and white political control was a constant theme in the writings of southern conservative whites during Reconstruction. There were, however, some white southerners who reverted back to the kind of paternalism forged during slavery. "The whites and blacks of the South have been life-long friends," reasoned the Raleigh *Sentinel:* "They know each other and we cannot doubt there is conservatism enough in both races to prevent and frown down any serious collisions or differences." A Virginia lawyer believed it was the duty of the superior race to act with patience, forbearance, and Christian charity to blacks. Even the often rabidly racist editor of the Tuscaloosa *Independent Monitor* saw the whites as natural allies of the freedmen, "those whose interests are more nearly identified with theirs than those of any other persons on this continent." Perhaps as a means of drawing the freedmen away from the Republican Party, southern whites appealed to a common history and destiny. "These among them

---

37. *Wilcox County News,* September 1, 1868; Richmond *Dispatch,* quoted in Columbia (South Carolina) *Daily Phoenix,* June 14, 1868; *Southern Argus,* August 1, 1869; Wilmington (North Carolina) *Journal,* April 24, 1868. See also Mobile *Daily Advertiser and Register,* October 18, 1867.

who know any thing of all," wrote a Georgia editor, "know that the best friends they have had heretofore or will have hereafter are the whites of the South, and that as long as the two races occupy this country in common, their interests are and must be identical." Reflecting the necessity of black labor to southern planters, the Mobile *Daily Advertiser and Register* claimed that both blacks and whites in the South were attached to the soil. These racial views anticipated the arguments of "New Departure" Democrats during the later years of Reconstruction.[38]

Manifestations of ethnic nationalism thus appeared among the Fenians, southern whites, and African American freedpeople during Reconstruction. To varying degrees, each group expressed a recognition of racial differences, constructed an ethnic history of past greatness and future fulfillment, and framed political conflicts in ethnic terms. Yet categories of race or ethnicity never became the dominant mode for expressing nationalist impulses, for powerful currents were working against separatism along these lines. Chief among these was the inclination, still common in the 1860s, to think of freedom and independence along universalist lines. Nonetheless, ethnic nationalism might well have provided communities of freedmen, Irish Americans, and southern whites with a means of mitigating internal conflict and even asserting the dominance of a particular group within that community.[39]

Historians are now well aware that African American society in the post–Civil War South was far from monolithic. The interests of free urban blacks often conflicted with those of former plantation slaves. In such heavily black states as South Carolina and Louisiana, these two groups fought over issues of civil rights and economic reform. Although the evidence is far from conclusive, the connection between the free black elite and an incipient black nationalism is suggestive. Most

---

38. Raleigh *Sentinel*, March 27, 1867; John Lyon to A. B. Springs, September 22, 1865, Springs Family Papers, Southern Historical Collection, University of North Carolina, Chapel Hill, North Carolina; Tuscaloosa *Independent Monitor*, October 9, 1867; *Southern Watchman*, March 27, 1867; Mobile *Daily Advertiser and Register*, January 30, 1868.

39. A major theme in more recent literature on nationalism suggests that it is often a ideological construct created by a small group as a means of asserting dominance and creating unity on their hegemonic terms. See Hutchinson and Smith, *Nationalism*.

of the testimony quoted in this chapter comes from the writings of black leaders and editors who had emerged from the free antebellum black community. Henry Turner, for example, was born free and became a minister and organizer for the Republican Party in Georgia. He was also a delegate to that state's 1867–1868 constitutional convention. Francis L. Cardozo, also freeborn, was president of the South Carolina Union League. In particular, the editors of African American newspapers during Reconstruction emerged from the antebellum free black elite. James M. Simms was born a slave but purchased his freedom in 1857. During Reconstruction, Simms helped organize Union Leagues in Georgia, spoke on behalf of the Republican Congressional Committee in 1867, and edited the *Southern Radical and Freedmen's Journal* (later called the *Freemen's Standard*) in Savannah. John Menard, elected to Congress in 1868, was the editor of *Free South* published in New Orleans. Pinckney B. S. Pinchback, a prominent African American leader in Reconstruction Louisiana, was another freeborn black and co-owner of the New Orleans *Louisianian*. Since urban black elites often faced challenges to their leadership from former slaves, nationalism might have been one way of preserving their high political and social status.[40]

The relationship between ethnic nationalism and internal conflict within the Irish American community is also suggestive, though more complex. Historians have presented conflicting interpretations of nineteenth-century Irish American nationalism. Thomas N. Brown has argued that it reflected a generally middle-class orientation as immigrants sought assimilation into the mainstream of American bourgeois society. In contrast, Kerby Miller contends that Irish American nationalism represented a deep attachment to the native culture of Ireland and an alienation from the host culture of America. He argues that the Fenians and later Irish American nationalists had a strong appeal among the urban working classes. Similarly, other historians have shown the close connection between Irish American nationalism and labor radicalism.

---

40. The biographical information in this paragraph was culled from Foner, *Freedom's Lawmakers*. On intraracial conflict, see Foner, *Reconstruction*, 397, and Thomas Holt, *Black over White: Negro Political Leadership in South Carolina during Reconstruction* (Urbana: Univ. of Illinois Press, 1977).

Both arguments can find support in the Fenian movement in the United States, as suggested by the differences between John Mitchel of the *Irish Citizen* and the more liberal Michael Scanlon of the *Irish Republic*. Also, the tensions that emerged in the Irish American community between a bourgeoisie in control of community institutional networks and labor activists more amenable to radical politics became more manifest in the 1870s after Fenianism had made its real impact.[41]

Finally, internal divisions also plagued southern whites during Reconstruction, though once again the conflicts surfaced more during the late 1870s. At the end of the Civil War, a sizable contingent of Unionists harbored deep class resentments born in intrastate sectional divisions and aggravated by certain Confederate policies and actions. During Radical Reconstruction, the major conflict between whites was political—white Republicans battling Conservatives/Democrats. In addition, deep structural economic and social changes were generating friction. New forms of exchange and dependency created class conflict between planters and yeomen, especially in areas of cotton and tobacco production. The commercialization of the southern countryside also led to a new bourgeoisie of merchants and railroad promoters whose interests were not always compatible with the planter class. Adherence to the belief in a white republic could defuse these conflicts and further the interests of the conservative planter and business elite. After all, the promise of white supremacy to unite whites and erase class conflict had long been and would continue to be a central theme in southern history.[42]

41. Miller, *Emigrants and Exiles*, 307, 337–342, 523–524. See also Thomas N. Brown, *Irish-American Nationalism, 1870–1890* (Philadelphia: J. B. Lippincott Company, 1966).

42. The literature on economic change in the postwar South is enormous, but Foner provides a reliable and brief summary in *Reconstruction*, 392–411.

5
Civic Nationalism

Francis Lieber was a likely spokesman for nineteenth-century American nationalism. As an immigrant, he brought to the United States the currents of European Romantic nationalism. As a young boy growing up in Germany, Lieber watched with tears as Napoleon's troops invaded his beloved but humiliated homeland. He was later inspired to fight for Greek independence, only to become disillusioned with the revolutionaries there. Lieber immigrated to America in 1826, where his academic career took him to South Carolina College and later to Columbia University.[1]

The Civil War presented Lieber with an opportunity to revisit the subject of nationalism. He contributed to the Union cause in a variety of ways, sending two sons to the Union army (one of whom lost an arm at Fort Donelson), drafting the guidelines for the Union army's first codification of military law, and writing patriotic pamphlets for the Loyal Publication Society. Guided by his own theories of nationalism, Lieber advocated the expansion of federal power during the Civil War. He supported Lincoln's wartime suspension of civil liberties, the confiscation of slave property from slaveowners, and conscription.[2]

---

1. The fullest biography of Lieber is Frank Freidel, *Francis Lieber: Nineteenth-Century Liberal* (1947; reprint, Gloucester, Mass: Peter Smith, 1968). Phillip S. Paluden provides a briefer account of his life in *A Covenant with Death: The Constitution, Law, and Equality in the Civil War Era* (Urbana: Univ. of Illinois Press, 1975), 61–64. For an analysis of his ideas of nationalism, see Paluden, *A Covenant with Death*, 64–108; David Herbert Donald, *Liberty and Union* (Lexington: D. C. Heath, 1978), 217–219; and Merle Curti, *The Growth of American Thought*, 2nd ed. (New York: Harper and Row, 1951), 482–483. See also the comment of Boston League member Alexander H. Bullock in Melinda Lawson, "'A Profound National Devotion': The Civil War Union Leagues and the Construction of a New National Patriotism," *Civil War History* 48 (December 2002): 358. Lawson's interpretation of Civil War nationalism corresponds closely with the one presented here.

2. Donald, *Liberty and Union*, 217–218; Freidel, *Francis Lieber*, 343–344; Paluden, *A Covenant with Death*, 91–94.

Francis Lieber well represents the civic nationalism that characterized the Republican Party in the Civil War era. More than any other factor, Republican nationalism set the boundaries for the separatist aspirations of freedpeople, southern whites, and Irish Americans. Wartime and immediate postwar nationalism provided African Americans the chance to achieve freedom, civil rights, and equality. They therefore supported a Republican-dominated national state, framed their arguments in the language of the American republican tradition, and adopted the symbolism of American nationality. In almost direct contrast, southern whites defined themselves in opposition to the nationalism of Reconstruction. Ironically, their collective sense of alienation from American civic nationalism did not preclude their desire to return to and even dominate American political values and institutions. The Fenian movement, too, adopted the discourse of republicanism and often saw the United States as a model for a republic. America provided the setting in which Fenians forged their distinctive diaspora nationalism. In America, an Irish "nation" could materialize that would one day restore Irish nationality to Ireland. Republican nationalism encouraged nationalist aspirations along civic rather than ethnic lines. It is thus a fitting subject to culminate this study.

The roots of Reconstruction nationalism lay in the Civil War. To boost flagging northern morale, groups like the Loyal Publication Society and the Board of Publications of the Philadelphia Union League disseminated a series of pamphlets that defined the meaning of the war and the Union. According to historian George M. Fredrickson, northern propaganda augured a shift in American thinking from individualism and anti-institutionalism toward a conservative organic sense of community. In this transition, nationalism in the North became identified with a conservative elite that valued order and distrusted democracy.[3]

---

3. On the rise of nationalism in the context of American thought, see George M. Fredrickson, *The Inner Civil War: Northern Intellectuals and the Crisis of the Union* (New York: Harper and Row, 1965), especially chapter 12, and Susan-Mary Grant and Peter J. Parish, eds., *Legacy of Disunion: The Enduring Significance of the American Civil War* (Baton Rouge: Louisiana State Univ. Press, 2003), 116–133, 188–206. On northern propaganda, see Frank Freidel, "The Loyal Publication Society: A Pro-Union Propaganda Agency,"

Postwar American nationalism was closely tied to the Republican Party. With a Republican administration and Congress fresh from Union victory, it was easy for patriotism to become synonymous with partisanship. Party leaders were only too glad to point out that the continued security of the Union and justice to the former slaves depended on Republican electoral success. Although Republicans were divided over economic issues (such as the tariff) and a number of questions of reconstruction (such as confiscation), they shared a common belief in the supremacy of the Union, the institutionalization of democratic ideals and practices in a national state, and the special destiny of the United States to lead the world toward republican principles.[4]

Republican spokesmen in the Reconstruction South were effusive in their devotion to American nationalism. "As the nation rises more and more rapidly in wealth and strength, as it exalts itself more and more decidedly above the great nations of the world," predicted the Wilmington *Daily Post,* "the sentiment of nationality will become more and more decided among our people; and the political party which devotes itself to national ideas will become more and more vigorous and formidable." A northern supporter of Republican Reconstruction in Tuscaloosa, Alabama, confided to a friend that the love of his country

---

Mississippi Valley Historical Review 26 (December 1939): 359–376; Frank Freidel, "Introduction," *Union Pamphlets of the Civil War, 1861–1865,* 2 vols. (Cambridge, Mass.: Belknap Press of Harvard Univ. Press, 1967); and Lawson, "'A Profound National Devotion.'" The best summary of the rise of an industrial state can be found in Eric Foner, *Reconstruction: America's Unfinished Revolution, 1863–1877* (New York: Harper and Row, 1988), 1–34.

4. American nationalism during the mid-nineteenth century remains curiously understudied. Older but still valuable works include Paul Nagel, *One Nation Indivisible: The Union in American Thought, 1776–1861* (New York: Oxford Univ. Press, 1964); Paul Nagel, *This Sacred Trust: American Nationality, 1798–1898* (New York: Oxford Univ. Press, 1971); Fred Somkin, *Unquiet Eagle: Memory and Desire in the Idea of American Freedom, 1815–1860* (Ithaca: Cornell Univ. Press, 1964); and Major L. Wilson, *Space, Time, and Freedom: The Quest for Nationality and the Irrepressible Conflict, 1815–1861* (Westport, Conn.: Greenwood Press, 1974). For a more recent study, see Melinda Lawson, *Patriot Fires: Forging a New American Nationalism in the Civil War North* (Lawrence: Univ. Press of Kansas, 2002). On the postwar Republicans, see Hans Trefousse, *The Radical Republicans: Lincoln's Vanguard for Racial Justice* (1968; reprint, Baton Rouge: Louisiana State Univ. Press, 1975), and Heather Cox Richardson, *The Death of Reconstruction: Race, Labor, and Politics in the Post-Civil War North, 1865–1901* (Cambridge, Mass.: Harvard Univ. Press, 2001).

"is with me a passion, & Sometimes I fear it has become an object of Idolatry." Southern Republicans saw their party as the bastion of patriotism. According to the Houston *Union*, a true Republican displayed an "unselfish and devoted love to his whole country, without regard to any particular section."[5]

Republican nationalists during Reconstruction drew upon the antebellum idea of America as a Redeemer Nation providentially destined to spread freedom throughout the world. "As God has given a common destiny to the States constituting the American Republic," insisted the *Georgia Republican*, "we are ordained to fulfill one mission among the nations by living up to the cardinal principles of our system." A Republican editor from Tennessee boasted similarly that republican influences would "continue to radiate from this great source and center—the United States, until free government will be established throughout the world." Union Leagues in the South joined in this nationalist chorus. The Green Creek Council Union League in North Carolina declared itself "uncompromisingly attached to the government of the United States and to the Union of the States thereof."[6]

African American freedmen were also swept up in the tide of postwar nationalism. "When I behold these Star-Spangled banners," confessed a black Union League organizer in North Carolina, "spreading in beauty above an assemblage of people without regard to race or color, this motto of 'Union, Liberty, Equality' carried into practical application, sir, upon this the first occasion in the State of North Carolina, my heart swells with emotions, which can scarcely find intelligible utterance!" Black Republicans closely followed their white brethren in linking American nationalism to their party. In an address to the people of Alabama, a freedmen's convention explained that they were Republicans because "we love the Union, the stars and stripes, the national colors, and the whole country—North as well as South." Even the idea of a Redeemer Nation found its way into black political rhetoric. As Henry M.

5. Wilmington *Daily Post*, February 6, 1870; D. Woodruff to Wager Swayne, July 6, 1867, Wager Swayne Papers, Alabama Department of Archives and History, Montgomery, Alabama; Houston *Union*, January 11, 1869.

6. Augusta *Georgia Republican*, July 2, 1870; Atlanta *New Era*, September 30, 1865; Wilmington *Daily Post*, August 11, 1867.

Turner of Georgia explained: "This great Continent slept in the cradle of undisturbance for thousands of years. God seemed to have held it back for some important purpose, while Asia, Africa, and Europe were the world's theatres, and men of all sizes, colors and languages were playing out the drama of life. While nations were rising on the one hand and crumbling on the other, America laid quietly beneath her green bowers and blooming foliage." Most African American leaders in the Reconstruction South thus closely identified with the normative Republican nationalism.[7]

Freedpeople manifested their attachment to American nationalism through the use of political iconography. Symbols and images had a special resonance for the majority of ex-slaves, for whom literacy had been forbidden under slavery. Union League members often likened their cause to that of the American Revolution, which had for decades been a means of seeking political legitimacy. In its organizational handbook, the Union League of America stated it was formed "for the purpose of perpetuating the liberties for which our fathers fought." The state Union League of North Carolina affirmed the mission of its parent organization: "Its object and aims are only to promote the teachings of WASHINGTON, FRANKLIN, HAMILTON, JEFFERSON, JACKSON, and other immortal spirits of our beloved UNION." Newly emancipated slaves likened their struggle for the right to vote to the Revolutionary fight for liberty. Freedmen in Georgia insisted that "taxation without representation is contrary to the fundamental principles which govern republican countries." A meeting of freedmen in Edgecomb County, North Carolina, thought similarly that it was "dramatically opposed to Republican institutions to tax us for the support and expense of the Government, and at the same time deny us the right of representation."[8]

---

7. Raleigh *Tri-Weekly Standard,* March 28, 1867; Montgomery *Daily State Sentinel,* May 21, 1867; *Colored American,* January 13, 1866.

8. Walter L. Fleming, ed., *Documentary History of Reconstruction: Political, Military, Social, Religious, Educational, and Industrial, 1865–1906* (1907; reprint, New York: McGraw-Hill, 1966), 2:10; Asheville *Pioneer,* August 29, 1867; *Proceedings of the Freedmen's Convention of Georgia, Assembled at Augusta, January 10th, 1866* (Augusta: Loyal Georgian Office, 1866), 18; *Journal of Freedom,* October 28, 1865.

The Declaration of Independence was a particularly strong symbol for Republican leaders, black and white. Speaking at the Texas constitutional convention, A. T. Monroe explained that the Leagues "inculcated the principles of the glorious chart of our liberties, the Declaration of Independence." The Union League of North Carolina agreed that their political creed was found in the Declaration and Constitution. The Declaration became a staple in southern Republican political iconography. It was read at July Fourth celebrations in Charleston and Augusta. A group of South Carolina blacks petitioned Congress for equal rights in the name of the Declaration of Independence. A Republican editor in North Carolina nicely summed up the meaning of the Revolution for Republican Reconstruction in the South: "The children of the men who laid the cornerstone of the temple of American liberty," declared the Raleigh *Tri-Weekly Standard*, "have thus completed the work of their ancestors."[9]

Other icons of American nationality were popular during Reconstruction. The name of Abraham Lincoln became a common symbol of emancipation. Freedmen meeting in Fayetteville, North Carolina, called Lincoln "the humblest instrument of Almighty God to declare us free." There was a black Union Lincoln Association that participated in a Lincoln birthday celebration in 1868. A Fourth of July observance in Charleston brought out black political organizations, such as the Lincoln Light Infantry and the Lincoln Republican Guards. A portrait of Lincoln hung at a New Year's celebration of emancipation in Charleston in 1866. The American flag was a more prevalent and powerful symbol of American nationalism. "We love the flag," proclaimed the Union League of North Carolina, "because it is the symbol of the national majesty and glory." In a speech to the Union Republican Convention at Huntsville, north Alabama Unionist David C. Humphries told his listeners to look to the American flag, "the stars and stripes that are familiar to you, that have been triumphant on five-hundred battlefields—this is your flag, and you must to-day feel and acknowledge its protecting

9. San Antonio *Daily Express*, January 16, 1869; *Loyal Georgian* (Augusta), February 15, 1868; Savannah *Morning News*, July 8, 1869; Charleston *Advocate*, February 23, 1867; Raleigh *Tri-Weekly Standard*, July 2, 1867. For further references to the Declaration of Independence, see Charleston *Daily News*, October 22, 1868, and the speech of A. J. Ransier in the Charleston *Daily Republican*, August 20, 1870.

power." The flag seemed to possess particularly great significance for African Americans. It stood outside the park of a mass Republican meeting for freedpeople in Savannah. African Americans marching in a July Fourth parade in Natchez, Mississippi, saluted the flag as they passed by. As one white observer of a July Fourth celebration in Alabama explained, blacks wanted a flag "as some of them had firmly marched under and had a kind of weakness for it."[10]

July Fourth, which served as another political icon, also tied freedmen to Republican civic nationalism. Throughout the antebellum era, this holiday had become a powerful expression of American nationalism in both the North and the South. Henry M. Turner of Georgia had recognized the hollowness of Independence Day for those Americans in bondage: "The Fourth of July—memorable in the history of our nation as the great day of independence to its countrymen—had no claims upon our sympathies." After emancipation, however, African Americans used the holiday to affirm their membership in the body politic. In Alabama, blacks made great preparations for July Fourth by requesting banners, fifes and drums, and a flag from local Republicans. In Natchez, Mississippi, a large procession of Union Leaguers and other blacks were "all decorated with ribbons, and many carrying flags." Freedpeople in Macon, Georgia, marched on horseback and foot to a nearby arbor where they heard religious and patriotic speeches, and after which they enjoyed a picnic. In Savannah, a local League was presented with a hand-sewn American flag on July 4, 1867.[11]

---

10. Raleigh *Tri-Weekly Standard*, March 26, 1867; *Freeman's Standard*, February 15, 1868; Savannah *Morning News*, July 8, 1869; Keowee (South Carolina) *Courier*, January 13, 1866. For a white Republican allusion to Lincoln, see the Raleigh *Tri-Weekly Standard*, March 28, 1867. *Loyal Georgian* (Augusta), February 15, 1868; *Daily State Sentinel*, May 25, 1867; Savannah *Daily News and Herald*, May 28, 1868; Natchez *Democrat*, July 6, 1867; Charles C. Colton, M. G. Candre (?) to F. Adams, [July 1867?], Wager Swayne Papers, Alabama Department of Archives and History, Montgomery, Alabama. See also the resolution of a Republican meeting in Forsyth County, North Carolina, in Raleigh *Tri-Weekly Standard*, July 2, 1867.

11. *Colored American*, January 13, 1866; Charles C. Colton, M. G. Candre (?) to F. Adams [July 1867?] Wager Swayne Papers, Alabama Department of Archives and History, Montgomery, Alabama; Natchez *Democrat*, July 6, 1867; Macon *Daily Telegraph*, July 6, 1866; Savannah *Daily News and Herald*, July 3, 1867.

Most Republicans in the South embraced the annual celebration of American independence. For a correspondent to an Athens, Tennessee, newspaper, the "national anniversary of our republic" was an "august day! Consecrated to freedom throughout the civilized world, wherever liberty has a resting place, enshrined in every American patriot's heart, by a thousand glorious traditions hallowed, around which cluster ten thousand precious memories of better and brighter days." To the editor of the Republican *Daily New Era* of Atlanta, July Fourth was "a day ever held in glorious remembrance by the venerated Fathers who founded the government—Washington, Adams, Jefferson, Madison, and their compatriots." African Americans in the Reconstruction South thus placed themselves firmly in the political culture of postwar American nationalism. They saw their present struggle to secure the fruits of liberty as part of a long and sacred tradition of American freedom.[12]

Southern whites, on the other hand, forged their collective identity in opposition to Republican nationalism. Nowhere was this more evident than in the manner in which they spurned the leading national holiday. "The Fourth of July," lamented the Richmond *Enquirer and Examiner* in 1868, "having ceased to be of the slightest interest to the white people of the south, like a worn-out pair of breeches, it has fallen into Cuffee's hands." Yet southern whites revealed their underlying attachment to American nationalism by accepting the holiday even as they used it to express their own sense of political estrangement. As Independence Day approached, a Georgia editor explained that "we are an unrepresented people, and have no more voice in national affairs than though we were Cossacks or Kaffirs . . . we should not quietly surrender our rights in the celebration of an event, commemorative in a great degree of the prowess and success of Southern rebels, in the first great Revolution." The Edgefield *Advertiser* of South Carolina felt that the "sack-cloth of humiliation" would be an appropriate dress for its readers to celebrate July Fourth. If southern whites failed to see the irony,

12. Athens (Tennessee) *Republican,* July 12, 1867; Atlanta *Daily New Era,* July 4, 1868. See also Graves [?] to Wager Swayne, July 9, 1867, Wager Swayne Papers, Alabama Department of Archives and History, Montgomery, Alabama. On the meaning of July Fourth in the antebellum era, see Len Travers, *Celebrating the Fourth: Independence Day and the Rites of Nationalism in the Early Republic* (Amherst: Univ. of Massachusetts Press, 1997).

they saw with particular clarity how their former slaves had taken their place in the mainstream of American nationalism. The Macon *Telegraph* blandly reported that July Fourth was "unenthusiastically celebrated" as the "negroes had Independence Day to themselves." [13]

The rejection of July Fourth was not the only sign that southern separatism re-emerged during Reconstruction. Several unreconstructed southerners maintained that a distinctive *southern* nationalism had indeed survived the Civil War. H. Rives Pollard, editor of the *Southern Opinion* of Richmond, claimed that in "nations, as to individuals, there is an inner as well as outer life, and whatever there was noble or elevated in us in the times gone by, we may still cherish, still cultivate in the times that are to come." Anticipating the views of later historians, the editor of the Tuscaloosa *Independent Monitor* claimed that southern nationalism was born in the Civil War: "Four terrible years and victory welded the States together. The cause was won. We emerged from the contest still vigorous." A Mississippi editor commended the soldiers who had fallen "in our struggle for separate nationality." The continued vitality of southern nationalism carried with it the antebellum belief in an irrepressible conflict between the North and South. H. Rives Pollard, for instance, maintained that the South "can yet preserve its moral and intellectual distinctiveness as a people." In the ethnic categories of the time, he explained that the South "must not cease to be the children of the Cavaliers, to ape the prim precision of the Puritans and mould our language upon the nasal abominations of New England." The Demopolis *New Era* of Alabama insisted that "the gulf which separates the two people in sympathy and feelings is wider than that between Lazarus and Dives, so impossible is it to whip a people into love and loyalty." [14]

In contrasting ways then, southern whites and blacks used the symbols of American nationalism to define their identity and their place in

---

13. Richmond *Enquirer and Examiner*, July 6, 1868; Macon *Daily Telegraph*, July 1, 1866; Edgefield (South Carolina) *Advertiser*, July 3, 1867; Macon *Daily Telegraph*, July 6, 1866. See also the *Southern Standard*, July 3, 1869.

14. *Southern Opinion* (Richmond), June 15, 1867; Tuscaloosa *Independent Monitor*, October 16, 1867; Natchez *Democrat*, July 11, 1867; *Southern Opinion* (Richmond), June 15, 1867; Demopolis (Alabama) *New Era*, May 18, 1866. See also *Southern Standard*, February 27, 1869.

Reconstruction politics. Republican nationalism was instrumental in yet another way for these groups. The Union victory and the challenges of Reconstruction led thoughtful northerners such as Francis Lieber to reconsider the meaning of nationalism. Their efforts yielded a heightened emphasis on the organic nature of the nation and a defense of a strong national government, providing a new vocabulary for southern whites and freedpeople seeking political self-determination and ethnic autonomy.

The organic nature of the American nation was well articulated by the Episcopalian scholar Elisha Mulford, whose 1870 book *The Nation* achieved great prestige in the United States. Abandoning the assumptions of Jeffersonian liberalism, Mulford argued that the natural and political rights were institutionalized in the state: "The government is the institution in which the sovereignty of the nation is realized." In particular, the right of citizenship—an issue of especial importance to all three groups in this study—was an organic and national one. As Mulford explained, "for it is only in the being of the nation that freedom becomes real." Mulford's ideas were reflected in Republican writings during Reconstruction. Lieber spoke in terms of "institutional liberty," while New England educator and reformer Orestes Brownson located sovereignty in the organic people. The Athens *Republican*, voice of the local Union League, also believed that the "interest of individuals should always be subservient to that of the whole country, and whoever stands in the way should be put aside—openly and legitimately." [15]

Many Republican spokesmen believed that the Civil War had created an American nation that would absorb different peoples. Through this process, American nationalism would be more civic than ethnic. "No element of race will ever make us a nation," explained Wendell Phillips in 1869. "No technicality and peculiarity will make us a nation." Instead, ideals and principles were the foundation of the American na-

---

15. Herbert W. Schneider, *A History of American Philosophy* (New York: Columbia Univ. Press, 1946), 185; Elisha Mulford, *The Nation: The Foundations of Civil Order and Political Life in the United States* (1870; reprint, Boston: Houghton, Mifflin, 1883), 142, 128; Fredrickson, *The Inner Civil War*, 190; Harold Hyman, ed., *The Radical Republicans and Reconstruction, 1861–1870* (Indianapolis: Bobbs Merrill, 1967), 480; Athens (Tennessee) *Republican*, September 13, 1867; December 26, 1867.

tion: "under that one and that impartial law all creeds and all tongues and all races shall be gathered with an equal protection." American nationalism thus rested upon and required cultural homogeneity. In 1865, journalist and Union veteran William Mason Grosvenor wrote: "Heterogeneous populations, hostile systems, and irreconcilable ideas had only been placed in contact, and held to bare juxta-position by a constitutional compact. No chemical union had ever taken place; for that the white-hot crucible of civil war was found necessary. To keep up the fire until antagonistic elements are refined away and a perfect union is effected is needful, and is the deliberate purpose of the nation, expressed in the late election." A Republican newspaper in the South agreed that since the war had ended, there was "one country, one flag, one Union. Political and social harmony is absolutely essential." The editor of the Wilmington *Daily Post,* a leading Republican newspaper in North Carolina, agreed that "although we are composed of different races, we speak one language, and claim as the foundation of the nation certain common principles."[16]

The power of the national state was another central principle of Republican nationalism that influenced the ideologies promoted by Fenians, southern whites, and freedpeople. The Civil War had firmly established the supremacy of the Union over states' rights. In an essay significantly entitled "Are We a Nation?" Republican senator Charles Sumner of Massachusetts declared that "*local sovereignty,* whether in the name of State or prince, is out of place and incongruous under a government truly national." A Georgia editor announced that his Republican newspaper "vindicates the supremacy of the National over State Governments." A meeting of North Carolina Republicans agreed with these assessments and resolved that one of the fundamental creeds of their party was "the indissolubility of the American Union."[17] Robert M. Douglas, speaking to a Republican mass meeting in Smithfield, North Carolina, explained further: "Call it consolidation, centralization, or

16. Hyman, ed., *Radical Republicans and Reconstruction,* 497, 154; Atlanta *Daily New Era,* January 14, 1868; Wilmington *Daily Post,* August 16, 1867.

17. George Frisbie Hoar, ed., *Charles Sumner: His Complete Works,* vol. 16 (Boston: Lee and Shepard, 1900), 13; Augusta *Georgia Republican,* July 2, 1870; Atlanta *Daily New Era,* July 19, 1868.

what you will, the United States has a strong government to maintain its authority and enforce its laws." He urged his listeners to "respect and obey its authority from a natural regard for law and order." During Reconstruction, many white southerners dissented from this view of a northern hegemonic nationalism. "In a Confederation the independent members may well be diverse but under consolidation there must be homogeneity," reasoned John Lyon, a lawyer from Petersburg, Virginia. Southerners, "as the weaker party must *perforce* adapt ourselves, or else be moulded by the hand of power, to suit the exigencies of the new dispensation. We will be *Yankeeized*."[18]

Unlike conservative southern whites or the freedmen, the Fenians did not collectively define themselves in relationship to postwar Republican nationalism. Rather, they saw the Irish nation as a people in exile whose national destiny would be fulfilled upon the overthrow of English rule in Ireland. The major motif in Fenian nationalism was this idea of a diaspora. A Fenian speaker in Houston referred to the Irish as "an exiled race." D. O. Sullivan, editor of the New York *Irish People*, spoke of "the Irish nation, at home and in exile." In their 1865 address to Irish Americans, Fenian leaders explained that Ireland was "the portion of the world decreed in the economy of Providence to be the dwelling place of your race, and deprived of it you are a people without a country." Fenianism was about "the resurrection of a nationality that has lain prostrate for three hundred years." Voicing a common theme in Fenian literature, Irishmen in Connecticut claimed "that they cherish the faith in their nationality and their efforts to restore it."[19]

18. Robert M. Douglas, *Speech of Col. Robert M. Douglas, of Washington, D.C., Delivered at a Republican Mass Meeting Held at Smithfield, N.C., July 12th, 1870* (Raleigh: "Standard" Steam Book and Job Press, 1870), 8; John Lyon to A. B. Springs, Springs Family Papers, Southern Historical Collection, University of North Carolina, Chapel Hill, North Carolina.

19. Quoted in *Irish People*, March 9, 1867; *Proceedings of the Senate and House of Representatives of the Fenian Brotherhood, in Joint Convention at Philadelphia, PA, November 24, 25, 26, 27, 28, & 29, 1868* (New York: D. W. Lee, 1868), 41; *Proceedings of the Second National Congress of the Fenian Brotherhood, held in Cincinnati, Ohio, January, 1865* (Philadelphia: James Gibbons, 1865), 46, 13; Buffalo *Fenian Volunteer*, December 14, 1867. See also *Irish Citizen*, May 16, 1868.

Fenian national identity rested upon the belief that Ireland had once been a nation, but that its nationalism had been destroyed by the English. Like Irish immigrants themselves, the Irish nation was in exile and waiting to be redeemed after centuries of lying dormant. The establishment of an Irish republic was therefore not so much an act of creation as one of restoration. Fenians meeting in East Weymouth, Massachusetts, for instance, spoke of the "redemption of Ireland." W. R. Roberts, addressing an audience at Cooper Union Institute in New York City, urged Fenians to struggle for the "redemption of their native land." A correspondent to the New York *Irish People* characterized Ireland as an "oppressed nationality." Irish American leader John Mitchel, in an essay on "Ancient Celtic Laws of Ireland," described a "remarkable nationality, undaunted, although convulsed under secular oppression, and now, preparing, with unceasing devotion, to resume the prestige of its former glory." The *Irish Citizen* insisted that the leading thought of all Irishmen was "to repeal the Conquest, and rear up again the Irish Nation upon its own soil."[20]

A future Irish republic would rest on the principle of liberty. Thomas Lavan, speaking to a St. Patrick's Day celebration in Cleveland, described the "Gospel" of Fenianism as "self-government and independence for poor, impoverished, down-trodden Ireland. In a word it is liberty, liberty for all classes and all creeds." The Emmet Circle of Blairstown, Iowa, argued similarly that the goal of the Fenian movement was not only the overthrow of English rule but the "erection, in its stead, of a government founded upon the broad and immutable principles of liberty, equality, and equal justice to all men, be they white or black, English or Irish, American or Mexican." Michael Scanlon, editor of the *Irish Republic,* suggested that a statue of liberty be placed in the temple of Irish nationality. In elaborating on the meaning of liberty, Fenian leaders relied heavily on the discourse of eighteenth-century

---

20. *Irish People*, February 25, 1867; W. R. Roberts, *Lecture by W. R. Roberts, Delivered Before the Fenian Brotherhood of New York, at Cooper Institute, on Wednesday, Sept. 27th, 1865* (New York: J. Croft, 1865), 22; *Irish People*, July 13, 1867; New York *Citizen*, March 10, 1866; *Irish Citizen*, October 19, 1867. I am indebted to a former colleague at Denison for suggesting that "diaspora nationalism" was a useful concept to understand the Fenian view of an Irish nation.

republicanism that had figured so prominently in the era of the American Revolution and Early Republic. In an address to Irish Americans, the Fourth National Congress of the Fenian Brotherhood announced that "we bow to no man's tyrant whim—that we are men, FREE-MEN, who both know and appreciate the value of Republican liberty." Echoing Thomas Paine, some Fenians insisted that Irish independence would mean the abolition of monarchy in England. One Fenian sympathizer stationed with the U.S. Army in the Utah Territory wrote to the *Irish Republic* that it was the work of Fenians "to destroy the last vestige of monarchical government in Great Britain."[21]

The Fenian construction of an Irish republic was envisioned for the future: it was a state to be achieved. Fenian leaders often pointed out that the Irish had to prepare themselves for republican nationhood. The Fenian Brotherhood of Philadelphia, in an address to the Irish in Pennsylvania, explained that "nationalities, like individuals, must pass through a fiery ordeal; as gold, they must be purified, to wipe away the stains of their political degradation, and to fit them to take their place in the great family of nations." The contentious Fenians must unify, John Mitchel urged, so that they would be ready for nationality when the opportunity arose. It was thus the mission of the Fenian movement to prepare the Irish people for nationhood. "As a people we must, first of all," explained the *Irish Republic*, "*be educated in the principles and practices of true liberty*. We must be made fit for freedom before we can be free." William H. Grace, speaking before a Fenian audience at Independence, Iowa, portrayed Fenianism as "a National school of cultivation and purification to the Irish race." The importance of a nationalistic education explains the call for Fenian reading rooms that cropped up in the Irish American press during the late 1860s. Reflecting the republican notion of an educated citizenry, the *Irish Republic* called for every Fenian circle to establish a reading room on the assumption "that an intelligent people cannot be enslaved, nor a people who are not intelligent become

21. Cleveland *Morning Leader*, March 19, 1866; *Irish Republic*, July 6, 1867; quotation from *Irish Republic*, February 6, 1869; *Proceedings of the Fourth National Congress of the Fenian Brotherhood, at Pittsburgh, Pa., February, 1866, with the Constitution of the F.B., and Addenda Thereto* (New York: J. Croft, 1866), 27; *Irish Citizen*, November 2, 1867; *Irish Republic*, August 10, 1867.

free." "Make your people once a reading people," insisted J. P. Hadnett at the formation of the Fenian Literary Society, "and England and hell cannot keep them in slavery." One Fenian correspondent from St. Louis, in endorsing reading rooms, stated simply that "KNOWLEDGE IS POWER— EDUCATE THAT YOU MAY BE FREE."[22]

The attempt to construct an Irish national identity within the context of postwar American nationalism raised a thorny problem for Fenian leaders. Could a nation in exile also exist as a nation within the United States? Some Fenians argued that the Irish in America constituted a separate nation. "For there is now another Ireland," explained the editor of the *Irish Republic*, "in existence and at work—the free Ireland of America—to accomplish the national deliverance." The editor of the New York *Irish People* also spoke of an "Irish nation in America." Yet not all Fenians believed that the Irish in America constituted a nation within a nation. Once again, John Mitchel stood in opposition to Michael Scanlon. In a lecture to the Brooklyn Academy of Music, the editor of the *Irish Citizen* explained: "I have sometimes heard it said 'We are an Irish nation in America.' But no; politically we are part of the American nation." Using constitutional language that harkened back to the Revolutionary era, Mitchel claimed that the "Fenian *Imperium in Imperio* was an anomaly." Mitchel might have rejected the notion of an Irish nation within America because of his own strategies of national liberation. An Irish nation in America could not proclaim itself as a belligerent nor have its own government, making it less able to wage war against England.[23]

---

22. *Address of the Fenian Brotherhood of Philadelphia, to Irishmen and Friends of Ireland in Pennsylvania* (broadside, 1866?), Fenian Brotherhood Papers, Philadelphia Archdiocesan Historical Research Center; *Irish Citizen,* October 19, 1867; *Irish Republic,* May 18, 1867; August 31, 1867; June 29, 1867; July 21, 1867; September 28, 1867. Another writer to the *Irish Republic* believed: "Could we teach them to think less of the saloon, and more of the reading-room, we would be accomplishing much towards making them strong for the inevitable conflict" (see *Irish Republic,* May 25, 1867). For more on reading rooms, see the *Irish Republic,* October 15, 1867. For parallel information on reading clubs among German immigrants, see Hartmut Keil and John B. Jentz, eds., *German Workers in Chicago: A Documentary History of Working-Class Culture from 1850 to World War I* (Urbana: Univ. of Illinois Press, 1988), 250–252.

23. *Irish Republic,* May 4, 1867; *Irish People,* February 16, 1867; *Irish Citizen,* February 8, 1868; February 22, 1868; June 13, 1868.

The theme of restoration, central to Fenian Irish American nationalism, also appears in the writings of southern white conservatives during Reconstruction. During the presidential election of 1868, southern whites believed that in opposing Reconstruction they were only attempting to restore true constitutional government to the United States. The Young Men's Democratic Club of Whistler, Alabama, argued that the successful return of the Democrats to power in 1868 "will restore to us our constitutional rights and liberties." The Seymour and Blair Club of Bayou La Batre claimed similarly that Democratic organization will help "to assist in restoring the government of the United States, which by a series of aggressive and unconstitutional measures has been already revolutionized, and its authority usurped by a fraction of the same, styling itself a Congress, transforming its boastful protection of the citizen into a civil engineering of systematic oppression." The nomination of the Democratic ticket was "the harbinger of a peaceful restoration of the Government to the true principles of the Constitution of '87, and its patriotic purposes and intention." The claim of restoration to defend an assertion of southern interests was not dissimilar to the position secessionists had made earlier in the decade. In 1860–1861, southern fire-eaters insisted that disunion would rescue true republican government from a Republican-dominated nation.[24]

The issue of suffrage best illustrates how the separatist efforts of freedmen, Fenians, and southern whites were channeled into the discourse of American civic nationalism. In the years after the Civil War, the question of suffrage became one of the most prominent and divisive issues in American public life. During the congressional debates over Reconstruction policy, Illinois Republican John A. Rawlins insisted that the right to vote "is the only sure protection to person and property. It gives one a voice in government, secures to him respect, and insures him the equal benefits of the law." African Americans, with some of their Re-

---

24. Mobile *Daily Advertiser and Register,* September 16, 1868; September 5, 1868. The notion of national redemption made sense to at least one African American leader in the Reconstruction South. A black newspaper from Savannah saw as one of his paper's missions the "redemption of the race" (*Freeman's Standard,* February 15, 1868).

publican allies, insisted that true freedom and citizenship included the right to vote. Their efforts culminated in 1870 in the adoption of the Fifteenth Amendment. Behind enfranchisement stood the more fundamental question of citizenship—who would be included in the body politic—which had arisen with the social, economic, and political transformations of the Civil War era. Political machines, which developed in response to the rapid urbanization and industrialization of American life, brought increasing numbers of immigrants and workers into the political process. Benjamin Butler in Massachusetts and Roscoe Conkling in New York, for example, created powerful political machines by carefully manipulating federal patronage and responding to the needs of working-class constituencies. In reaction to these developments and to the many instances of political corruption in the postwar era, conservative northern elites began to voice serious questions about the future course of American politics. Increasingly anxious about the fitness of immigrants and laborers for citizenship, they created reform clubs to help stem the tide of democratic participation.[25]

For all three groups in this study, the right to vote came to signify membership in the American body politic. Suffrage was central to black political struggles during Reconstruction. The Reconstruction Acts of March 1867 entitled African American males to vote for delegates to state constitutional conventions. Black delegates to the South Carolina

---

25. Hyman, ed., *Radical Republicans and Reconstruction*, 395. On the women's suffrage issue during Reconstruction, see Ellen Carol DuBois, *Feminism and Suffrage: The Emergence of an Independent Women's Movement in America, 1848–1869* (Ithaca: Cornell Univ. Press, 1978); and Ellen Carol DuBois, "Outgrowing the Compact of the Fathers: Equal Rights, Woman Suffrage, and the United States Constitution, 1820–1878," *Journal of American History* 74 (December 1987): 836–862. An excellent recent study that emphasizes the postwar anti-democratic impulse is Sven Beckert, *The Monied Metropolis: New York City and the Consolidation of the American Bourgeoisie, 1850–1896* (New York: Cambridge Univ. Press, 2001), but see also John G. Sproat, *"The Best Men": Liberal Reformers in the Gilded Age* (New York: Oxford Univ. Press, 1968), chapter 3. On the rise of political machines after the Civil War, see Samuel Shapiro, "'Aristocracy, Mud, and Vituperation': The Butler-Dana Campaign in Essex County in 1868," *New England Quarterly* 31 (September 1958): 340–362; William D. Mallam, "Butlerism in Massachusetts," *New England Quarterly* 33 (June 1960): 186–206; and William Hartman, "The New York Custom House: Seat of Spoils Politics," *New York History* 34 (April 1953): 149–163.

convention of 1868 referred to the vote as "the inherent right of man" and "our chief means for self defense."[26] African American leaders in the Reconstruction South placed suffrage at the top of their political agenda. The *Journal of Freedom*, a black newspaper published in Raleigh, North Carolina, made "the truly republican principle of Universal suffrage" the main issue in its first editorial in 1865. "The theory of our government," the editor explained, "is the 'consent of the governed,' as expressed through the ballot-box in their votes for rulers." He believed that "every citizen . . . should be allowed a voice in making laws to which he is amenable." Another black newspaper, the *New Era* of Fort Smith, Arkansas, similarly supported the "extension of suffrage to all loyal men, irrespective of race or color." George Cox, a black who served in the Alabama state legislature, insisted that the right to vote was "that privilege of freedom and manhood."[27]

African Americans defended the right to vote on the grounds of racial justice. "The whole question of manhood suffrage is a simple one," insisted the editor of the *Colored Tennessean*, "and is, if men will look at it from the simple and human stand point of a wise equity, entirely disconnected with any question of the races being able to live together." The *Colored American* hoped that "all will acknowledge the justice of their enfranchisement, and wonder that it was not bestowed before." Black leaders defended their right to vote on deeply imbedded principles in the American political tradition. A gathering of freedmen in Athens, Alabama, in 1866 resolved that universal suffrage rested upon the republican principle that "all just governments are founded on the consent

---

26. Quoted in Joel Williamson, *After Slavery: The Negro in South Carolina during Reconstruction, 1861–1877* (1965: New York: Norton, 1975), 337. See also Forest *Register* (Scott County, Mississippi), May 1, 1869. For the suffrage struggle on a national level, see William Gillette, *The Right to Vote: Politics and the Passage of the Fifteenth Amendment* (Baltimore: Johns Hopkins Univ. Press, 1965), and Xi Wang, *The Trial of Democracy: Black Suffrage and Northern Republicans, 1860–1910* (Athens: Univ. of Georgia Press, 1997).

27. *Journal of Freedom*, September 30, 1865; Fort Smith (Arkansas) *New Era*, quoted in *Journal of Freedom*, October 14, 1865; *Daily State Sentinel*, June 24, 1867. For an early petition for black suffrage, see Ira Berlin, et al., eds., *Freedom: A Documentary History of Emancipation, 1861–1867: Series II: The Black Military Experience* (Cambridge: Cambridge Univ. Press, 1982), 811–818.

of the governed." A similar meeting in Davidson County, North Carolina, a year later declared that the franchise allowed them "the glorious privilege of making the choice of those who are to rule over us." The local Union League of Decatur, Alabama, supported the right to vote as "the inestimable privilege of sharing equally with other loyal citizens the right to choose our rulers." African American leaders offered other, more practical reasons for the vote. A correspondent to the New Orleans *Tribune* believed that universal suffrage was the "only hope and surety of peace; that inevitable, all wise and lasting deliverance." F. L. Cardozo of South Carolina told a meeting of the Union League that suffrage would be a means of protecting their freedom. To the radical New Orleans *Tribune,* universal suffrage would be a way of finally "annihilating the slave power." [28]

Freedmen saw the close connection between voting, civil freedom, and citizenship. "We are living in an important era in the history of the world," declared some Georgia freedmen. "A large number of our citizens were, but a few months since, held in bondage; now, that they are freemen they are entitled to all the rights of citizenship." John W. Menard of New Orleans, the first African American to speak before Congress, also argued that blacks had "only one great common interest pending in this contest, and that is to secure forever our common rights and privileges of citizenship in the organic law of the land." To the New Orleans *Tribune,* the right to vote was "inherent to citizenship." At public meetings held in Monroe and Clarke counties in Alabama, freedmen were told similarly that citizenship involved the franchise. Their right

---

28. *Colored Tennessean,* August 12, 1865; *Colored American,* March 16, 1867; Huntsville *Advocate,* March 21, 1866; Raleigh *Tri-Weekly Standard,* April 4, 1867; see also New Orleans *Tribune,* October 5, 1866; Raleigh *Tri-Weekly Standard,* April 16, 1867; New Orleans *Tribune,* September 4, 1866; F. L. Cardozo, *Address before the Grand Council of the Union League at Their Annual Meeting, held July 27, 1870 by Hon. F. L. Cardozo, President* (Columbia, S.C.: John W. Denny, 1870), 15; New Orleans *Tribune,* September 22, 1866.

A Freedmen's Bureau official in Alabama noticed that the freedmen "are generally alive on the question of registration, and, I think, understand the matter pretty thoroughly" (George Tracy to O. D. Kinsman, July 1, 1867, Wager Swayne Papers, Alabama Department of Archives and History, Montgomery, Alabama).

to vote was confirmed in the Fifteenth Amendment to the U.S. Constitution, ratified in 1870, although the implementing legislation was never strong enough to grant them true equal citizenship.[29]

Despite the passage of the Fifteenth Amendment, the national Republican Party was divided over the issue of black suffrage. Prominent Radicals in the party supported enfranchisement for the freedmen. "In the right to vote," explained Carl Schurz, "he would find the best permanent protection against oppressive class-legislation, as well as against individual persecution." The Second District Republican Convention in Alabama endorsed the action of Congress "to secure the right of suffrage to every American citizen impartially." David Humphries, speaking to the Union Republican Convention in Huntsville, Alabama, insisted that the idea of qualified suffrage was "incompatible with true ideas of republican government." According to one student of the Fifteenth Amendment, the majority of Republicans after the war were opposed to enfranchising former slaves. Besides the usual racist justifications, moderate Republicans were hesitant to use federal power to enforce voting rights and feared that black suffrage would raise troublesome questions about voting discrimination in the North. George Templeton Strong of New York considered enfranchising the blacks a problem "full of difficulties and conflicting rights." An Ohio Republican believed that agitation of the suffrage question would bring harm to the party. In the South, the Shelbyville *Republican* of Tennessee believed that universal suffrage was "unwise and inexpedient." Qualified suffrage, on the other hand, "would produce no convulsions or violence, when universal might, and would fail to be any stimulus to the negro to improve." Black suffrage had made little progress in the North during the early years of Reconstruction. Only five states, all in New England, granted equal voting rights to blacks.[30]

---

29. *Colored American*, December 30, 1865; *Free South*, February 15, 1868; New Orleans *Tribune*, September 13, 1866; Samuel Gardner to O. D. Kinsman, July 23, 1867, in Wager Swayne Papers, Alabama Department of Archives and History, Montgomery, Alabama. On J. W. Menard, see Eric Foner, *Freedom's Lawmakers: A Directory of Black Officeholders during Reconstruction*, rev. ed. (Baton Rouge: Louisiana State Univ. Press, 1996), 148.

30. Hyman, ed., *Radical Republicans and Reconstruction*, 297 (see also 88 and 271); Mobile *Nationalist*, June 11, 1869; *Daily State Sentinel*, June 25, 1867; Gillette, *The Right to Vote*,

Southern white conservatives saw black suffrage as a "crime against the civilization of the age." For southern whites, granting the vote to the freedmen was the logical culmination and most devastating consequence of Radical Reconstruction. "The interests of the white race," warned a Mississippi newspaper, "are nothing compared with the grand scheme of making Sambo a voter. It is through him that this yoke of oppression is to be kept upon your necks." The Austin *Daily State Gazette* thought black suffrage was "incompatible with the public safety." With some justification, southern whites believed that northern Republicans were enfranchising the freedmen to maintain their political hegemony over the nation. "Their last hope now is in a lease of power through negro supremacy," protested the Democratic *Independent Monitor*. It was plain to a South Carolina editor "that these States must be reconstructed if the dominant party retain its sway, and this the present movement has for its object." A Savannah man argued that the grand object of Reconstruction was to "give the Radical party control of Congress by means of the negro votes of the South." A newspaper from Jefferson, Texas, warned that the Radicals needed the votes of blacks to help them in the 1868 presidential election. The belief that the Republicans were seeking political hegemony through the black vote was well summarized by the Austin *Daily State Gazette:* "But now, when the radical purposes are well known and understood—when the violations of law, the frauds and swindling are patent and not even denied, it is time for all good conservative people to unite and prevent, if possible, the domination of the negro and the degradation and ruin of the whole country, North and South."[31]

31; Wang, *The Trial of Democracy*, 22; Foner, *Reconstruction*, 222; Shelbyville (Tennessee) *Republican*, October 19, 1866.

31. Forrest Cooper, "Reconstruction in Scott County," *Publications of the Mississippi Historical Society* 13 (1913), 215; *Weekly Panola Star*, May 9, 1868; Austin *Daily State Gazette*, November 15, 1867; Tuscaloosa *Independent Monitor*, October 16, 1867; Laurensville *Herald*, February 24, 1871; New York *Citizen*, August 24, 1867; *Semi-Weekly Jimpleuite* (Jefferson, Texas), May 12, 1868; Austin *Daily State Gazette*, October 23, 1867. See also the *Alabama Beacon*, May 25, 1867; the comments of J. C. Brahan of Kirkwood, Mississippi, quoted in the *Weekly Panola Star*, August 1, 1868; and George Marshall (?) to William W. Holden [June 1868], "Correspondence 1868" folder, William W. Holden Miscellaneous Papers, North Carolina Division of Archives and History, Raleigh, North Carolina. Forrest G. Wood, *Black Scare: The Racist Response to Emancipation and Reconstruction* (Berkeley: Univ.

The right to vote was also a major concern of southern whites who faced a variety of forms of disfranchisement during Reconstruction. The third section of the Fourteenth Amendment, adopted as part of Congressional Reconstruction, imposed disabilities against former Confederates. The disfranchisement of former Confederates was an important and controversial issue in the constitutional conventions held in the Reconstructed states during 1867 and 1868. Disfranchisement varied from state to state, the most far-reaching occurring in Alabama, Arkansas, and Louisiana. It received its greatest support from those former Unionists in the upcountry or nonplantation areas of the South who harbored great resentment against their own proscription during the Civil War. The discussion of political disabilities surfaced often during the early years of Reconstruction and was clearly one of the grounds for conservative white opposition to Radical regimes in the South. "I was once a voter," explained Democratic senator James Campbell of South Carolina: "It was my birthright my ancestors under Washington and his compeers thought they had forever secured the right to their descendants. It has been taken from me." A Florida editor claimed that the enfranchisement of blacks put the liberties of white men in jeopardy. The Memphis *Daily Avalanche* complained with more fear than reality that Republican Reconstruction has "deprived eighty thousand white men of the right to vote—that right which is the only defense of the liberties both of blacks and whites."[32]

Southern whites saw behind their disfranchisement covert Republican plans for partisan and racial dominance. To Jonathan Worth, North

---

of California Press, 1970), 107–120, provides a discussion of the southern white response to black enfranchisement.

32. William A. Dunning, *Reconstruction, Political and Economic, 1865–1877* (1907; reprint, Harper and Row, 1962), 125; Foner, *Reconstruction*, 324; [James B. Campbell], *Two Letters from the Hon. James B. Campbell, U.S. Senator Elect from South Carolina, on Public Affairs, and Our Duties to the Colored Race* (Charleston: Walker, Evans, and Cogswell, 1868), 11; Jacksonville *Mercury*, January 18, 1868; Memphis *Daily Avalanche*, May 17, 1867. On the connection between the lack of access to political power and the emergence of white violence during Reconstruction, see George C. Rable, *But There Was No Peace: The Role of Violence in the Politics of Reconstruction* (Athens: Univ. of Georgia Press, 1984), especially 81.

Carolina Republicans were looking "to the disenfranchisement of the great body of the whites and the enfranchisement of [all] the negroes, whereby the negroes would become the dominant political power in the State." One Mississippian believed that the main object of the 1868 constitution was "to exclude the whites from the possession of that influence in local government to which their numbers, their wealth, and their mental and moral status entitle them." Southern whites did not need to complain for too long. Congress repealed the so-called "ironclad" oath in 1871, and the General Amnesty Act of 1872 removed disabilities from all but a few ex-Confederates.[33]

Denying the suffrage to former Confederates posed thorny problems for the Republican Party in the South. It not only contradicted their commitment to universal manhood suffrage—their great appeal among the freedmen—but also undercut much-needed political support among southern whites. According to one informed student of Reconstruction politics, most northern Republicans opposed a proscriptive policy toward whites. Conservative Republicans in the South also saw the dangers of white disfranchisement. In the intraparty struggle in Virginia between Gilbert C. Walker and Henry H. Wells, the *Independent Republican* of Richmond assured its readers that the supporters of Walker "seek not, by State test oaths and disenfranchising laws, to crush their neighbors, and keep alive heart burnings." Yet many Republicans in the South recognized the critical importance of disfranchisement in securing the political rights of former Unionists and former slaves. A local Union League in Galveston considered universal amnesty "dangerous, imprudent and unwise—antagonistic to the wise and prudent mea-

---

33. J. G. de Roulhac Hamilton, ed., *The Correspondence of Jonathan Worth*, 2 vols. (Raleigh: Edwards and Broughton Print Company, 1909), 2:865; *Weekly Panola Star*, May 30, 1868; Foner, *Reconstruction*, 324; Dunning, *Reconstruction*, 202. See also the "Address from the Chairman of the Democratic State Executive Committee," reprinted in the *Weekly Panola Star*, May 9, 1868. One historian maintains that the disfranchisement of whites could have been a decisive factor in Radical victories in Mississippi, Louisiana, and South Carolina (William A. Russ Jr., "Registration and Disfranchisement under Radical Reconstruction," *Mississippi Valley Historical Review* 21 [September 1934]: 163–180).

sures of reconstruction adopted by the Congress of the United States." A meeting of the Union Leagues of Alabama insisted similarly that the disabilities imposed by Congress on former Confederates should not be removed without the consent of the state Leagues.[34]

This perspective on enfranchisement also underscores the significance of the debate over citizenship sparked by the Fenian controversy in Ireland and America. In the late 1860s, Fenianism was one of several factors creating tensions in the diplomatic relationship between Great Britain and the United States. Britain's insistence that the United States help prevent Fenian military incursions into Canada provided a convenient opportunity for American statesmen to emphasize Britain's violation of neutrality laws during the Civil War through the building of Confederate raiders like the *Alabama*. In 1866, some Irish Americans were jailed in Ireland for participating in Fenian uprisings. Their incarceration raised the question of naturalization, which became a point of contention between the two nations in the postwar era. At issue was the difficulty of distinguishing between a naturalized American citizen born in Ireland and an American citizen of Irish descent born in the United States. The British clung to the doctrine of the inalienability of citizenship, the position that a British citizen could not transfer allegiance from one country to another. (Put simply, "Once an Englishman, always an Englishman.") In reply, American secretary of state William H. Seward argued that naturalization following residence in the United States for five years was sufficient to change one's nationality. In 1865 and 1866, Fenians called upon the American government to protect Irish American citizens in Ireland. The Knights of St. Patrick, meeting in New York, resolved that "American citizens, whether native or adopted, are not British subjects, and if accused of crime in Great Britain or Ireland, have a right to be tried as aliens, and not as Englishmen, by the species of jury provided for aliens." The British finally

---

34. Michael Les Benedict, "The Politics of Reconstruction," in *American Political History: Essays on the State of the Discipline*, ed. John F. Marzalak and Wilson D. Miscamble, C.S.C. (Notre Dame: Univ. of Notre Dame Press, 1997), 64; Richmond (Virginia) *Independent Republican*, May 1, 1869; San Antonio *Daily Express*, December 27, 1868; Montgomery *Daily Mail*, April 17, 1867. See also the comments of Thaddeus Stevens in Hyman, ed., *Radical Republicans and Reconstruction*, 374.

recognized the right of naturalization in the Treaty of Washington of 1871.³⁵

Suffrage embodied the fullest manifestation of citizenship, another central issue of the Civil War era. Emancipation and the ratification of the Thirteenth Amendment formally ended slavery but did not confer citizenship on African Americans. In its infamous *Dred Scott* decision (1857), the Supreme Court denied that blacks had ever been or could be citizens of an American state for purposes of granting federal court jurisdiction. The Fourteenth Amendment, which granted both federal and state citizenship to all persons born or naturalized in the United States, essentially made former slaves American citizens and extended citizenship to naturalized immigrants as well. The issue of citizenship during Reconstruction also involved women as well as immigrants. Women were excluded from the Fourteenth Amendment's provision providing for a reduction of congressional representation because of disfranchisement, while military service had earlier offered the opportunity for citizenship to Irish and German immigrants who enlisted in the Union army. The debates over suffrage during Reconstruction emboldened the movement for women's right to vote.³⁶

The question of citizenship was a crucial one for freedmen, southern whites, and the Fenians, for it was the most tangible way of ensur-

---

35. Thomas A. Bailey, *A Diplomatic History of the American People*, 10th ed. (Englewood Cliffs, N.J., Prentice Hall, 1980), 376; Brian Jenkins, *Fenians and Anglo-American Relations during Reconstruction* (Ithaca: Cornell Univ. Press, 1969), 264; *Irish Citizen*, January 18, 1868; see also *Irish Citizen*, August 22, 1868, and the Cleveland *Morning Leader*, January 1, 1868. For the important context of postwar Anglo-American relations, see Charles S. Campbell, *The Transformation of American Foreign Relations, 1865–1900* (New York: Harper and Row, 1976), chapter 2, and the authoritative Allan Nevins, *Hamilton Fish: An Inner History of the Grant Administration* (New York: Dodd, Mead, 1936), especially chapter 16.

36. On citizenship, see James H. Kettner, *The Development of American Citizenship, 1608–1870* (Chapel Hill: Published for the Institute of Early American History and Culture, Williamsburg, Va., by the Univ. of North Carolina Press, 1978). Foner, *Reconstruction*, 251–261. David Herbert Donald, Jean Harvey Baker, and Michael F. Holt, *The Civil War and Reconstruction* (New York: Norton, 2001), 543–550, provide the best brief discussion of the Fourteenth Amendment, although the legal literature on the subject is quite large. On the campaign for women's suffrage, see DuBois, *Feminism and Suffrage*.

ing their place in American political society. Blacks in the Reconstruction South fought primarily for civil rights, voting privileges, and an end to discrimination and segregation. Facing disfranchisement for the first time, many southern whites waged a vigorous fight to regain their political privileges. The Fenians, drawn largely from Irish American urban communities, saw their political power increase in the postwar era. In response to the growing enfranchisement of groups such as immigrants, laborers, and freedmen, powerful voices sought to stem the tide of democratization. The era of Reconstruction witnessed troublesome questions about the meaning of citizenship that demarcated as much as any other factor the nationalist aspirations of all three groups. Whether it was inclusion in the American political order or in a separate republic, citizenship for freedmen, southern whites, and Fenians became the defining mark of nationality.

Reflecting contemporary political beliefs, African American leaders in the South realized that citizenship entailed certain demands and responsibilities. "By being free," George Cox told a group of Alabama freedmen, "we are not discharged from the obligations of citizens. With citizenship our responsibilities begin. We stand erect before the world as men, and we must improve our mental and moral qualities so as to enable us to take care of ourselves in this race of life." Citizenship was a status to be attained with preparation. Recently enfranchised freedmen in Greensboro, Alabama, recognized their own need "to be guided by a sincere sense of duty and an exalted patriotism, such as should ever animate those who presume to take part in the government of their country." The *Journal of Freedom* remained confident, however, that "with a proper use of the strength of character developed by the Freedmen in their new surroundings, they will eventually take their proper place in our political arena as *men*."[37]

Southern white opponents of Reconstruction were not as sanguine as was this African American editor. They insisted that the freedman was unfit for citizenship. "Is the nation to centre all its future hopes upon the ability of the black man to govern it?" asked the doubtful edi-

37. *Daily State Sentinel*, June 24, 1867; *Alabama Beacon*, May 25, 1867; *Journal of Freedom*, September 30, 1865.

tor of the Tuscaloosa *Independent Monitor:* "Are we expected, in the light of the intelligence of this century, to believe that any body of men, be they the Congress of the United States or a body of mythological gods, can, by a simple legislative fiat, lift the negro from barbarism to the summit of civilization?" The *Southern Argus* maintained that the Radical Party "universally enfranchised a class which is neither fitted by education, past associations, or native intellect, to exercise so responsible and delicate a privilege as the elective franchise." Reacting to recent riots in Wilmington, the conservative paper in that city said that it "renders such citizenship in direct conflict with the welfare of the country." In a petition to Congress, some "white people of Alabama" explained that blacks "are in the main, ignorant generally, wholly unacquainted with the principles of free governments, improvident, disinclined to work, credulous, yet suspicious, untruthful, incapable of self-restraint, and easily impelled by want, or invited by false and specious counsels, into folly and crime."³⁸

Southern freedmen and Republicans responded to these charges by claiming that education would prepare blacks for citizenship. "In a commonwealth where universal suffrage makes every man a lawgiver," explained the *Daily Austin Republican,* "a general diffusion of knowledge is needed, to enact and sustain good laws, and to favor a right public opinion." States had public schools since "intelligence is indispensable to republican safety and growth." The *Southern Republican* of Demopolis, Alabama, believed that universal suffrage demanded universal education. Another Alabama Republican editor thought that knowledge was necessary for the freedmen now that they had gained the right to vote: "the children must be taught that they may become good citizens in the future." General Davis Tillson, commander of the Freedmen's Bureau in Georgia, told a group of freedmen that "the great mass of your people have need to make use of the opportunities of education—now for the first time afforded them—before they can with advantage to themselves and safety to the country be entrusted with such rights." The Norfolk

---

38. Tuscaloosa *Independent Monitor,* October 16, 1867; *Southern Argus,* June 19, 1869; Wilmington (North Carolina) *Journal,* June 26, 1868; Mobile *Daily Advertiser and Register,* February 19, 1868.

Republican was optimistic that with the right to vote, freedmen would become educated, and "step out into the light, into civilization, and give strength to the strong power of a people's government."[39]

Emerging in these discussions of black citizenship was a conservative and elitist anti-democratic strain that had long lain under the surface of American republicanism. From James Madison in the 1780s to Chancellor James Kent in the 1820s, dedicated republicans worried about the ability of the people to govern themselves. Jacksonian democracy had partially and temporarily obscured these fears. But Reconstruction witnessed a renewed and more aggressive belief in the rule of the "best men." The Democratic Charleston *Daily News* laid bare this assumption: "We can yet rule the State as it was ruled of old—by intelligence and worth." Give the franchise to blacks and "non-taxpaying voters," warned the chairman of the Mississippi Democratic State Executive Committee, and "your constitutional liberty is forever at an end." This elitist, anti-democratic principle was even endorsed by a black editor. The *Colored American* of Augusta explained that the immigrant should be excluded from participation in government "because not being native born, he is ignorant of our institutions of government, and must understand them before he can participate in them." This sentiment could perhaps justify the disfranchisement of whites: "How many thousands are there of enfranchised *white* voters who know no more about the qualification of a candidate for office, but what they gather from word of mouth and in the political debate of the barroom."[40]

Similar assumptions surfaced in the objections of conservative southern whites to their disfranchisement. "The continued imposition of disabilities upon our best, our trusted men," argued North Carolina congressman Plato Durham, "is regarded as nothing more than an effort to keep in position and place men of inferior talents, and to deprive the public of the services of men who could perhaps rescue the State governments from their present condition." Durham defined the

39. *Daily Austin Republican,* June 5, 1868; *Southern Republican,* March 3, 1869; *Alabama State Journal,* February 6, 1869; *Proceedings of the Freedmen's Convention of Georgia,* 8–9; Raleigh *Tri-Weekly Standard,* March 26, 1867.

40. Charleston *Daily News,* October 15, 1868; *Weekly Panola Star,* May 9, 1868; *Colored American,* January 13, 1866.

"best people" as "the property owners of the country, the men representing the intelligence of the country." A correspondent from Nashville expressed his concern that the Radical leadership in his state would "deprive 80,000 of our best men of citizenship, and place the heels of 45,000 ignorant freedmen on our necks." Armistead Burt of South Carolina, speaking at the state Democratic convention, saw white disfranchisement in similar terms: "I say that a more arrant and infamous spoiliation of a class was never designed by any country on the face of the earth." A North Carolinian made the southern white fear of democracy explicit: "The tendency is to ignore virtue and property and intelligence—and to put the powers of government into the hands of mere numbers.... The majority in all times and in all countries are improvident and without property. Agrarianism and anarchy must be the result of this ultra democracy."[41]

Thus in one way or another, the ability of Irish immigrants, freedmen, and former Confederates to vote and become citizens was questioned. The concern with democracy that underlay much of the discussion of suffrage and citizenship during Reconstruction reflected a more fundamental cultural, social, and political shift in the United States. The Civil War had strengthened certain conservative and anti-democratic forces in American life.

In a retreat from the humanitarian and anti-institutional reform of the antebellum years, northern intellectuals increasingly stressed the combined forces of law and religion to bring order to society and urged that democratic impulses must be held in check. Such men as journalist E. L. Godkin, Democratic leader Samuel J. Tilden, and economist David Wells began to articulate a philosophy of the "best men" that often explicitly supported restrictions on democracy. Groups like the Citizen's Association in New York proposed to limit suffrage through educational requirements and systems of "minority representation." The New York *Journal of Commerce* made these anti-democratic beliefs explicit in 1869: "The tendency among thoughtful men who desire honesty, economy,

---

41. KKK Hearings, North Carolina, page 313; *Wilcox County News,* August 16, 1867; Charleston *Daily News,* April 6, 1868; Hamilton, ed., *Correspondence of Jonathan Worth,* 2:1155.

and a good deal of intelligence in legislation is towards a restriction of the right of suffrage considerably inside its present limits." According to one historian, this impulse "gained its impetus from their efforts to limit the political influence of those social groups that had been mobilized during the Civil War, most particularly northern workers and southern freedpeople."[42]

In the South, anti-democratic sentiments can be glimpsed in a series of taxpayers' conventions held in the region during the later years of Reconstruction. Florida was the first to hold a taxpayers' convention, in 1870. A similar gathering met in South Carolina in May 1871. Later that year, 217 delegates representing ninety-four counties met at a taxpayers' convention in Texas. In Louisiana a Tax Resisting Association appeared in 1872, followed by a Citizens' Reform Association in 1874. Mississippi held its taxpayers' meeting in 1875. Taxpayer conventions were ostensibly called to protest the high rate of taxation and state expenditures of Radical regimes and hence pushed for financial retrenchment and reform. Echoing many of the concerns of northern urban elites, these meetings also assailed against political corruption. The purported object of the South Carolina meeting, for instance, was to "rebuke corruption in high places." The Citizens' Reform Association of Louisiana promised to work "zealously against official corruption" in that state. Most historians see these taxpayer meetings as a front to oust the Republicans from power and reinstate Conservative/Democratic rule. As one astute (if grammatically challenged) observer shared with the governor of South Carolina, "thars good deel of talk a mong the Democrats har about their Citizen's party . . . but we fear the woolf is in the sheep skin. They are the same kind of Creatures but they have Changed their boaast butonst and again the war out the old boat and then the good old

---

42. Fredrickson, *The Inner Civil War*, 185; Sproat, *"The Best Men,"* remains the best place to begin understanding this Liberal mindset. Foner, *Reconstruction*, 488–494; Beckert, *The Monied Metropolis*, 184–185; Foner, *Reconstruction*, 493; Beckert, *The Monied Metropolis*, 230. See also Lawson, "'A Profound National Devotion," 354–355. It should be noted that similar arguments against Home Rule for the Irish were being made in England. See the short but suggestive article by Joseph M. Heron Jr., "The Use of the American Civil War in the Debate over Irish Home Rule," *American Historical Review* 69 (July 1964): 1022–1026.

Democrat poles out his head and we Can get a Look at his Deformed principals."[43]

These taxpayers' meetings revealed elitist, anti-democratic currents similar to the ones circulating in the post–Civil War North. The Charleston *Mercury*, for example, claimed that the South Carolina taxpayers' convention was composed of men "most distinguished for learning, judgment, prudence, and statesmanship." In observing the taxpayers' convention in Florida, C. B. Wilder from Boston found many of the delegates to be "respectable, old-fashioned, and intelligent men." In contrast, claimed Wilder, "one-half of the colored and white are unfit, for they are ignorant, and do not know what is for their best interests." The Louisiana Taxpayers' Association claimed that Republican officeholders in that state represented "neither the intelligence, honesty, nor material interests of the parish." Interestingly, the taxpayers' movement in the South searched for the same kinds of electoral formulas being explored by conservative urban elites in the North to gain and keep power. One South Carolina newspaper supported a form of voting that would "enable the property-holders to elect a fair proportion of Representatives from every county in the State."[44]

Civic nationalism was the most powerful force shaping the aspirations of Fenians, southern whites, and African Americans. Freedpeople appropriated postwar Republican nationalism because it best served their political interests and expressed their desire for self-determination and ethnic autonomy. The Fenians adopted several elements of American nationalism; republicanism in particular became the key concept in en-

---

43. E. T. Miller, "State Finances of Texas during Reconstruction," *Texas State Historical Association Quarterly* 14 (October 1910): 95; Charleston *News*, quoted in Tallahassee *Sentinel*, May 20, 1871; Tallahassee *Sentinel*, May 13, 1871; Alexandria (Louisiana) *Caucasian*, June 27, 1874; Tucker to Robert K. Scott, May 17, 1870, Robert K. Scott Papers, Ohio Historical Society, Columbus, Ohio. Significantly, Liberals like Godkin joined in attacking the corruption of Carpetbag governments in the South (Sproat, *"The Best Men,"* 34). A majority of Florida's convention were Democrats or Conservatives (KKK Hearings, Florida, page 219).

44. Quoted in Tallahassee *Sentinel*, May 20, 1871; KKK Hearings, Florida, page 247, 257; Alexandria *Caucasian*, June 27, 1874; Keowee (South Carolina) *Courier*, May 5, 1871.

visioning an Irish republic. For southern whites, Republican nationalism defined the terms of Reconstruction against which they forged their efforts at self-determination.

Reconstruction witnessed a conflict between civic and ethnic nationalism. The organicism of American nationalism might have discouraged separatist impulses based on ethnicity. The kind of nationality envisioned by Lieber, Mulford, and others rested upon an assumption of a high degree of homogeneity. Different races and nationalities would be subsumed under the institutions of liberty. Indeed, postwar nationalism could have been a response to the increasing heterogeneity of American society. There was also a tension between republicanism and postwar nationalism. The Declaration of Independence, cited so often by African Americans, and the Fenian idea of a republic both rested on a contract theory of government rejected by Lieber and Mulford. The normative nationalism represented by the Republican Party thus channeled separatist impulses along the lines of civic nationalism while discouraging them along ethnic lines.

Conclusion

After the Battle of Ridgeway, American Fenians continued to see an invasion of Canada as a means of attacking Britain. In 1870, John O'Neil led another expedition—with a smaller force of about two hundred men—across the border. This time the Canadian militia was prepared and repulsed the Fenian invaders. The "Battle of Eccles Hill" was a humiliating defeat for the Fenians. Not one Canadian soldier had been wounded or killed. Moreover, O'Neil was captured by U.S. marshals for violation of the neutrality laws. He was found guilty and sentenced to two years' imprisonment, although President Ulysses S. Grant commuted his sentence. O'Neil apparently could not shake his Fenian fever. He led one more abortive attempt to invade Manitoba a year later. Afterward, O'Neil settled in Nebraska, where he died in 1878.[1]

The fate of the Fenian movement in the United States paralleled that of John O'Neil. The Brotherhood in New York was so broke by 1870 that they could not even pay for a telegram sent from the Canadian front. John O'Mahoney, one of the founding fathers of the Fenian movement, died in poverty in a small, unheated room in New York City in 1877. The Fenian Brotherhood officially disbanded in 1886. Yet the spirit lived on. John Phillip Holland of New Jersey, one of the last Fenian holdouts, devised a plan to harass British shipping by sending underwater boats to destroy English ships. Holland built a few prototypes of what would later become the submarine. It would be the Germans in 1914, however, who would successfully attack English shipping with torpedoes.[2]

Irish American nationalism persevered through the Clan na Gael, a more secret association founded in 1867 by Jerome J. Collins. Like the

---

1. W. S. Neidhardt, *Fenianism in North America* (University Park: Pennsylvania State Univ. Press, 1975), 120–121.

2. Ibid., 123–130.

Fenians, they were dedicated to using force to achieve Irish independence and established a Skirmishing Fund to finance terroristic activities. One of their members was Terence V. Powderly, future leader of the Knights of Labor. During the 1880s, Irish American nationalists continued to follow the lead of their Irish brethren. Charles Stewart Parnell led a "New Departure" movement, which stressed constitutional reform through the Parliamentary Party in Ireland. Michael Davitt centered nationalist efforts around land reform, organizing the Land League of Ireland in 1879. An American Land League was established in 1880 and became quite popular during the early part of that decade. On Easter 1916, Irish nationalists staged a revolt against British rule. A few years later, Ireland was divided between a northern part that remained British and a south that became an independent Irish republic.[3]

The Union Leagues, after their peak years of 1867–1869, also went into decline. They gradually dissolved after they had achieved their primary function of mobilizing black voters into the Republican Party. In Georgia, they began to disintegrate after the 1868 election and had virtually disappeared by the early 1870s. James Justice, a Republican lawyer and state legislator in North Carolina, believed that the Leagues died out after 1868. Similarly, Essie Harris, a black North Carolinian, claimed in 1871 that the Leagues broke up "some two years [ago]—may be more." This chronological pattern seems to fit other states as well. At the Ku Klux Klan hearings in 1871, future Democratic leader John B. Gordon of Georgia said he had heard nothing about the Union Leagues

---

3. Thomas N. Brown, *Irish-American Nationalism, 1870–1890* (Philadelphia: J. B. Lippincott, 1966), 65–69; Florence E. Gibson, *The Attitudes of the New York Irish Toward State and National Affairs, 1848–1892* (New York: Columbia Univ. Press, 1951), 330–335. The course of Irish nationalism during the rest of the nineteenth century can be followed in Norman D. Palmer, *The Land League Crisis* (1940; reprint, New York: Octagon Books, 1978); Paul Bew, *Land and the National Question in Ireland, 1858–82* (Dublin: Gill and Macmillan, 1978); James S. Donnelly, *The Land and the People of Nineteenth-Century Cork: The Rural Economy and the Land Question* (London: Routledge and Kegan Paul, 1975); Conor Cruise O'Brien, *Parnell and His Party, 1880–1890* (Oxford: Clarendon Press, 1957); and T. W. Moody, *Michael Davitt and Irish Revolution, 1846–82* (Oxford: Clarendon Press, 1981). See also the valuable essay by Eric Foner, "Class, Ethnicity, and Radicalism in the Gilded Age: The Land League and Irish-America," in *Politics and Ideology in the Age of the Civil War* (New York: Oxford Univ. Press, 1980).

for a few years. Native white Republican John R. Smith, editor of the Meridian *Chronicle,* told a similar congressional committee that the Mississippi Leagues "were pretty well lost sight of since the fall of 1869." By the 1870s there was little evidence of League activities.[4]

Yet Union League efforts continued. The national organization revived its interest in southern affairs in the late 1870s, publicizing the plight of the African American in the post-Redemption South. Remnants of the League in the South continued to work for civil rights during the 1880s. In Louisiana, they were active in promoting Kansas immigration. More important, the tradition of black political participation that owed so much to the Union Leagues did not die after Reconstruction. Even if state power lay in Democratic hands, blacks served in county and state offices throughout the South during the 1870s and 1880s. From 1876 to 1890, sixty-nine African Americans served in the Mississippi House of Representatives. When expedient, southern blacks joined independent parties, such as the Greenbackers, Readjusters, and Populists, to gain access to political power. In addition, regional strongholds of black political power like North Carolina's Second Congressional District and Fort Bend in Texas remained. By the end of the nineteenth century, however, it became clear that for several generations black political participation in the South was at an end. Henry Cabot Lodge's Federal Elections bill of 1890 never became law. That same year, the constitutional convention of Mississippi inaugurated a series of measures to deny African Americans the vote, variations of which were later adopted by many southern states. By 1894, Congress had repealed all its protection of federal elections. Disfranchisement, accompanied by segregation, set the pattern of southern race relations well into the twentieth century.[5]

---

4. Roberta F. Carson, "The Loyal League in Georgia," *Georgia Historical Quarterly* 20 (June 1936): 152; KKK Hearings, North Carolina, pages 145, 100; KKK Hearings, Georgia, vol. 1, page 345; KKK Hearings, Mississippi, vol. 1, page 77. On the other hand, a student of Reconstruction in Scott County, Mississippi, notes League activity after 1871 (see Forrest Cooper, "Reconstruction in Scott County," *Publications of the Mississippi Historical Society* 13 [1913]: 123).

5. Michael W. Fitzgerald, *The Union League Movement in the Deep South: Politics and Agricultural Change during Reconstruction* (Baton Rouge: Louisiana State Univ. Press, 1989), 235–238; Steven Hahn, *A Nation under Our Feet: Black Political Struggles in the Rural South*

The escalating violence of the Ku Klux Klan in the late 1860s finally drove the Republican-dominated Congress into taking action. In 1870 and 1871, it passed a series of Enforcement Acts to protect black voting rights. In April 1871, Congress enacted a more sweeping Ku Klux Klan Act that made certain crimes punishable under federal law. Attorney General Amos T. Akerman and Solicitor General Benjamin Bristow vigorously pursued prosecution under these laws. Hundreds of Klan members were indicted and imprisoned in North Carolina. Federal troops were sent into South Carolina. These measures were effective in curbing Klan violence for the remainder of Reconstruction, but a tradition of white terrorism against blacks and Republicans had been set. In the late summer of 1874, White Leagues dedicated to the violent overthrow of Republican governments arose in Louisiana and Mississippi. In Red River Parish in Louisiana, White League violence was responsible for the murders of three relatives of Republican political leader Marshall H. Twitchell. In New Orleans, the Crescent City White League proved crucial to driving Republican governor William P. Kellogg out of office. The White Leagues and Ku Klux Klan faded in the historical record during the remainder of the nineteenth century, though terroristic attacks on southern blacks persisted.[6]

At the turn of the twentieth century, the Ku Klux Klan of Reconstruction enjoyed a kind of cultural rebirth. Historian Walter L. Fleming spoke appreciatively of the Klan, and Thomas Dixon's novel *The Clansman* and the film it inspired, *The Birth of a Nation*, glorified the Klan and sanitized its violent past. In 1915, an Atlanta lawyer, no doubt inspired by the movie, took a group of men up to Stone Moun-

---

from Slavery to the Great Migration (Cambridge, Mass.: Belknap Press of Harvard Univ. Press, 2003), 386; Vernon Wharton, *The Negro in Mississippi, 1865–1890* (1947; reprint, New York: Harper and Row, 1965), 202, 205; Hahn, *A Nation under Our Feet*, 394–395.

6. Eric Foner, *Reconstruction: America's Unfinished Revolution, 1863–1877* (New York: Harper and Row, 1988), 454–457, 550–551; Hahn, *A Nation under Our Feet*, 295–302. On events in Louisiana, see Ted Tunnell, *Crucible of Reconstruction: War, Radicalism, and Race in Louisiana, 1862–1877* (Baton Rouge: Louisiana State Univ. Press, 1984), and H. Oscar Lestage Jr., "The White League in Louisiana and Its Participation in Reconstruction Riots," *Louisiana Historical Quarterly* 18 (July 1935): 617–695.

tain on Thanksgiving night, burned a cross, and founded the second Ku Klux Klan.[7]

Viewed in comparative perspective, the history of the Fenians, freedmen, and conservative southern whites in the late 1860s suggests some new meanings for Reconstruction. The post–Civil War era occupied a distinctive stage in the history of Irish American nationalism and the racial consciousness of whites and blacks in the South. The period was characterized by semi-secret, fraternal, paramilitary societies: the Fenian Brotherhood, the Union Leagues, and the Ku Klux Klan. They had similar structures and adopted common elements of a political culture centering on countersubversion. The politics of Reconstruction strongly influenced all three groups, and the hegemonic force of Republican nationalism set limits to the separatist aspirations of southern whites, freedpeople, and Fenians. With a discourse largely informed by republicanism, it encouraged separatism along civic rather than ethnic or class lines. The common recourse among the three groups to the political language of republicanism—the language of liberty, slavery, democracy, and aristocracy—also suggests that Reconstruction was far more rooted in the political culture of the early nineteenth century than has been previously recognized. In this way, Reconstruction was a period that looked as much backward to the early nineteenth century as it did forward to the industrial capitalism of the Gilded Age.

The history of the Fenians, freedmen, and southern whites also shows that democracy and citizenship were central issues of Reconstruction. The process of emancipation—the end of slavery, the transition to free labor, and the rise of African American politics in the South—and the economic, political, and constitutional reintegration of the United States were at the core of Reconstruction. What needs emphasis, however, is that the Civil War was a modernizing and liberalizing experience that unintentionally raised the aspirations of groups who had recently been marginalized from the mainstream of American

---

7. Allen W. Trelease, *White Terror: The Ku Klux Klan Conspiracy and Southern Reconstruction* (1971; rpr. Baton Rouge: Louisiana State Univ. Press, 1995), 421–422.

political power. Reconstruction, as I have tried to suggest in this book, provided the primary context in which these struggles over autonomy and hegemony took place and helped determine their outcome. Thus, it might not be far-fetched to claim that Carl Becker's famous phrase regarding the American Revolution—that it was not so much a question of home rule but who should rule at home—applies equally well to American Reconstruction.

Bibliography

Manuscript Collections

Alabama Department of Archives and History, Montgomery
Dallas County (Ala.) Political Scrapbook.
Dustan, Charles William. Papers.
Huntsville Republican Club (Ala.) Minutes, 1876.
Knights of the White Camelia. Notebook, ca. 1867.
Moore, Joshua Burns. Diary, 1860–1874.
Perry, Sally Randle. Diary, 1867–1868.
Reconstruction Era Political Records, 1868–1878.
Swayne, Governor Wager, Administration Files, Reconstruction Correspondence, Folders 18–28.

East Tennessee Historical Society, Knoxville
Houk, Leonidas Campbell. Papers.
Nelson, T. A. R. Papers, McClung Collection.
Union League of Maryville. Minutes of Meetings. McClung Collection.

Filson Historical Society, Louisville, Kentucky
Bristow, Benjamin Helm. Letters, 1874–1876.
Bruner, John B. Papers.
Haycroft, Samuel, Jr. Transcribed Journal, 1849–1878.
Hill Family. Correspondence, 1852–1873.
Jefferson, John F. Diary, 1867.
McElroy, Hugh. Diary, 1865–1877.
Sanders Family Papers.
Winn-Cook Papers.

Florida Historical Society, Cocoa
A Record of the Proceedings of the Union Republican Club of Jacksonville, Florida.

Georgia Department of Archives and History, Atlanta
Bullock, Rufus Brown. Executive Department Correspondence.
Conley, Benjamin. Papers, 1839–1875.
Reconstruction Papers.

Georgia Historical Society, Savannah
Waring, Joseph Frederick. Papers.

Hargrett Rare Book and Manuscript Library, University of Georgia, Athens
Denton, Lyman W., M.D. "The Ku Klux Klan and the Days of Reconstruction, or In the Shadow of the Kennesaw." Typescript.
Farrow, Henry Patillo. Papers.
Ku Klux Klan File.

Louisiana State University Archives, Baton Rouge
Bowman (James P. and Family). Papers.
DeClaret (Alexandre E. and Family) Papers.
Ellis (E. John, Thomas C. W., and Family) Papers.
Rives, Mary Elizabeth Carter. Diary, 1865–1900.

Mississippi Department of Archives and History, Jackson
Alcorn, J. L. Governor's Papers.
Alcorn (James L. and Family) Papers.
Ames, Adelbert. Governor's Office. Correspondence and Papers, 1868–1870.
Anderson, E. H. "A Memoir on Reconstruction in Yazoo City."
Carter, Martha A. "Oral History."
Forbes (Spooner) Diary.
Golding (John Reid II) Letter.
Harper (Annie E.) Manuscript.
Hopkins, Edward Randolph. "Some Reminiscences of Lowndes County History."
Lyon, James A. Journal.
Metcalfe Family Papers.
Nicholson (Flavellus G.) Diary-Journal.
Rainwater, P. L. Collection.
Strickland, Belle. Diary.

New York Historical Society, New York
Fontaine, Rev. Edward. "Missionary Labor on the Lower Coast of Louisiana among the Creoles, Negroes & Chinese."

North Carolina Division of Archives and History, Raleigh
Douglas, Robert Martin. Papers.
Harris, James Henry. Papers.
Hawthorne, Sally. "Memories."
Holden, William W. Governor's Papers.
Lusk, Virgil S. File.
Reconstruction File.

Ohio Historical Society, Columbus
Schenk, Robert. Papers (Microfilm).
Scott, Robert K. Papers.

Perkins Library, Duke University, Durham
Bryant, John Emory. Papers.
Chaffin, Washington Sandford. Papers.
Ku Klux Klan Papers.
Wellborn, Joel Romulus. Papers.

Philadelphia Archdiocesan Historical Research Center
Fenian Brotherhood Papers, 1857–1870.

Rare Book and Manuscript Library, Columbia University, New York
Union League Constitution.

South Carolina Department of Archives and History, Columbia
Orr, James L. Governor's Papers.
Scott, Robert K. Governor's Papers.

South Caroliniana Library, University of South Carolina, Columbia
Deas, Elias Horry. Papers.
Jenkins Papers.
Keitt, Ellison Summerfield. 1867–1876 Newspaper Clippings.
Kincaid-Anderson Family Papers.
Reconstruction Scrapbook. Clippings, 1865–1867.
Stoeber, Edward M. Papers.

Southern Historical Collection, University of North Carolina, Chapel Hill
Brower Family Papers.
Clarke, William J. Diary, 1868–1876.
Day, William Alburtus. Book of Recollections and Miscellany.
Fitzgerald, Robert G. Diary.

Howell, Robert Philip. Memoirs.
Lineburger, Thomas James. Diary.
Long, Jacob A. Recollections.
Schenck, David. Papers.
Springs Family Papers.
Turner Papers.
Warmoth, Henry Clay. Papers.

Tennessee Historical Society, Nashville
Brownlow, James P. Papers.

Tennessee State Library and Archives, Nashville
Brownlow, Gov. William G. Petitions, 1865–1869.
Hughes, Archelaus Madison. Diary, 1867–1884.
Mooney, W. D. "Ku Klux Klan."
Senter, Dewitt C. Governor's Papers. Special Subjects.

GOVERNMENT DOCUMENTS AND PUBLICATIONS

42nd Congress, 2nd Session. House of Representatives. Report No. 22, pt. 3. *Testimony Taken by the Joint Select Committee to Inquire into the Condition of Affairs in the Insurrectionary States.* Washington, D.C., 1872.

Proceedings in the Ku Klux Trials, at Columbia, S.C., in the United States Circuit Court, November Term, 1871. Columbia: Republican Printing Company, 1872.

NEWSPAPERS AND PERIODICALS

Alabama Beacon, 1867
Alabama State Journal, 1869
Alexandria (Louisiana) *Caucasian*, 1874
American Freedman, 1866
American Union (Harrisonburg, Virginia), 1867–1868
Arkansas Freeman
Asheville *Pioneer*, 1867
Ashtabula *Sentinel*, 1867
Athens (Tennessee) *Republican*, 1867
Atlanta *Daily New Era*, 1868
Austin *Daily State Gazette*, 1867
Beaufort *Republican*, 1870
Boston *Commonwealth*, 1867
Brownsville *Republican*, 1867

Buffalo *Fenian Volunteer*, 1867
Carolina *Times*, 1869
Central Georgian, 1868
Charleston *Advocate*, 1867
Charleston *Daily Courier*, 1867
Charleston *Daily News*, 1867–1868
Charleston *Daily Republican*, 1869
Chicago *Irish Republic*, 1867–1868
Cleveland *Morning Leader*, 1865–1867
Colored American (Augusta), 1865–1866
Columbia (South Carolina) *Daily Phoenix*
Daily Austin Republican, 1868, 1870
Daily Republican (Charleston), 1869
Daily Sentinel (Raleigh, North Carolina), 1867
Daily State Sentinel (Raleigh, North Carolina), 1867
East Alabama Monitor, 1868–1869
Edgefield (South Carolina) *Advertiser*, 1867
Flake's Daily Bulletin, 1867
Forest *Register* (Scott County, Mississippi), 1867
Free Citizen (Orangeburg, South Carolina), 1875
Freeman's Standard (Savannah), 1868
Free Press (Charleston), 1868
Free South (New Orleans), 1868
Galveston *Weekly News*, 1867
Great Republic (Washington, D.C.), 1866
Greenville *Republican*, 1871
Houston *Union*, 1869
Jacksonville (Alabama) *Republican*, 1867
Journal of Freedom (Raleigh, North Carolina), 1865
Keowee (South Carolina) *Courier*, 1870
The Ku-Klux (Mississippi), 1871
Laurensville (South Carolina) *Herald*, 1868–1871
Loyal Georgian (Augusta), 1866–1868
Macon *Daily Telegraph*, 1867–1868
Macon *Georgia Journal and Messenger*
Maryville (Tennessee) *Republican*, 1867–1868
Memphis *Daily Post*, 1868
Messenger and Advertiser (Troy, Alabama), 1869
Mobile *Daily Advertiser and Register*, 1867–1868

Mobile *Nationalist*, 1869
Montgomery *Daily State Sentinel*, 1867+
Nashville *Union and Dispatch*, 1867
Natchez *Democrat*, 1867
National Antislavery Standard, 1866–1867
National *Republican* (Augusta), 1868
New-Berne *Daily Republican*, 1868
Newbern *Journal of Commerce*, 1867
New Bern (North Carolina) *Republican*, 1867
New Orleans *Weekly Republican*, 1867–1868
New South (Port Royal), 1866
New York *Citizen*, 1866–1868
New York *Freeman's Journal and Catholic Register*, 1867
New York *Irish Citizen*, 1867–1868
New York *Irish People*, 1867
New York *Tribune*, 1865–1867
Opelika (Alabama) *Era and Whig*, 1871
Philadelphia *Catholic Herald and Visitor*, 1861
Philadelphia *Public Ledger*, 1866
Pittsburgh *Catholic*, 1867
The Radical (New Bern, North Carolina), [1867?]
Richmond *Enquirer and Examiner*, 1867
Richmond *Whig and Public Advertiser*, 1867
Rural Carolinian, 1869–1870
San Antonio *Daily Express*, 1868–1869
San Francisco *Irish Nationalist*, 1873
Savannah *Daily News and Herald*, 1867–1869
Savannah *Daily Republican*, 1867
Savannah *Morning News*, 1868–1869
Savannah *National Republican*, 1865–1866
Selma *Press*, 1869–1870
South Carolina Leader, 1865
South Carolina Republican, 1868–1869
Southern Argus (Selma, Alabama), 1869
Southern Field and Factory, 1871
Southern Opinion (Richmond, Virginia), 1867
Southern Planter, 1867
Southern Republican (Demopolis, Alabama), 1869

Southern Standard (Arkedelphia, Arkansas), 1869
Southern Watchman (Athens, Georgia), 1867
Tallahassee *Sentinel*, 1871
Talledega *Watch-Tower*, 1869–1870
Tri-Weekly Austin Republican, 1867–1868
Tuscaloosa *Independent Monitor*, 1867
Union Flag (Jonesboro, Tennessee), 1867
Vicksburg *Republican*, 1867
Weekly Floridian (Tallahassee)
Weekly Mississippi Pilot, 1867–1869
Weekly Panola Star, 1868
Wilcox County News (Alabama), 1867–1868
Wilmington (North Carolina) *Daily Post*, 1867
Wilmington (North Carolina) *Journal*, 1868
Yorkville (South Carolina) *Enquirer*, 1870

CONTEMPORARY PUBLICATIONS AND PUBLISHED DOCUMENTS

Address of the Union League of Philadelphia, to the Citizens of Pennsylvania, with the Preamble and Resolutions, Adopted in General Meeting, August 26th, 1868. Philadelphia: King and Baird, n.d.

Alexander, Thomas B., ed. "Persistent Whiggery in Mississippi: The Hinds County Gazette." *Journal of Mississippi History* 23 (April 1961): 71–93.

Barnhart, John D., ed. "Reconstruction on the Lower Mississippi." *Mississippi Valley Historical Review* 21 (December 1934): 387–396.

Berlin, Ira, et al., eds. *Freedom: A Documentary History of Emancipation, 1861–1867: Series II: The Black Military Experience.* Cambridge: Cambridge Univ. Press, 1982.

Boutwell, George S. *Reconstruction: Its True Basis. Speech of Hon. George S. Boutwell, at Weymouth, Mass., July 4, 1865.* Boston: Wright and Potter, 1865.

Brackenridge, Alexander. *Address Delivered before the Friends of Ireland; at an Adjourned Meeting of the Repeal Association, Held at the Washington Coffee House, Pittsburgh, Dec. 11, 1841.* Pittsburgh: Office of American Manufacturer, [1841?].

Byrnes, T. A. *Address to the Citizens of the 16th Senatorial District.* N.p., n.d.

[Campbell, James B.]. *Two Letters from the Hon. James B. Campbell, U.S. Senator Elect from South Carolina, on Public Affairs, and our Duties to the Colored Race.* Charleston: Walker, Evans and Cogswell, 1868.

Campbell, William A., cont. "A Freedmen's Bureau Diary by George Wagner." Parts 1 and 2. *Georgia Historical Quarterly* 48 (June 1964): 196–214; (September 1964): 333–360.

Cardozo, F. L. *Address before the Grand Council of the Union Leagues at Their Annual Meeting, held July 27, 1870, by Hon. F. L. Cardozo, President.* Columbia, S.C.: John W. Denny, 1870.

[Constitutional Club of Mobile]. *Roll of the Black Dupes and White Renegades who Voted in Mobile City and County for the Menagerie Constitution, for the State of Alabama.* Mobile: Book and Job Office of the Mobile Daily Register, 1868.

Correspondence Relating to the Fenian Invasion, and the Rebellion of the Southern States. Ottawa: Hunter, Rose, and Company, 1869.

Declaration of Principles, By the Representatives of the Fenian Brotherhood, in Congress Assembled. Cleveland: N.p., 1867.

Douglas, Robert M. *Speech of Col. Robert M. Douglas, of Washington, D.C., Delivered at a Republican Mass Meeting Held at Smithfield, N.C., July 12th, 1870.* Raleigh: "Standard" Steam Book and Job Press, 1870.

Dykema, Frank E., ed. "An Effort to Attract Dutch Colonists to Alabama, 1869." *Journal of Southern History* 14 (May 1948): 247–261.

The Fenian's Progress: A Vision. New York: John Bradburn, 1865.

First Annual Convention of the Irish National Land League held at Buffalo, New York, January 12th and 13th, 1881. Richmond: P. Keenan, 1881.

Fleming, Walter L., ed. *Documentary History of Reconstruction: Political, Military, Social, Religious, Educational, and Industrial, 1865–1906.* 2 vols. 1907. Reprint, New York, McGraw-Hill, 1966.

———. *Union League Documents.* Morgantown, W.Va.: n.p., 1904.

Freidel, Frank, ed. *Union Pamphlets of the Civil War, 1861–1865.* 2 vols. Cambridge, Mass.: Belknap Press of Harvard Univ. Press, 1967.

Gibbons, James. *Address of the Executive Committee of the Senate, F.B. to the Officers and Members of the F.B.* New York: n.p., 1870.

Glicksburg, Charles I., ed. "Letters of William Cullen Bryant from Florida." *Florida Historical Quarterly* 14 (April 1936): 255–274.

Hamilton, J. G. de Roulhac, ed. *The Correspondence of Jonathan Worth.* 2 vols. Raleigh: Edwards and Broughton Printing Company, 1909.

———, ed. *The Papers of Randolph Abbott Shotwell*, vol. 2. Raleigh: North Carolina Historical Commission, 1931.

———, ed. *The Papers of Thomas Ruffin.* 4 vols. Raleigh: Edwards and Broughton Printing Company, 1920.

Harwood, W. S. "Secret Societies in America." *North American Review* 164 (May 1897): 620–623.

Hoar, George Frisbie, ed. *Charles Sumner: His Complete Works*, vol. 16. Boston: Lee and Shepard, 1900.

Houzeau, Jean-Charles. *My Passage at the New Orleans Tribune: A Memoir of the Civil War Era*. Edited by David C. Rankin. Translated by Gerard F. Denault. Baton Rouge: Louisiana State Univ. Press, 1984.

Hunt, Gaillard, cont. "Letter of William Henry Trescot on Reconstruction in South Carolina, 1867." *American Historical Review* 15 (1910): 574–582.

Hyman, Harold, ed. *The Radical Republicans and Reconstruction, 1861–1870*. Indianapolis: Bobbs Merrill, 1967.

Kollock, Susan, ed. "Letters of the Kollock and Allied Families, 1826–1884," part 4. *Georgia Historical Quarterly* 34 (December 1950): 313–327.

Lawrence, Alexander A., ed. "Some Letters from Henry C. Wayne to Hamilton Fish." *Georgia Historical Quarterly* 43 (December 1959): 391–409.

Leigh, Frances Butler. *Ten Years on a Georgia Plantation Since the War*. Savannah: Beehive Press, 1992.

Leland, John. *A Voice from South Carolina*. Charleston: Walker, Evans and Cogswell, 1879.

Mahaffey, Joseph H., ed. "Carl Schurz's Letters from the South." *Georgia Historical Quarterly* 35 (September 1951): 222–256.

Marchione, William P., Jr., ed. "Go South, Young Man! Reconstructionist Letters of a Massachusetts Yankee." *South Carolina Historical Magazine* 80 (January 1979): 18–35.

Marquette, C. C., ed. "Letters of a Yankee Sugar Planter." *Journal of Southern History* 6 (November 1940): 521–546.

McPherson, Elizabeth G., ed., "Letters from North Carolina to Andrew Johnson." *North Carolina Historical Review* 27 (July 1950): 336–363; (October 1950): 462–490.

Moore, William A. *Law and Order v. Kuklux Violence: Speech of Col. Wm. A. Moore, of Chowan, Delivered in the House of Representatives, January 19, 1870*. N.p., n.d.

Morton, Richard L., ed. "Life in Virginia, by a 'Yankee Teacher,' Margaret Newbold Thorpe." *Virginia Magazine of History and Biography* 64 (April 1958): 180–207.

Muggleston, William F., ed. "The Freedmen's Bureau and Reconstruction in Virginia: The Diary of Marcus Sterling Hopkins, a Union Officer." *Virginia Magazine of History and Biography* 86 (January 1978): 45–102.

Mulford, Elisha. *The Nation: The Foundations of Civil Order and Political Life in the United States*. 1870. Reprint, Boston: Houghton, Mifflin, 1883.

Nevins, Allan, and Milton Halsey Thomas, eds. *The Diary of George Templeton Strong*. 4 vols. New York: Macmillan, 1952.

North Carolina Republican State Executive Committee Facts and Figures. N.p., n.d.

[O'Neil, John]. *Address to the Officers and Members of the Fenian Brotherhood.* New York: n.p., 1868.

Osborn, George C., ed. "Letters of a Carpetbagger in Florida, 1866–1869." *Florida Historical Quarterly* 36 (January 1958): 237–285.

Padgett, James A., ed. "Reconstruction Letters from North Carolina." *North Carolina Historical Review* 18 (April 1941): 171–195; (July 1941): 278–300; (October 1941): 373–398; 19 (January 1942): 59–94; (April 1943): 187–208; (July 1942): 280–302.

———, ed. "Some Letters of George Stanton Denison, 1854–1866: Observations of a Yankee on Conditions in Louisiana and Texas." *Louisiana Historical Quarterly* 23 (October 1940): 1132–1240.

Phillips, Samuel F. *Speech of Mr. Samuel F. Phillips, at Concord, Cabanis County, July 4th, 1870.* Raleigh: "Standard" Steam Book and Job Print, 1870.

Proceedings of the First General Convention of the Fenian Brotherhood of the Pacific Coast, Held in San Francisco, California, September 1864. San Francisco: George W. Stevens and Company, 1864.

Proceedings of the Fourth National Congress of the Fenian Brotherhood, at Pittsburgh, Pa., February, 1866, with the Constitution of the F.B., and Addenda Thereto. New York: J. Croft, 1866.

Proceedings of the Freedmen's Convention of Georgia, Assembled at Augusta, January 10th, 1866. Augusta: Loyal Georgian Office, 1866.

Proceedings of the National Council of the Union League of America at its Sixth Annual Session, held in the City of Washington, D.C., on Tuesday and Wednesday, March 2d and 3rd, 1869. N.p., 1869.

Proceedings of the Republican District Convention, Fifth District, North Carolina, Held at Greensboro, N.C., Sept. 18th, 1868. N.p., n.d.

Proceedings of the Second National Congress of the Fenian Brotherhood, held in Cincinnati, Ohio, January, 1865. Philadelphia: James Gibbons, 1865.

Proceedings of the Senate and House of Representatives of the Fenian Brotherhood, in Joint Convention, at Philadelphia, PA., November 24, 25, 26, 27, 28 & 29, 1868. New York: D. W. Lee, 1868.

Proceedings of the Sixth National Congress of the Fenian Brotherhood, Held in New York City, 21st–25th August, 1867. New York: O'Sullivan, McBride and Marrot, 1868.

Rainwater, Percy L., ed. "The Autobiography of Benjamin Grubb Humphreys, August 26, 1808–December 20, 1882." *Mississippi Valley Historical Review* 21 (September 1934): 231–255.

———, ed. "Letters of James Lusk Alcorn." *Journal of Southern History* 3 (May 1937): 196–211.

Raper, Horace, ed. *The Papers of William Woods Holden*, vol. 1, *1841–1868*. Raleigh: Division of Archives and History, 2000.

Report of the Joint Committee on Outrages. Montgomery: Jno. G. Stokes and Co., 1868.

*Revised and Amended Prescript of the Order of the * * * . . . .* Pulaski, Tenn., 1868.

Richardson, Joe, ed. "A Northerner Reports on Florida: 1866." *Florida Historical Quarterly* 40 (April 1962): 381–390.

Roberts, W. R. *Lecture by W. R. Roberts, Delivered Before the Fenian Brotherhood of New York, at Cooper Institute, on Wednesday, Sept. 27th, 1865*. New York: J. Croft, 1865.

Robertson, James I., ed. "The Diary of Dolly Lunt Burge, Part VIII" [1866–1879]. *Georgia Historical Quarterly* 46 (March 1962): 59–78.

Stephen's Fenian Songster, Containing all the Heart-Stirring and Patriotic Ballads and Songs, as Sung at the Meeting of the Fenian Brotherhood. New York: Wm. H. Murphy, 1866.

Sterling, Dorothy, ed. *The Trouble They Seen: Black People Tell the Story of Reconstruction*. Garden City, N.Y.: Doubleday, 1976.

Stevens, Thaddeus. *Reconstruction. Speech of the Hon. Thaddeus Stevens, Delivered in the City of Lancaster, September 7th, 1865*. Lancaster: Examiner and Herald Print, 1865.

Stevenson, Mary, comp. *The Diary of Clarissa Adger, Bowen. 1865* . . . Pendleton, S.C.: Published by the Research and Publication Committee Foundation for Historic Restoration in Pendleton Area, 1973.

Steward, Edgar A., ed. "The Journal of James Mallory, 1834–1877." *Alabama Review* 14 (July 1961): 219–232.

Stone, James H. "L. Q. C. Lamar's Letters to Edward Donaldson Clark, 1868–1885, Part I: 1868–1873." *Journal of Mississippi History* 35 (February 1973): 65–75.

Third Annual Convention of the Irish National Land League and First Convention of the Irish National League of America, held at Philadelphia, PA. April 25th, 26th, and 27th, 1883. Buffalo: Union and Times Print, 1883.

To the State Centres, Centres, and Members of the Fenian Brotherhood of North America. New York: O' Sullivan and McBride, 1866.

Wells, Carol, ed. *War, Reconstruction and Redemption on Red River: The Memoirs of Dosia Williams Moore*. Ruston, La.: McGinty Publications, 1990.

Wheeler, T. B. "Reminiscences of Reconstruction in Texas." *The Quarterly of the Texas State Historical Association* 11 (1907): 56–66.

Wight, Willard E., ed. "Reconstruction in Georgia: Three Letters by Edwin G. Higbee." *Georgia Historical Quarterly* 41 (March 1957): 81–89.

[Williams, Henry Llewellyn]. *The Fenian Chief; or, the Martyr of '65.* New York: Robert M. DeWitt, 1865.

SECONDARY SOURCES

Books

Abbott, Richard H. *For Free Press and Equal Rights: Republican Newspapers in the Reconstruction South*, edited by John W. Quist. Athens: Univ. of Georgia Press, 2004.

———. *The Republican Party and the South, 1855–1877.* Chapel Hill: Univ. of North Carolina Press, 1986.

Alexander, Thomas B. *Political Reconstruction in Tennessee.* 1950. Reprint, New York: Russell and Russell, 1968.

Allen, James S. *Reconstruction: The Battle for Democracy, 1865–1876.* New York: International Publishers, 1937.

Anbinder, Tyler. *Nativism and Slavery: The Northern Know-Nothings and the Politics of the 1850s.* New York: Oxford Univ. Press, 1992.

Anderson, Eric, and Alfred A. Moss, Jr., eds. *The Facts of Reconstruction: Essays in Honor of John Hope Franklin.* Baton Rouge: Louisiana State Univ. Press, 1991.

Bailey, Thomas A. *A Diplomatic History of the American People*, 10th ed. Englewood Cliffs: Prentice Hall, 1980.

Bailyn, Bernard, et al. *The Great Republic: A History of the American People*, 4th ed. Lexington, Mass: D. C. Heath, 1992.

Barney, William L. *The Secessionist Impulse: Alabama and Mississippi in 1860.* Princeton: Princeton Univ. Press, 1974.

Beckert, Sven. *The Monied Metropolis: New York City and the Consolidation of the American Bourgeoisie, 1850–1896.* New York: Cambridge Univ. Press, 2001.

Benedict, Michael Les. *The Compromise of Principle: Congressional Republicans and Reconstruction, 1863–1869.* New York: Norton, 1974.

Benzel, Richard Franklin. *Yankee Leviathan: The Origins of Central State Authority in America, 1859–1877.* Cambridge: Cambridge Univ. Press, 1990.

Berlin, Ira, Joseph P. Reidy, and Leslie S. Rowland, eds. *Freedom's Soldiers: The Black Military Experience in the Civil War.* Cambridge: Cambridge Univ. Press, 1998.

Berlin, Ira, and Philip D. Morgan, eds. *Cultivation and Culture: Labor and the Shaping of Slave Life in the Americas.* Charlottesville: Univ. of Virginia Press, 1993.
Bernstein, Iver. *The New York City Draft Riots: Their Significance for American Society and Politics in the Age of the Civil War.* New York: Oxford Univ. Press, 1990.
Bew, Paul. *Land and the National Question in Ireland, 1858–82.* Dublin: Gill and Macmillan, 1978.
Billington, Ray Allen. *The Protestant Crusade, 1800–1860: A Study in the Origins of American Nativism.* 1938. Reprint, Chicago: Quadrangle Books, 1964.
Brown, Canter, Jr., *Ossian Bingley Hart: Florida's Loyalist Reconstruction Governor.* Baton Rouge: Louisiana State Univ. Press, 1997.
Brown, Dee Alexander. *Bury My Heart at Wounded Knee: An Indian History of the American West.* New York: Holt, Rinehart, and Winston, 1970.
Brown, Thomas N. *Irish-American Nationalism, 1870–1890.* Philadelphia: J. B. Lippincott, 1966.
Buck, Solon. *The Granger Movement: A Study of Agricultural Organization and Its Political, Economic, and Social Manifestations, 1870–1880.* Cambridge, Mass.: Harvard Univ. Press, 1933.
Bullock, Steven C. *Revolutionary Brotherhood: Freemasonry and the Transformation of the American Social Order, 1730–1840.* Chapel Hill: Univ. of North Carolina Press, 1996.
Callow, Alexander B., Jr. *The Tweed Ring.* New York: Oxford Univ. Press, 1966.
Campbell, Charles S. *The Transformation of American Foreign Relations, 1865–1900.* New York: Harper and Row, 1976.
Carter, Dan T. *When the War Was Over: The Failure of Self-Reconstruction in the South, 1865–1867.* Baton Rouge: Louisiana State Univ. Press, 1985.
Coclanis, Peter A. *The Shadow of a Dream: Economic Life and Death in the South Carolina Low Country, 1670–1920.* New York: Oxford Univ. Press, 1989.
Cohen, Mitchell. *Zion and State: Nation, Class, and the Shaping of Modern Israel.* New York: Columbia Univ. Press, 1992.
Commons, John R., et al. *History of Labour in the United States,* vol. 2. New York: Macmillan, 1921.
Connor, Walker. *Ethnonationalism: The Quest for Understanding.* Princeton: Princeton Univ. Press, 1994.
———. *The National Question in Marxist-Leninist Theory and Strategy.* Princeton: Princeton Univ. Press, 1984.
Cook, Adrian. *The Alabama Claims: American Politics and Anglo-American Relations, 1865–1872.* Ithaca: Cornell Univ. Press, 1975.

———. *The Armies of the Street: The New York City Draft Riots of 1863*. Lexington: Univ. Press of Kentucky, 1974.

Cooper, Frederick, Rebecca Scott, and Thomas Holt, eds. *Beyond Slavery: Explorations of Race, Labor, and Citizenship in Postemancipation Societies*. Chapel Hill: Univ. of North Carolina Press, 2000.

Cooper, William J., Jr. *The South and the Politics of Slavery, 1828–1856*. Baton Rouge: Louisiana State Univ. Press, 1978.

Cooper, William J., Jr., and Thomas E. Terrill. *The American South: A History*. New York: Knopf, 1990.

Coulter, E. Merton. *The Civil War and Readjustment in Kentucky*. Chapel Hill: Univ. of North Carolina Press, 1926.

———. *The South during Reconstruction, 1865–1877*. Baton Rouge: Louisiana State Univ. Press, 1947.

———. *William G. Brownlow, Fighting Parson of the Southern Highlands*. Chapel Hill: Univ. of North Carolina Press, 1937.

Crenshaw, Ollinger. *The Slave States in the Presidential Election of 1860*. 1945. Reprint, Gloucester, Mass.: Peter Smith, 1969.

Current, Richard. *Those Terrible Carpetbaggers*. New York: Oxford Univ. Press, 1988.

Curry, Richard O., ed. *Radicalism, Racism and Party Realignment: The Border States during Reconstruction*. Baltimore: Johns Hopkins Univ. Press, 1969.

Curti, Merle. *The Growth of American Thought*, 2nd ed. New York: Harper and Row, 1951.

D'Arcy, William. *The Fenian Movement in the United States, 1858–1886*. Washington, D.C.: Catholic Univ. Press, 1947.

Davis, David Brion. *The Slave Power Conspiracy and the Paranoid Style*. Baton Rouge: Louisiana State Univ. Press, 1969.

———, ed. *The Fear of Conspiracy: Images of Un-American Subversion from the Revolution to the Present*. Ithaca: Cornell Univ. Press, 1971.

Davis, William Watson. *The Civil War and Reconstruction in Florida*. New York: Columbia Univ. Press, 1913.

Dolan, Jay P. *The Immigrant Church: New York's Irish and German Catholics, 1815–1865*. Baltimore: Johns Hopkins Univ. Press, 1975.

Donald, David. *Charles Sumner and the Rights of Man*. New York: Knopf, 1970.

Donald, David Herbert. *Liberty and Union*. Lexington, Mass.: D. C. Heath, 1978.

Donald, David Herbert, Jean Harvey Baker, and Michael F. Holt. *The Civil War and Reconstruction*. New York: Norton, 2001.

Donnelly, James S. *The Land and the People of Nineteenth-Century Cork: The Rural Economy and the Land Question*. London: Routledge and Kegan Paul, 1975.

Drago, Edmund L. *Black Politicians and Reconstruction in Georgia: A Splendid Failure*. Baton Rouge: Louisiana State Univ. Press, 1982.

DuBois, Ellen Carol. *Feminism and Suffrage: The Emergence of an Independent Women's Movement in America, 1848–1869*. Ithaca: Cornell Univ. Press, 1978.

Du Bois, W. E. B. *Black Reconstruction in America, 1860–1880*. 1935. Reprint, New York: Atheneum, 1975.

Duncan, Russell. *Freedom's Shore: Tunis Campbell and the Georgia Freedmen*. Athens: Univ. of Georgia Press, 1986.

Dunning, William A. *Reconstruction, Political and Economic, 1865–1877*. 1907. Reprint, New York: Harper and Row, 1962.

Durrill, Wayne. *War of Another Kind: A Southern Community in the Great Rebellion*. New York: Oxford Univ. Press, 1990.

Ernst, Robert. *Immigrant Life in New York City, 1825–1863*. 1949. Reprint, New York: Syracuse Univ. Press, 1994.

Evans, W. McKee. *Ballots and Fence Rails: Reconstruction on the Lower Cape Fear*. Chapel Hill: Univ. of North Carolina Press, 1966.

Fite, Emerson David. *The Presidential Campaign of 1860*. 1911. Reprint, Port Washington, N.Y.: Kennikat Press, 1967.

Fitzgerald, Michael W. *The Union League Movement in the Deep South: Politics and Agricultural Change during Reconstruction*. Baton Rouge: Louisiana State Univ. Press, 1989.

Fleming, Walter L. *Civil War and Reconstruction in Alabama*. New York: Columbia Univ. Press, 1905.

——. *The Sequel of Appomattox: A Chronicle of the Reunion of the States*. Toronto: Glasgow, Brook, 1919.

Foner, Eric. *Freedom's Lawmakers: A Directory of Black Officeholders during Reconstruction*, rev. ed. Baton Rouge: Louisiana State Univ. Press, 1996.

——. *Free Soil, Free Labor, Free Men: The Ideology of the Republican Party Before the Civil War*. New York: Oxford Univ. Press, 1970.

——. *Nothing but Freedom: Emancipation and Its Legacy*. Baton Rouge: Louisiana State Univ. Press, 1983.

——. *Reconstruction: America's Unfinished Revolution, 1863–1877*. New York: Harper and Row, 1988.

Foster, Gaines M. *Ghosts of the Confederacy: Defeat, the Lost Cause, and the Emergence of the New South*. New York: Oxford Univ. Press, 1988.

——. *Moral Reconstruction: Christian Lobbyists and the Federal Legislation of Morality, 1865–1920*. Chapel Hill: Univ. of North Carolina Press, 2002.

Fredrickson, George M. *The Inner Civil War: Northern Intellectuals and the Crisis of the Union.* New York: Harper and Row, 1965.

Freehling, William. *The Road to Disunion,* vol. 1, *Secessionists at Bay, 1776–1854.* New York: Oxford Univ. Press, 1990.

Freidel, Frank. *Francis Lieber: Nineteenth-Century Liberal.* 1947. Reprint, Gloucester, Mass.: Peter Smith, 1968.

Garner, James W. *Reconstruction in Mississippi.* 1901. Reprint, Baton Rouge: Louisiana State Univ. Press, 1968.

Genovese, Eugene D. *Roll, Jordan, Roll: The World the Slaves Made.* New York: Pantheon, 1974.

Gibson, Florence E. *The Attitudes of the New York Irish Toward State and National Affairs, 1848–1892.* New York: Columbia Univ. Press, 1951.

Gillette, William. *The Right to Vote: Politics and the Passage of the Fifteenth Amendment.* Baltimore: Johns Hopkins Univ. Press, 1965.

Gleeson, David T. *The Irish in the South, 1815–1877.* Chapel Hill: Univ. of North Carolina Press, 2001.

Gordon, Michael A. *The Orange Riots: Irish Political Violence in New York City, 1870 and 1871.* Ithaca: Cornell Univ. Press, 1993.

Grant, Susan-Mary. *North over South: Northern Nationalism and American Identity in the Antebellum Era.* Lawrence: Univ. of Kansas Press, 2000.

Grant, Susan-Mary, and Peter J. Parish, eds. *Legacy of Disunion: The Enduring Significance of the American Civil War.* Baton Rouge: Louisiana State Univ. Press, 2003.

Green, Constance M. *Holyoke, Massachusetts: A Case History of the Industrial Revolution in America.* New Haven: Yale Univ. Press, 1939.

Greenfield, Liah. *Nationalism: Five Roads to Modernity.* Cambridge, Mass.: Harvard Univ. Press, 1992.

Gwynn, Stephen. *History of Ireland.* New York: Macmillan, 1923.

Hadden, Sally E. *Slave Patrols: Law and Violence in Virginia and the Carolinas.* Cambridge, Mass.: Harvard Univ. Press, 2001.

Hahn, Steven. *A Nation under Our Feet: Black Political Struggles in the Rural South from Slavery to the Great Migration.* Cambridge, Mass.: Belknap Press of Harvard Univ. Press, 2003.

———. *The Roots of Southern Populism: Yeoman Farmers and the Transformation of the Georgia Upcountry, 1850–1890.* New York: Oxford Univ. Press, 1983.

Handlin, Oscar. *Boston's Immigrants, 1790–1880,* Fiftieth Anniversary Edition. Cambridge, Mass.: Belknap Press of Harvard Univ. Press, 1991.

Harding, Vincent. *There Is a River: The Black Struggle for Freedom in America.* New York: Harcourt, Brace, and Company, 1981.

Harris, William C. *The Day of the Carpetbagger: Republican Reconstruction in Mississippi*. Baton Rouge: Louisiana State Univ. Press, 1979.

———. *William Woods Holden: Firebrand of North Carolina Politics*. Baton Rouge: Louisiana State Univ. Press, 1987.

Haskins, James. *Pinckney Benton Stewart Pinchback*. New York: Macmillan, 1974.

Hermann, Janet S. *The Pursuit of a Dream*. New York: Oxford Univ. Press, 1981.

Hibbard, Benjamin Horace. *A History of the Public Land Policies*. New York: Macmillan, 1924.

Higham, John. *From Boundlessness to Consolidation*. Ann Arbor, Mich.: Clements Library, 1969.

Hobsbawm, Eric J. *The Age of Capital, 1848–1875*. New York: Scribner, 1975.

Hofstader, Richard. *The Paranoid Style in American Politics*. New York: Knopf, 1964.

Holt, Thomas. *Black over White: Negro Political Leadership in South Carolina during Reconstruction*. Urbana: Univ. of Illinois Press, 1977.

Horn, Stanley F. *Invisible Empire: The Story of the Ku Klux Klan, 1866–1871*. 1939. Reprint, Cos Cob, Conn.: John E. Edwards, 1969.

Hoxie, Frederick, ed. *Encyclopedia of North American Indians*. Boston: Houghton Mifflin, 1996.

Huston, Reeve. *Land and Freedom: Rural Society, Popular Protest, and Party Politics in Antebellum New York*. New York: Oxford Univ. Press, 2000.

Hutchinson, John, and Anthony D. Smith, eds. *Ethnicity*. New York: Oxford Univ. Press, 1996.

———, eds. *Nationalism*. New York: Oxford Univ. Press, 1994.

Ignatiev, Noel. *How the Irish Became White*. New York: Routledge, 1995.

Jenkins, Brian. *Fenians and Anglo-American Relations during Reconstruction*. Ithaca: Cornell Univ. Press, 1969.

Jones, Wilson Jeremiah, ed. *Classical Black Nationalism: From the American Revolution to Marcus Garvey*. New York: New York Univ. Press, 1996.

Joyner, Charles W. *Down By the Riverside: A South Carolina Slave Community*. Urbana: Univ. of Illinois Press, 1984.

Keil, Hartmut, and John B. Jentz, eds. *German Workers in Chicago: A Documentary History of Working-Class Culture from 1850 to World War I*. Urbana: Univ. of Illinois Press, 1988.

Kelly, Patrick J. *Creating a National Home: Building the Veterans' Welfare State, 1860–1900*. Cambridge, Mass.: Harvard Univ. Press, 1997.

Kenny, Kevin. *Making Sense of the Molly Maguires*. New York: Oxford Univ. Press, 1988.

Kettner, James H. *The Development of American Citizenship, 1608–1870.* Chapel Hill: Published for the Institute of Early American History and Culture, Williamsburg, Virginia, by the Univ. of North Carolina Press, 1978.

Klement, Frank. *The Copperheads in the Middle West.* Chicago: Univ. of Chicago Press, 1960.

Kolchin, Peter. *A Sphinx on the American Land: The Nineteenth-Century South in Comparative Perspective.* Baton Rouge: Louisiana State Univ. Press, 2003.

Lanza, Michael L. *Agrarianism and Reconstruction Politics: The Southern Homestead Act.* Baton Rouge: Louisiana State Univ. Press, 1990.

Lawson, Melinda. *Patriot Fires: Forging a New American Nationalism in the Civil War North.* Lawrence: Univ. Press of Kansas, 2002.

Lowe, Richard. *Republicans and Reconstruction in Virginia, 1856–70.* Charlottesville: Univ. Press of Virginia, 1991.

Maddex, Jack P. *The Virginia Conservatives, 1867–1879: A Study in Reconstruction Politics.* Chapel Hill: Univ. of North Carolina Press, 1970.

McConnell, Stuart. *Glorious Contentment: The Grand Army of the Republic, 1865–1900.* Chapel Hill: Univ. of North Carolina Press, 1992.

McCurdy, Charles W. *The Anti-Rent Era in New York Law and Politics, 1839–1865.* Chapel Hill: Univ. of North Carolina Press, 2001.

McFeely, William. *Yankee Stepfather: General O. O. Howard and the Freedmen.* New Haven: Yale Univ. Press, 1968.

McGlynn, Frank, and Seymour Drescher, eds. *The Meaning of Freedom: Economics, Politics, and Culture after Slavery.* Pittsburgh: Univ. of Pittsburgh Press, 1992.

McPherson, James M. *Ordeal by Fire: The Civil War and Reconstruction.* New York: Knopf, 1982.

Miller, Kerby A. *Emigrants and Exiles: Ireland and the Irish Exodus to North America.* New York: Oxford Univ. Press, 1985.

Miller, Randall, Harry S. Stout, and Charles Reagan Wilson, eds. *Religion and the American Civil War.* New York: Oxford Univ. Press, 1998.

Moneyhon, Carl H. *The Impact of the Civil War and Reconstruction on Arkansas: Persistence in the Midst of Ruin.* Baton Rouge: Louisiana State Univ. Press, 1994.

———. *Texas after the Civil War: The Struggle of Reconstruction.* College Station: Texas A & M Univ. Press, 2004.

Montgomery, David. *Beyond Equality: Labor and the Radical Republicans, 1862–1872.* 1967. Reprint, Urbana: Univ. of Illinois Press, 1981.

Moody, T. W. *Michael Davitt and Irish Revolution, 1846–82.* Oxford: Clarendon Press, 1981.

Morgan, Philip D. *Slave Counterpoint: Black Culture in the Eighteenth-Century Chesapeake and Lowcountry*. Chapel Hill: Published for the Omohundro Institute of Early American History and Culture, Williamsburg, Va., by the Univ. of North Carolina Press, 1998.

Morris, Richard B., ed. *Encyclopedia of American History*, Bicentennial Edition. New York: Harper and Row, 1976.

Mushkat, Jerome. *The Reconstruction of the New York Democracy, 1861–1874*. Rutherford: Fairleigh Dickinson Univ. Press, 1981.

Nagel, Paul. *One Nation Indivisible: The Union in American Thought, 1776–1861*. New York: Oxford Univ. Press, 1964.

———. *This Sacred Trust: American Nationality, 1798–1898*. New York: Oxford Univ. Press, 1971.

Nathans, Elizabeth Studley. *Losing the Peace: Georgia Republicans and Reconstruction, 1865–1871*. Baton Rouge: Louisiana State Univ. Press, 1968.

Neely, Mark, Jr. *The Union Divided: Party Conflict in the Civil War North*. Cambridge, Mass.: Harvard Univ. Press, 2002.

Neidhardt, W. S. *Fenianism in North America*. University Park: Pennsylvania State Univ. Press, 1975.

Nevins, Allan. *The Emergence of Modern America, 1865–1878*. New York: Macmillan, 1927.

———. *Hamilton Fish: An Inner History of the Grant Administration*. New York: Dodd, Mead, 1936.

Nunn, W. C. *Texas under the Carpetbaggers*. Austin: Univ. of Texas Press, 1962.

O'Brien, Conor Cruise. *Parnell and His Party, 1880–1890*. Oxford: Clarendon Press, 1957.

Ó Broin, León. *Fenian Fever: An Anglo-American Dilemma*. New York: New York Univ. Press, 1971.

Olsen, Otto, ed. *Reconstruction and Redemption in the South*. Baton Rouge: Louisiana State Univ. Press, 1980.

Oubre, Claude F. *Forty Acres and a Mule: The Freedmen's Bureau and Black Land Ownership*. Baton Rouge: Louisiana State Univ. Press, 1978.

Palmer, Norman D. *The Irish Land League Crisis*. 1940. Reprint, New York: Octagon Books, 1978.

Paluden, Phillip S. *A Covenant with Death: The Constitution, Law, and Equality in the Civil War Era*. Urbana: Univ. of Illinois Press, 1975.

Paolino, Ernest M. *The Foundations of the American Empire: William Henry Seward and U.S. Foreign Policy*. Ithaca: Cornell Univ. Press, 1973.

Patterson, Joe Smith. *The Republican Expansionists of the Early Reconstruction Era*. Chicago: Univ. of Chicago Libraries, 1933.

Patton, James Welch. *Unionism and Reconstruction in Tennessee, 1860–1869.* Chapel Hill: Univ. of North Carolina Press, 1934.

Pereyra, Lillian A. *James Lusk Alcorn: Persistent Whig.* Baton Rouge: Louisiana State Univ. Press, 1966.

Perman, Michael. *Reunion without Compromise: The South and Reconstruction, 1865–1868.* Cambridge: Cambridge Univ. Press, 1973.

———. *The Road to Redemption: Southern Politics, 1869–1879.* Chapel Hill: Univ. of North Carolina Press, 1984.

Potter, David M. *The South and the Sectional Conflict.* Baton Rouge: Louisiana State Univ. Press, 1968.

Rabinowitz, Howard, ed. *Southern Black Leaders of the Reconstruction Era.* Urbana: Univ. of Illinois Press, 1982.

Rable, George C. *But There Was No Peace: The Role of Violence in the Politics of Reconstruction.* Athens: Univ. of Georgia Press, 1984.

Ransom, Roger L., and Richard Sutch. *One Kind of Freedom: The Economic Consequences of Emancipation.* Cambridge: Cambridge Univ. Press, 1977.

Reidy, Joseph P. *From Slavery to Agrarian Capitalism in the Cotton Plantation South: Central Georgia, 1800–1880.* Chapel Hill: Univ. of North Carolina Press, 1992.

Richardson, Heather Cox. *The Death of Reconstruction: Race, Labor, and Politics in the Post-Civil War North, 1865–1901.* Cambridge, Mass.: Harvard Univ. Press, 2001.

———. *The Greatest Nation of the Earth: Republican Economic Policies during the Civil War.* Cambridge, Mass.: Harvard Univ. Press, 1997.

Robbins, Roy. *Our Landed Heritage: The Public Domain, 1776–1936.* Princeton: Princeton Univ. Press, 1942.

Rodrigue, John C. *Reconstruction in the Cane Fields: From Slavery to Free Labor in Louisiana's Sugar Parishes, 1862–1880.* Baton Rouge: Louisiana State Univ. Press, 2001.

Rogers, William Warren, Jr. *Black Belt Scalawag: Charles Hays and the Southern Republicans in the Era of Reconstruction.* Athens: Univ. of Georgia Press, 1993.

Rubin, Anne Sarah. *A Shattered Nation: The Rise and Fall of the Confederacy, 1861–1868.* Chapel Hill: Univ. of North Carolina Press, 2005.

Sanders, Elizabeth. *Roots of Reform: Farmers, Workers, and the American State, 1877–1917.* Chicago: Univ. of Chicago Press, 1999.

Saville, Julie. *The Work of Reconstruction: From Slave to Wage Laborer in South Carolina, 1860–1870.* New York: Cambridge Univ. Press, 1994.

Saxton, Alexander. *The Indispensable Enemy: Labor and the Anti-Chinese Movement in California.* Berkeley: Univ. of California Press, 1971.

Schmidt, James D. *Free to Work: Labor Law, Emancipation, and Reconstruction, 1815–1880.* Athens: Univ. of Georgia Press, 1998.

Schneider, Herbert W. *A History of American Philosophy.* New York: Columbia Univ. Press, 1946.

Schneirov, Richard. *Labor and Urban Politics: Class Conflict and the Origins of Modern Liberalism in Chicago, 1864–97.* Urbana: Univ. of Illinois Press, 1998.

Seip, Terry L. *The South Returns to Congress: Men, Economic Measures, and Intersectional Relationships, 1868–1879.* Baton Rouge: Louisiana State Univ. Press, 1983.

Shanks, Henry T. *The Secession Movement in Virginia, 1847–1861.* 1934. Reprint, New York: AMS Press, 1971.

Shippee, Lester. *Canadian-American Relations, 1850–1875.* New Haven: Yale Univ. Press, 1939.

Shofner, Jerrell H. *Nor Is It Over Yet: Florida in the Era of Reconstruction, 1863–1877.* Gainesville: Univ. Presses of Florida, 1974.

Simkins, Francis Butler, and Robert Woody. *South Carolina during Reconstruction.* 1932. Reprint, Gloucester, Mass.: Peter Smith, 1966.

Simpson, Craig D. *A Good Southerner: The Life of Henry A. Wise of Virginia.* Chapel Hill: Univ. of North Carolina Press, 1985.

Singletary, Otis A. *Negro Militia and Reconstruction.* Austin: Univ. of Texas Press, 1957.

Smith, Anthony D., ed. *Nationalist Movements.* London: Macmillan, 1976.

Somkin, Fred. *Unquiet Eagle: Memory and Desire in the Idea of American Freedom, 1815–1860.* Ithaca: Cornell Univ. Press, 1964.

Sproat, John G. *"The Best Men": Liberal Reformers in the Gilded Age.* New York: Oxford Univ. Press, 1968.

Stanley, Amy Dru. *From Bondage to Contract: Wage Labor, Marriage, and the Market in the Age of Slave Emancipation.* New York: Cambridge Univ. Press, 1998.

Staples, Thomas S. *Reconstruction in Arkansas, 1862–1874.* New York: Columbia Univ. Press, 1923.

Steele, E. D. *Irish Land and British Politics: Tenant-Right and Nationality, 1865–1870.* Cambridge: Cambridge Univ. Press, 1974.

Still, Bayrd. *Milwaukee: The History of a City.* Madison: State Historical Society of Wisconsin, 1965.

Storey, Margaret. *Loyalty and Loss: Alabama's Unionists in the Civil War and Reconstruction.* Baton Rouge: Louisiana State Univ. Press, 2004.

Stuckey, Sterling. *Slave Culture: Nationalist Theory and the Foundations of Black America.* New York: Oxford Univ. Press, 1987.

Tansill, Charles Callan. *America and the Fight for Irish Freedom, 1866–1922.* New York: Devin-Adair, 1957.

Tatum, Georgia Lee. *Disloyalty in the Confederacy.* Chapel Hill: Univ. of North Carolina Press, 1934.

Taylor, Joe Gray. *Louisiana Reconstructed, 1863–1877.* Baton Rouge: Louisiana State Univ. Press, 1974.

Thompson, C. Mildred. *Reconstruction in Georgia: Economic, Social, and Political, 1865–1872.* New York: Columbia Univ. Press, 1915.

Thompson, Mattie Thomas. *History of Barbour County, Alabama.* Eufaula, Ala.: N.p., 1939.

Thornton, J. Mills, III. *Politics and Power in a Slave Society: Alabama, 1800–1860.* Baton Rouge: Louisiana State Univ. Press, 1978.

Travers, Len. *Celebrating the Fourth: Independence Day and the Rites of Nationalism in the Early Republic.* Amherst: Univ. of Massachusetts Press, 1997.

Trefousse, Hans L. *The Radical Republicans: Lincoln's Vanguard for Racial Justice.* 1968. Reprint, Baton Rouge: Louisiana State Univ. Press, 1975.

Trelease, Allen W. *White Terror: The Ku Klux Klan Conspiracy and Southern Reconstruction.* 1971; rpr. Baton Rouge: Louisiana State Univ. Press, 1995.

Tunnell, Ted. *Crucible of Reconstruction: War, Radicalism and Race in Louisiana, 1862–1877.* Baton Rouge: Louisiana State Univ. Press, 1984.

Walker, Mabel Gregory. *The Fenian Movement.* Colorado Springs: Ralph Myles Publisher, 1969.

Wang, Xi. *The Trial of Democracy: Black Suffrage and Northern Republicans, 1860–1910.* Athens: Univ. of Georgia Press, 1997.

Welke, Barbara Young. *Recasting American Liberty: Gender, Race, Law, and the Railroad Revolution, 1865–1920.* Cambridge: Cambridge Univ. Press, 2001.

West, Elliott. *The Contested Plains: Indians, Goldseekers, and the Rush to Colorado.* Lawrence: Univ. Press of Kansas, 1998.

Wharton, Vernon. *The Negro in Mississippi, 1865–1890.* 1947. Reprint, New York: Harper and Row, 1965.

Wiener, Jonathan. *Social Origins of the New South: Alabama, 1860–1885.* Baton Rouge: Louisiana State Univ. Press, 1978.

Wiggins, Sarah Woolfolk. *The Scalawag in Alabama Politics, 1865–1881.* Tuscaloosa: Univ. of Alabama Press, 1977.

Wilentz, Sean. *Chants Democratic: New York City and the Rise of the American Working Class, 1788–1850.* New York: Oxford Univ. Press, 1984.

Williams, Lou Falkner. *The Great South Carolina Ku Klux Klan Trials, 1871–1872.* Athens: Univ. of Georgia Press, 1996.

Williamson, Joel. *After Slavery: The Negro in South Carolina during Reconstruction, 1861–1877.* 1965. Reprint, New York: Norton, 1975.

Wilson, Major L. *Space, Time, and Freedom: The Quest for Nationality and the Irrepressible Conflict, 1815–1861.* Westport, Conn.: Greenwood Press, 1974.

Wood, Forrest G. *Black Scare: The Racist Response to Emancipation and Reconstruction.* Berkeley: Univ. of California Press, 1970.

Articles and Essays

Abney, M. G. "Reconstruction in Pontotoc County." *Publications of the Mississippi Historical Society* 11 (1910): 228–269.

Alexander, Thomas B. "Whiggery and Reconstruction in Tennessee." *Journal of Southern History* 16 (August 1950): 291–305.

Aptheker, Herbert. "South Carolina Negro Conventions, 1865." *Journal of Negro History* 31 (January 1946): 91–98.

Armstrong, Thomas F. "From Task Labor to Free Labor: The Transition Along Georgia's Rice Coast, 1820–1880." *Georgia Historical Quarterly* 64 (winter 1980): 432–447.

Auman, William T., and David S. Scarboro. "The Heroes of America in Civil War North Carolina." *North Carolina Historical Review* 58 (autumn 1981): 327–363.

Barnes, Johnny W. "The Political Activities of the Union League of America in North Carolina." *Quarterly Review of Higher Education among Negroes* 20, no. 4 (October 1952): 141–150.

Bates, James P., III. "The British High Commissioners at Washington in 1871." Massachusetts Historical Society *Proceedings* 65 (1932–1936): 339–357.

Baum, Dale. "The 'Irish Vote' and Party Politics in Massachusetts, 1860–1876." *Civil War History* 26 (June 1980): 117–141.

Belissary, C. G. "Tennessee and Immigration, 1865–1880." *Tennessee Historical Quarterly* 7 (1948): 229–248.

Bell, Howard H. "The Negro Emigration Movement, 1849–1854: A Phase of Negro Nationalism." *Phylon* 9 (summer 1959): 132–142.

Benedict, Michael Les. "The Politics of Reconstruction." In *American Political History: Essays on the State of the Discipline,* edited by John F. Marzalak and Wilson D. Miscamble, C.S.C. Notre Dame: Univ. of Notre Dame Press, 1997.

Bentley, George. "The Political Activity of the Freedmen's Bureau in Florida." *Florida Historical Quarterly* 28 (July 1949): 28–37.

Berthoff, Rowland. "Southern Attitudes Toward Immigration, 1865–1914." *Journal of Southern History* 17 (August 1951): 328–360.

Bethel, Elizabeth. "The Freedmen's Bureau in Alabama." *Journal of Southern History* 14 (February 1948): 49–92.
Braden, W. H. "Reconstruction in Lee County." *Publications of the Mississippi Historical Society* 10 (1907): 135–146.
Brock, Euline W. "Thomas W. Cardozo: Fallible Black Reconstruction Leader." *Journal of Southern History* 47 (May 1981): 183–206.
Brough, Charles Hillman. "The Clinton Riot." *Publications of the Mississippi Historical Society* 6 (1902): 53–64.
Brown, Ira V. "William D. Kelley and Radical Reconstruction." *Pennsylvania Magazine of History and Biography* 85 (July 1961): 316–329.
Brown, Julia C. "Reconstruction in Yalobusha and Grenada Counties." *Publications of the Mississippi Historical Society* 12 (1912): 214–282.
Brown, Thomas N. "The Origins and Character of Irish-American Nationalism." *Review of Politics* 18 (July 1956): 327–358.
Browne, F. Z. "Reconstruction in Oktibbeha County." *Publications of the Mississippi Historical Society* 13 (1913): 273–298.
Brundage, David. "Irish Land and American Workers: Class and Ethnicity in Denver, Colorado." In *"Struggle a Hard Battle": Essays on Working-Class Immigrants*, ed. Dirk Hoerder. DeKalb: Northern Illinois Univ. Press, 1986.
Calvert, Robert A., ed. "The Freedmen and Agricultural Prosperity." *Southwestern Historical Quarterly* 76 (April 1973): 461–471.
Carmichael, Maude. "Federal Experiments with Negro Labor on Abandoned Plantations in Arkansas, 1862–1865." *Arkansas Historical Quarterly* 1 (June 1942): 101–116.
Carson, Roberta F. "The Loyal League in Georgia." *Georgia Historical Quarterly* 20 (June 1936): 125–153.
Cimbala, Paul A. "The Freedmen's Bureau, the Freedmen, and Sherman's Grant in Reconstruction Georgia, 1865–1867." *Journal of Southern History* 55 (November 1989): 597–632.
———. "On the Front Line of Freedom: Freedmen's Bureau Officers and Agents in Reconstruction Georgia, 1865–1868." *Georgia Historical Quarterly* 76, no. 3 (fall 1992): 577–611.
Clark, Dennis. "Militants of the 1860's: The Philadelphia Fenians." *Pennsylvania Magazine of History and Biography* 95 (January 1971): 98–108.
Clark, Robert Carlton. "The Diplomatic Mission of Sir John Rose, 1871." *Pacific Northwest Quarterly* 27 (1936): 227–242.
Clawson, Mary Ann. "Fraternal Orders and Class Formation in the Nineteenth-Century United States." *Comparative Studies in Society and History* 27 (October 1985): 672–695.

Clifton, James M. "Twilight Comes to the Rice Kingdom: Postbellum Rice Culture on the South Atlantic Coast." *Georgia Historical Quarterly* 62 (summer 1978): 146–154.

Cook, Adrian. "Failure of a Mission: Reverdy Johnson in London, 1868–1869." *Maryland Historical Magazine* 61 (June 1996): 120–146.

Cooper, Forrest. "Reconstruction in Scott County." *Publications of the Mississippi Historical Society* 13 (1913): 99–221.

Coulter, E. Merton. "Cudjo Frye's Insurrection." *Georgia Historical Quarterly* 38 (September 1954): 213–235.

Cox, John, and LaWanda Cox. "General O.O. Howard and the 'Misrepresented Bureau.'" *Journal of Southern History* 19 (November 1953): 427–456.

Crane, J. Michael. "Controlling the Night: Perceptions of the Slave Patrol in Mississippi." *Journal of Mississippi History* 61 (summer 1999): 119–136.

Dante, Harris. "Western Attitudes and Reconstruction Politics in Illinois, 1865–1872." *Journal of the Illinois State Historical Society* 49 (summer 1956): 149–162.

Davis, David Brion. "Some Themes of Countersubversion: An Analysis of Anti-Masonic, Anti-Catholic, and Anti-Mormon Literature." *Mississippi Valley Historical Review* 47 (September 1960): 205–224.

Dozer, Donald Marquand. "Anti-Expansionism during the Johnson Administration." *Pacific Historical Review* 12 (1943): 253–276.

DuBois, Ellen Carol. "Outgrowing the Compact of the Fathers: Equal Rights, Woman Suffrage, and the United States Constitution, 1820–1878." *Journal of American History* 74 (December 1987): 836–862.

Engelsman, John C. "The Freedmen's Bureau in Louisiana." *Louisiana Historical Quarterly* 32 (January 1949): 145–224.

Fels, Rendig. "American Business Cycles, 1865–1879." *American Economic Review* 41 (June 1951): 325–349.

Ferguson, James S. "The Grange and Farmer Education in Mississippi." *Journal of Southern History* 8 (November 1942): 497–512.

Fitzgerald, Michael W. "The Ku Klux Klan: Property Crime and the Plantation System in Reconstruction Alabama." *Agricultural History* 71 (spring 1997): 186–206.

———. "Railroad Subsidies and Black Aspirations: The Politics of Economic Development in Reconstruction Mobile, 1865–1879." *Civil War History* 39 (September 1993): 240–256.

Fleming, Walter. "The Formation of the Union League in Alabama." *Gulf States Historical Magazine* 2 (September 1903): 73–87.

Foner, Eric. "Class, Ethnicity, and Radicalism in the Gilded Age: The Land League and Irish-America." In *Politics and Ideology in the Age of the Civil War.* New York: Oxford Univ. Press, 1980.

———. "Politics and Ideology in the Shaping of Reconstruction: The Constitutional Conventions of 1867–1869." In *The Evolution of Southern Culture,* ed. Numan V. Bartley. Athens: Univ. of Georgia Press, 1988.

———. "Thaddeus Stevens, Confiscation, and Reconstruction." In *The Hofstader Aegis: A Memorial to Richard Hofstader,* ed. Stanley M. Elkins and Eric McKittrick. New York: Knopf, 1974.

Freidel, Frank. "The Loyal Publication Society: A Pro-Union Propaganda Agency." *Mississippi Valley Historical Review* 26 (December 1939): 359–376.

Futrell, Robert F. "Efforts of Mississippians to Encourage Immigration, 1865–1880." *Journal of Mississippi History* 20 (April 1958): 59–76.

Gates, Paul Wallace. "Federal Land Policy in the South, 1866–1888." *Journal of Southern History* 6 (August 1940): 303–330.

———. "The Homestead Law in an Incongruous Land System." *American Historical Review* 41 (July 1936): 652–681.

Green, James J. "American Catholics and the Irish Land League, 1879–1882." *Catholic Historical Review* 35 (April 1949): 19–42.

Hahn, Steven. "Class and State in Postemancipation Societies: Southern Planters in Comparative Perspective." *American Historical Review* 95 (February 1990): 75–98.

———. "'Extravagant Expectations' of Freedom: Rumour, Political Struggle, and the Christmas Insurrection Scare of 1865 in the American South." *Past and Present* 157 (November 1997): 122–159.

Hardy, W. H. "Recollections of Reconstruction in East and Southeast Mississippi." *Publications of the Mississippi Historical Society* 4 (1901): 105–132.

Harris, William C. "The Creed of the Carpetbagger: The Case of Mississippi." *Journal of Southern History* 40 (May 1974): 199–224.

Hartman, William. "The New York Custom House: Seat of Spoils Politics." *New York History* 34 (April 1953): 149–163.

Heard, George Alexander. "St. Simon's Island during the War Between the States." *Georgia Historical Quarterly* 22 (September 1938): 249–272.

Hennessey, Melinda. "Reconstruction Politics and the Military: The Eufaula Riot of 1874." *Alabama Historical Quarterly* 38 (summer 1976): 112–126.

Hernon, Joseph M., Jr. "The Use of the American Civil War in the Debate over Irish Home Rule." *American Historical Review* 69 (July 1964): 1022–1026.

Highsmith, William E. "Some Aspects of Reconstruction in the Heart of Louisiana." *Journal of Southern History* 13 (November 1947): 460–491.

Hodes, Martha. "The Sexualization of Reconstruction Politics: White Women and Black Men in the South after the Civil War." *Journal of the History of Sexuality* 3 (January 1993): 402–417.

Hoffman, Edwin D. "From Slavery to Self-Reliance: The Record of Achievement of the Freedmen of the Sea Island Region." *Journal of Negro History* 41 (January 1956): 8–42.

Hoffnagle, Warren. "The Southern Homestead Act: Its Origin and Operation." *Historian* 32 (August 1970): 612–629.

Jentz, John B., and Richard Schneirov. "Chicago's Fenian Fair of 1864: A Window into the Civil War as a Popular Political Awakening." *Labor's Heritage* 6 (winter 1995): 4–19.

John, Richard R. "Governmental Institutions as Agents of Change: Rethinking American Political Development in the Early Republic, 1787–1835." *Studies in American Political Development* 11 (fall 1997): 347–380.

Johnson, Benjamin S. "The Brooks-Baxter War." *Publications of the Arkansas Historical Association* 3 (1908): 122–174.

Keller, Morton. "The Politicos Reconsidered." *Perspectives in American History* 1 (1967): 401–408.

Kendel, Julia. "Reconstruction in Lafayette County." *Publications of the Mississippi Historical Society* 13 (1913): 223–272.

Kyle, John W. "Reconstruction in Panola County." *Publications of the Mississippi Historical Society* 12 (1912): 9–98.

Larkin, Emmet. "The Devotional Revolution in Ireland, 1850–1875." *American Historical Review* 77 (June 1972): 625–652.

Lawson, Melinda. "'A Profound National Devotion': The Civil War Union Leagues and the Construction of a New National Patriotism." *Civil War History* 48 (December 2002): 338–362.

Lestage, H. Oscar, Jr. "The White League in Louisiana and Its Participation in Reconstruction Riots." *Louisiana Historical Quarterly* 18 (July 1935): 617–695.

Lowenberg, Bert James. "Efforts of the South to Encourage Immigration, 1865–1900." *South Atlantic Quarterly* 33 (1934): 365–367.

Magee, Hattie. "Reconstruction in Lawrence and Jefferson Davis Counties." *Publications of the Mississippi Historical Society* 11 (1910): 163–204.

Mallam, William D. "Butlerism in Massachusetts." *New England Quarterly* 33 (June 1960): 186–206.

———. "The Grant-Butler Relationship." *Mississippi Valley Historical Review* 41 (September 1954): 259–276.

McKay, S. S. "Social Conditions in Texas in the 1870s." *West Texas Historical Association Year Book* 14 (October 1938): 32–52.

McNair, Cecil E. "Reconstruction in Bullock County." *Alabama Historical Quarterly* 15 (spring 1953): 75–124.

McPherson, James. "Was Blood Thicker Than Water? Ethnic and Civic Nationalism in the American Civil War." *Proceedings of the American Philosophical Society* 143 (March 1999): 102–108.

Meenaugh, Martin L. "Archbishop John Hughes and the New York Schools Controversy of 1840–43." *American Nineteenth-Century History* 5 (spring 2004): 34–65.

Miller, E. T. "State Finances of Texas during Reconstruction." Texas State Historical Association *Quarterly* 14 (October 1910): 87–112.

Miller, Kerby A. "Class, Culture, and Immigrant Group Identity in the United States: The Case of Irish-American Ethnicity." In *Immigration Reconsidered: History, Sociology, and Politics,* ed. Virginia Yans-McLoughlin. New York: Oxford Univ. Press, 1990.

Miller, Steven, Susan E. O'Donovan, John C. Rodrigue, and Leslie S. Rowland. "Between Emancipation and Enfranchisement: Law and the Political Mobilization of Black Southerners during Presidential Reconstruction, 1865–1877." *Chicago-Kent Law Review* 70 (1995): 1059–1077.

Mintz, Sidney W., and Douglas Hall. "The Origins of the Jamaican Internal Marketing System." *Yale University Publications in Anthropology* 57 (1960): 1–26.

Moneyhon, Carl. "The Impact of the Civil War in Arkansas: The Mississippi River Plantation Counties." *Arkansas Historical Quarterly* 51 (summer 1992): 105–119.

Montgomery, David M. "Radical Republicanism in Pennsylvania, 1866–1873." *Pennsylvania Magazine of History and Biography* 85 (October 1961): 439–457.

Morris-Crowther, Jayne. "An Economic Study of the Substantial Slaveholders of Orangeburg County, 1860–1880." *South Carolina Historical Magazine* 86 (October 1985): 296–314.

Morrow, R. L. "The Anglo-American Treaty of 1870." *American Historical Review* 39 (1934): 663–681.

Nichols, Irby C. "Reconstruction in DeSoto County." *Publications of the Mississippi Historical Society* 11 (1910): 295–316.

"Notes on Reconstruction in Tallahassee and Leon County, 1866–1876." *Florida Historical Society* 5 (January 1927): 153–158.

Osofsky, Gilbert. "Abolitionists, Irish Immigrants, and the Dilemmas of Romantic Nationalism." *American Historical Review* 80 (October 1975): 889–912.

Painter, Nell Irvin. "Martin R. Delany: Elitism and Black Nationalism." In *Black Leaders of the Nineteenth Century*, ed. Leon Litwack and August Meier. Urbana: Univ. of Illinois Press, 1988.

Peek, Ralph A. "Lawlessness in Florida, 1868–1871." *Florida Historical Quarterly* 40 (October 1961): 164–185.

Penningroth, Dylan. "Slavery, Freedom, and Social Claims to Property among African Americans in Liberty County, Georgia, 1850–1880." *Journal of American History* 84 (September 1997): 405–435.

Powell, Lawrence. "The American Land Company and Agency: John A. Andrew and the Northernization of the South." *Civil War History* 21 (December 1975): 293–308.

Puckett, E. F. "Reconstruction in Monroe County." *Publications of the Mississippi Historical Society* 11 (1910): 103–161.

Queener, Vernon M. "The East Tennessee Republicans as a Minority Party, 1870–1896." *East Tennessee Historical Society's Publications* 15 (1943): 49–73.

Randolph, Frederick. "Chinamen in Yankeedom: Anti-Unionism in Massachusetts in 1870." *American Historical Review* 53 (October 1947): 1–29.

Reynolds, Thomas J. "The Pope County Militia War." *Publications of the Arkansas Historical Association* 11 (1908): 174–199.

Richardson, Heather Cox. "North and West of Reconstruction: Studies in Political Economy." In *Reconstructions: New Perspectives on the Postbellum United States*, ed. Thomas J. Brown (New York: Oxford Univ. Press, 2006).

Robinson, Armstead L. "Beyond the Realm of Social Consensus: New Meanings of Reconstruction for American History." *Journal of American History* 68 (September 1981): 276–297.

Robson, Maureen M. "The Alabama Claims and the Anglo-American Reconciliation, 1865–1871." *Canadian Historical Review* 42 (March 1961): 1–22.

Rodrigue, John C. "Labor Militancy and Black Grassroots Political Mobilization in the Louisiana Sugar Region, 1865–1868." *Journal of Southern History* 67 (February 2001): 115–142.

Roediger, David. "Ira Stewart and the Anti-Slavery Origins of American Eight-Hour Theory." *Labor History* 27 (summer 1986): 410–426.

Russ, William A., Jr. "Registration and Disfranchisement under Radical Reconstruction." *Mississippi Valley Historical Review* 21 (September 1934): 163–180.

Saloutos, Theodore. "The Grange in the South, 1870–1877." *Journal of Southern History* 19 (November 1953): 473–487.

Sanborn, John Bell. "Some Political Aspects of Homestead Legislation." *American Historical Review* 6 (October 1900): 19–37.

Saville, Julie. "Rites and Power: Reflections on Slavery, Freedom and Political Ritual." *Slavery and Abolition* 20 (April 1999): 81–102.

Schwalm, Leslie A. "'Sweet Dreams of Freedom': Freedwomen's Reconstruction of Life and Labor in Lowcountry South Carolina." *Journal of Women's History* 9 (spring 1997): 9–38.

Scroggs, Jack B. "Carpetbagger Constitutional Reform in the South Atlantic States, 1867–1868." *Journal of Southern History* 27 (November 1961): 475–493.

Shannon, Fred. "The Homestead Act and the Labor Surplus." *American Historical Review* 41 (July 1936): 637–651.

Shapiro, Herbert. "The Ku Klux Klan during Reconstruction: The South Carolina Episode." *Journal of Negro History* 49 (January 1964): 34–55.

Shapiro, Samuel. "'Aristocracy, Mud, and Vituperation': The Butler-Dana Campaign in Essex County in 1868." *New England Quarterly* 31 (September 1958): 340–362.

———. "Problems of International Arbitrations: The Halifax Fisheries Commission of 1877." *Essex Institute Historical Collections* 95 (January 1959): 21–31.

Shortreed, Margaret. "The Antislavery Radicals: From Crusade to Revolution, 1840–1868." *Past and Present* 16 (November 1959): 65–85.

Shugg, Robert W. "Survival of the Plantation System in Louisiana." *Journal of Southern History* 3 (August 1937): 311–325.

Simkins, Francis B. "The Ku Klux Klan in South Carolina, 1868–1871." *Journal of Negro History* 12 (October 1927): 606–648.

———. "The Problems of South Carolina Agriculture after the Civil War." *North Carolina Historical Review* 7 (January 1930): 46–78.

Simmel, Georg. "The Sociology of Secrecy and of Secret Societies." *American Journal of Sociology* 11 (January 1906): 441–498.

Smith, George Winston. "Some Northern Wartime Attitudes Towards the Post-Civil War South." *Journal of Southern History* 10 (August 1944): 253–274.

Stanley, Amy Dru. "Beggars Can't Be Choosers: Compulsion and Contract in Postbellum America." *Journal of American History* 78 (March 1992): 1265–1293.

———. "Conjugal Bonds and Wage Labor: Rights of Contract in the Age of Emancipation." *Journal of American History* 75 (September 1988): 471–500.

Teal, Margaret E. "The Battle of Limeridge: Stories and Legends of the Fenian Raid, June 2, 1866, at Ridgeway, Ontario." 1976. Reprint, [Ridgeway, Ontario]: Bertie Historical Society: 1982.

Thornton, J. Mills, III. "Fiscal Policy and the Failure of Radical Reconstruction in the Lower South." In *Region, Race, and Reconstruction: Essays in Honor of C. Vann Woodward,* ed. Morgan Kousser and James M. McPherson. New York: Oxford Univ. Press, 1982.

Wagstaff, Thomas. "Call Your Old Master-'Master': Southern Political Leaders and Negro Labor during Presidential Reconstruction." *Labor History* 10 (summer 1969): 323–345.

Walsh, Victor. "A Fanatic Heart: The Cause of Irish-American Nationalism in Pittsburgh during the Gilded Age." *Journal of Social History* 15 (winter 1981): 187–204.

Warner, Donald F. "Drang Nach Norden: The United States and the Riel Rebellion." *Mississippi Valley Historical Review* 39 (March 1953): 693–712.

Watkins, Ruth. "Reconstruction in Newton County." *Publications of the Mississippi Historical Society* 11 (1910): 205–228.

Williams, Lou Falkner. "The South Carolina Ku Klux Klan Trials and the Enforcement of Federal Rights, 1871–1872." *Civil War History* 39 (March 1993): 47–66.

Williams, T. Harry. "The Louisiana Unification Movement of 1873." *Journal of Southern History* 11 (August 1945): 349–369.

Williamson, Edward C. "The Alabama Election of 1874." *Alabama Review* 17 (July 1964): 210–219.

Witty, Fred M. "Reconstruction in Carroll and Montgomery Counties." *Publication of the Mississippi Historical Society* 10 (1909): 115–134.

Wood, Gordon. "Conspiracy and the Paranoid Style: Causality and Deceit in the Eighteenth Century." *William and Mary Quarterly* 39 (July 1982): 401–441.

Woodman, Harold. "Sequel to Slavery: The New History Views the Postbellum South." *Journal of Southern History* 43 (November 1977): 523–554.

Woodward, C. Vann. "The Price of Freedom." In *What Was Freedom's Price?,* ed. David Sansing. Oxford: Univ. Press of Mississippi, 1978.

Woody, Robert H. "The Labor and Immigration Problem of South Carolina during Reconstruction." *Mississippi Valley Historical Review* 18 (September 1931): 195–212.

Worley, Ted R. "The Arkansas Peace Society of 1861: A Study in Mountain Unionism." *Journal of Southern History* 24 (November 1958): 445–456.

Yellowitz, Irwin. "Eight Hours and the Bricklayers' Strike of 1868." In *Essays in the History of New York City: A Memorial to Sidney Pomerantz,* ed. Irwin Yellowitz. Port Washington, N.Y.: Kennikat Press, 1978.

Zuczek, Richard M. "The Last Campaign of the Civil War: South Carolina and the Revolution of 1876." *Civil War History* 42 (March 1996): 18–31.

Dissertations and Theses

Bacon, Charles Madison. "A History of Hinds County, Mississippi, during Reconstruction, 1865–1875." Master's thesis, Mississippi College, 1959.

Owens, Susie L. "The Union Leagues of America: Political Activities in Tennessee, the Carolinas, and Virginia, 1865–1870." Ph.D. diss., New York University, 1943.

Index

Abbeville Court House, S.C., 26
Aberdeen, Miss., 67
Adams, Charles Francis, 47
African Americans, 6, 136–37; and American nationalism, 142–45; and citizenship, 164–66; comparison to Irish Americans, 14–15; and emigration from the South, 122–24; and ethnic nationalism, 116–24; and foreign immigration, 110–11; and land, 90–103; relations with Irish Americans, 15; and Republican Party, 20; on suffrage, 25, 155–58. *See also* Ogeechee uprising
Akerman, Amos T., 174
Alabama, 21, 24, 26, 32, 33, 34, 36, 39, 40, 41, 58, 59, 61, 63, 68, 78, 79, 85, 90, 93, 122, 132, 134, 135, 142, 144, 145, 147, 156, 157, 158, 160, 162, 164, 165
Alabama claims, 45, 48, 162
Alamance, N.C., 24
Albany, N.Y., 66
Alexandria *Gazette*, 118
American Democratic Association, 53
American Revolution, 143, 176
Ancient Order of the Hibernians, 51
Anthony, Susan B., 15
Arkansas, 22, 30, 31, 33, 76, 109, 150
Arkansas Freeman, 111
Arkansas River Valley Immigration Company, 109
Arkansas State Gazette, 132
Athens, Ala., 156
Athens, Ga., 42

Athens, Tenn., 146
Athens *Republican*, 21, 148
Atlanta, Ga., 42, 61, 73
Atlantic Monthly, 70
Augusta, Ga., 119, 144, 166
Augusta *Chronicle and Sentinel*, 91, 105
Austin *Daily State Gazette*, 33, 34, 97, 134, 159

Barnes, Thomas, 67
Baton Rouge, La., 121
Battle of Eccles Hill, 171
Baxley, George, 103
Bayou La Batre, Ala., 154
Beaufort, S.C., 100
Becker, Carl, 176
Bellville Farmers Association, 103
Benning, Henry 24
Birth of a Nation, The, 174
Black Reconstruction in America, 1860–1880, 84–85
Blairstown, Iowa, 151
Board of Publication, Philadelphia Union League, 57, 140
Booker, Colonel Alfred, 2
Boston, Mass., 52, 53, 64, 169
Boyd, James, 24
Bristow, Benjamin, 174
Brooklyn Academy of Music, 153
Brown, Albert Gallatin, 31
Brown, Thomas N., 137
Brownson, Orestes, 148
Bryant, John E., 29
Buffalo, N.Y., 65, 127

209

Bullock County, Ala., 3–5, 105
Burke, Richard, 39
Burnett, George P., 61
Burt, Armistead, 167
Butler, Benjamin, 155
Byrnes, T. A. 23

Caldwell, J. H., 40, 42
Campbell, George, 76
Campbell, James, 160
Campbell, Tunis, 103
Canada, 1–3, 171
Cape Elizabeth, Maine, 57
Carbonari, 55
Cardozo, Francis L., 58, 95, 97, 123, 137, 157
Carlin, David, 37
Catholic Church, 53, 77, 80, 86, 130, 131
Celtic language, 126–27
Celtic Literary Club, 127
Central and Auxiliary Constitutional Club, 36
Charleston, S.C., 27, 78, 144
Charleston *Advocate,* 90, 111
Charleston *Daily Courier,* 13, 32, 34
Charleston *Daily News,* 69, 166
Charleston *Daily Republican,* 23, 73, 95
Charleston *Mercury,* 105, 169
Charleston *News and Courier,* 35
Charlestown, Mass., 53
Chesnut, James, Jr., 13, 104
Chicago, Ill., 44, 127, 129
Chinese labor, 110, 114
Christy, John H., 42
Cincinnati, Ohio, 44
Citizen's Association, 167
Citizen's Reform Association, 168
Citizenship, 163–67: African American, 164–66; Irish American, 162–63. *See also* suffrage
civic nationalism: among African Americans, 8, 142–45. *See also* nationalism
Civil Rights Act of 1866, 8
Clan na Gael, 171

Clansman, The, 174
class: and Reconstruction historiography, 81; relationship to nationalism, 82–84
Clay Clubs, 35
Clayton, Powell, 33
Cleveland, 57, 65, 131, 151
Cleveland *Morning Leader,* 47, 48
Coleman, William, 84
Colfax, Schuyler, 44
Collins, Jerome J., 171
Colored American, 123, 133, 156, 166
Colored Tennessean, 111, 121, 123, 156
Columbus, Ga., 123
Columbus, Miss., 69
Condition, Elevation, Emigration and Destiny of the Colored People of the United States, The, 122
confiscation, 96–98, 139. *See also* land
Conkling, Roscoe, 155
Connecticut, 150
Connor, Walker, 10, 112
Constitutional Club of Mobile, 36, 78, 132
Cook, Wilson, 118
Cooper Institute, 44, 151
Copperheads, 50. *See also* secret societies
countersubversion, 77–80. *See also* secret societies
Cox, George, 94, 156, 164
Cromwell, Oliver, 86
Crystal Springs, Miss., 30
Cub Lake, Miss., 74

Daily Austin Republican, 165
Daily New Era, 146
Daily Newbern Commercial, 91
Daily Press, 70
Danbury, Conn., 57
Davis, Benjamin, 103
Davis, David Brion, 51n3, 80
Davis, Jefferson, 103
Davis Bend, Miss., 103
Davitt, Michael, 172
Dawson, Francis W., 35

Decatur, Ala., 157
Decatur, Ga., 68
Decatur, Miss., 69
Declaration of Independence, 144, 170
Deep River Union League, 21, 26, 57. See also Union Leagues.
Dell, Valentine, 22
democracy, 166–69
Democratic Party, 34–35, 43, 46, 53, 57, 97, 136, 138, 154, 166, 167, 172, 173; and Reconstruction, 19. See also Pineville Democratic Club; Tammany Hall
Democratic-Republican societies, 35
Demopolis, Ala., 165
Demopolis *New Era*, 147
Dennis, William, 5
Dibble, H. C., 22
disfranchisement, 160–62, 173. See also suffrage
Dixon, Thomas, 174
Donald, David Herbert, 7n10, 114n1
Douglas, Robert, 75, 149
Dred Scott (1857), 163
Du Bois, W. E. B., 81, 84
Dublin, Ireland, 87
Dulany, Martin, 118, 122, 126
Dunning, William A., 8, 70, 122
Durham, Plato, 166

East Weymouth, Mass., 151
Edgefield, S.C., 98
Edgefield *Advertiser*, 146
emancipation, 11, 163
Emmet Circle, 14, 56, 151
Enfield Union League, 27. See also Union Leagues
Enforcement Acts, 174
Era and Whig, 93
ethnic nationalism, 9, 114–16; among African Americans, 116–24; among Fenians, 124–31; among southern whites, 131–36
ethnicity. See ethnic nationalism
Exoduster movement, 117, 173

Farrow, Henry P., 26, 99
Federal Elections Bill (1890), 173
Federal Union, 78
Fenian Chief, The, or the Martyr of '65, 65, 89
Fenian Literary Society, 153
Fenians: at Battle of Ridgeway, 1–3; comparison to Ku Klux Klan, 13; comparison to southern whites, pp. 12–14; decline of, 171–72; and ethnic nationalism, 124–31; and Irish American nationalism, 150–53; and land, 86–90; organization, 55–57, 63; as paramilitary organization, 64–67; and the politics of Reconstruction, 43–48; as proto-state, 62–63
Fenian's Progress, The, 66, 72
Fifteenth Amendment, 155, 158
Fleming, Walter L., 174
Florida, 25, 38, 41, 75, 84, 96, 109, 160, 168, 169
Flourney, Robert, 29, 74
Foner, Eric, 81, 82
Forest *Register*, 76
Forrest, Nathan Bedford, 60, 61. See also Ku Klux Klan
Forsyth, C. D., 40
Forsyth, John, 35, 36
Fort Bend, Tex., 173
Fort Erie, 1, 18
Fort Smith *New Era*, 22, 156
Fort Valley, Ga., 69
Fortune, Emmanuel, 96
Fourteenth Amendment, 8, 160, 163
Franklin, Tenn., 69
Frazier, Garrison, 90
Fredrickson, George, 140
free soil ideology, 93–95. See also Republican Party; land
Free South, 137
Freedmen's Bureau, 95, 101; in Alabama, 4; in Georgia, 119, 165
Freeman's Standard, 20, 123, 137
Fullerton, James Scott, 100

212 Index

Galveston, Tex., 21, 161
Garnet, Henry Highland, 14
Gaston, N.C., 120
General Amnesty Act of 1872, 161
Genovese, Eugene D., 117n5, 120
Georgetown, S.C., 23
Georgia, 22, 23, 26, 30, 39, 40, 42, 43, 60, 61, 68, 69, 72, 74, 78, 91, 92, 95, 97, 100, 103, 105, 110, 111, 115, 119, 120, 136, 137, 143, 145, 146, 149, 157, 172
Georgia Equal Rights Association, 29
Georgia Republican, 142
Gibbons, James, 62
Glasgow, Ken., 41
Godkin, E.L., 167
Gordon, John B., 172
Goss, J. H., 37
Grace, William, 126, 152
Grand Army of the Republic, 15
Grange, 15, 105, 106
Grant, Susan-Mary, 7
Grant, Ulysses S., 44, 171
Great Famine, 87, 90, 128, 130
Green Creek Union League, 142. *See also* Union Leagues
Greenbackers, 104, 173
Greensboro, Ala., 164
Grosvenor, William Mason, 149

Hadnett, J. P., 131, 153
Hamburg Lodge, 58. *See also* Union Leagues
Harrington, James, 27
Harris, Essie, 23, 172
Harris, Rice E., 41
Hatcher, Burrell, 124
Heaton, David, 99
Hilton Head, S.C., 119
Hobsbawm, Eric, 115
Hoffman, John T., 47
Hofstader, Richard, 80
Holden, William W., 21, 27, 33
Holland, John Phillip, 171

Holyoke, Mass., 56
homestead exemptions, 95, 97
homestead laws, 95. *See also* land
Houston, Tex., 150
Houston Union, 142
Howard, O. O., 101
Howard, W. S., 64
Howell, Robert Philip, 43
Huggins, A. P., 67
Hughes, John, 130
Humphries, David C., 144, 158
Hungary, 130
Huntsville, Ala., 158

Idaho Territory, 56
Illinois, 57, 126, 154
Illinois State Register, 77
immigration, 52–54, 108–11, 128. *See also* Irish Americans; land
Independence, Iowa, 152
Independents, 104
Indiana, 57, 77, 96
Indians, Plains, 15, 114
Iowa, 126, 151
Ireland, 50
Irish American Republican Clubs, 44
Irish Americans, 6, 43–44, 52–54; comparison to African Americans, 14–15; nationalism among, 124–31, 150–53; and Reconstruction, 43–48; relations with African Americans, 15. *See also* Fenians; immigration
"Irish Brigade," 54
Irish Citizen, 4, 12, 55, 83, 87, 125, 126, 138, 151, 153
Irish Land League, 82, 83, 90, 172
Irish nationalism, 54–55. *See also* nationalism; Young Ireland
Irish Nationalist, 115, 125, 128
Irish People, 10, 44, 45, 46, 84, 87, 125, 126, 128, 129, 150, 151, 153
Irish Republic, 14, 44, 45, 56, 83, 88, 112, 125, 127, 128, 129, 131, 138, 151, 152, 153

Irish Revolutionary Brotherhood, 55. See also Fenians

Jackson, Miss., 70
Jackson *Clarion,* 74
Jacksonville, Fla., 40
Jacques, D. H., 106
Jefferson, Tex., 159
Jefferson, Thomas, 88, 106, 108, 148
John Mitchel Circle, 56
Johnson, Andrew, 3, 28, 44, 60, 95, 101, 107
Jonesboro *Union Flag,* 25
Journal of Freedom, 117, 119, 156, 164
Julian, George W., 96
July Fourth, 144–45, 146–47
Justice, James, 172

Keffer, John C., 99
Kellogg, William P., 174
Kenny, Kevin, 16
Kent, James, 166
Kentucky, 41
Keowee (S.C.) *Courier,* 109
Knights of Labor, 82, 172
Knights of St. Patrick, 162
Knights of the Golden Circle, 50, 77. See also secret societies
Know-Nothings, 50, 53, 77. See also nativism
Knoxville *Whig,* 75
Ku-Klux, 64
Ku Klux Klan: congressional committee on, 22, 37, 104, 122, 172 6; initiation rites of, 72; mentioned 12, 13, 18, 36, 132; at Meridian, 5–6; origins of, 59–61; as paramilitary organization, 67–68; as proto-state, 63–64; and racism, 37–38; as secret society, 72–77; use of iconography, 40–43; use of violence, 37–40
Ku Klux Klan Act, 174

Lafayette Springs, Miss., 69
Lakin, A. S., 40

Land: and Fenians, 86–90; in Ireland, 86–87; and nationalism, 111–12; in postwar South, 90–104; and Reconstruction historiography, 84–85; and southern whites, 101–8. *See also* confiscation; homestead; Ogeechee uprising
Langston, John, 99
Laurensville *Herald,* 79
Lavan, Thomas, 13, 46, 57, 131, 151
Lawson, Melinda, 7
Leon County Industrial and Immigration Association, 109
Liberia, 117, 122, 123
Lieber, Francis, 139–40, 148, 170
Limestone Ridge, Battle of. *See* Battle of Ridgeway
Lincoln, Abraham, 35, 139, 144
Lincoln Light Infantry, 144
Lincoln Republican Guards, 144
Lindsay, Robert B., 61, 134
Linton, Melton R., 92
Little Rock *Republican,* 111
Lodge, Henry Cabot, 173
Louisiana, 22, 104, 136, 137, 150, 168, 173, 174
Louisiana Taxpayers' Association, 169. *See also* taxpayer movements
Louisville, Ky., 55
Loyal Georgian, 29
Loyal Leagues. *See* Union Leagues
Loyal Publication Society, 57, 139, 140
Lusk, Virgil, 41
Luxemburg, Rosa, 82
Lynch, James, 110
Lynchburg, Va., 59
Lyon, John, 150

Mackey, E. W. M., 22
Macon, Ga., 29, 98, 145
Macon, Miss., 70
Macon *Daily Telegraph,* 32, 147
Macon *Georgia Journal and Messenger,* 133
Madison, James, 166

Maine, 59
Manitoba, 171
Marcus, Joshua, 70
Markham, William, 22
Marxism, 82, 84, 112
Maryville *Republican,* 28
Maryville Union League, 28. *See also* Union Leagues
Masons, 50, 80. *See also* secret societies
Massachusetts, 55, 75, 149, 155
Maximilian (emperor of Mexico), 47
McPherson, James, 9n14
Meade, General George, 2
Memphis, Tenn., 55, 75
Memphis *Appeal,* 59
Memphis *Daily Advocate,* 160
Menard, John W., 137, 157
Meridian, Miss., 5–6, 61, 69
Meridian *Chronicle,* 173
Methodist Episcopal Church, 84
Mexico, 47
Military Reconstruction Acts of 1867, 23. *See also* Reconstruction
Milledgeville *Recorder,* 31
Miller, Kerby, 137
Mills, Letty, 43
Milwaukee, 64, 131
Minneapolis *Tribune,* 46
Minute Men, 36
Mississippi, 25, 29, 30, 31, 36, 38, 39, 43, 58, 60, 61, 62, 67, 73, 74, 84, 85, 90, 91, 121, 134, 135, 147, 159, 161, 166, 168, 173, 174
Mitchel, John, 12, 44–45, 47, 55, 83, 88–89, 125, 127, 130, 138, 151, 152, 153
Mobile, Ala., 23, 36, 132
Mobile Central Constitutional Club, 36
Mobile *Daily Advertiser and Register,* 33, 34, 35, 136
Mobile *Nationalist,* 93, 121
Mobile *Register. See* Mobile *Daily Advertiser and Register*
Mobile *Tribune,* 105, 110

Molly Maguires. *See* Ancient Order of the Hibernians
Monck, Charles Stanley, 1
Monroe, A. T., 144
Monroe City, Miss., 38
Montana Territory, 56
Montgomery, Benjamin, 103
Montgomery, David, 81
Montgomery *Advertiser,* 78, 110
Montgomery *Daily State Sentinel,* 94
Montgomery *Mail,* 33, 98
Mooney, W. D., 72
Moore, Aaron, 5
Moore, B. F., 6
Moore, William A., 76
Moss, William, 41
Mulford, Elisha, 148, 170
Mullaly, John, 36

Nashville, Tenn., 62, 122, 167
Nashville *Gazette,* 132
Natchez, Miss., 145
Natchez *Democrat,* 24, 30, 99, 119
Nation, The, 148
Nation under Our Feet, A 7
National Women's Suffrage Association, 15
nationalism: and American Civil War, 7, 57–58, 140; in Confederacy, 7; in Europe, 7; in Ireland, 54–55; Irish American, 81; and land, 112–13; proto-nationalism, 9–10, 116n3; of Republican Party, 140–42, 148–50; and southern whites, 146–47. *See also* civic nationalism; ethnic nationalism; Irish American nationalism
Native Americans. *See* Plains Indians
nativism, 53–54, 130
naturalization, 162. *See also* citizenship
Nebraska, 171
Nelson, Joseph, 40
New Bern, N. C., 99
New Bern *Republican,* 97
New Hanover Agricultural Society, 109
New Jersey, 171

New Orleans, La., 55, 62, 115, 137
New Orleans *Louisianian,* 137
New Orleans *Tribune,* 14, 157
New York, 52, 53, 54, 57, 64, 89, 91, 126, 129, 151, 155, 158, 162, 167, 171; draft riots in, 54, 114
New York *Citizen,* 125, 127
New York *Herald,* 99
New York *Irish American,* 53
New York *Irish People. See Irish People*
New York *Journal of Commerce,* 167
New York Protestant Association, 53
New York *Tribune,* 90
Newberry, S. C. 41
newspapers, 35, 137
Newtown, Miss., 69
Newtown, Willoughby, 107
Norfolk *Journal,* 94
Norfolk *Republican,* 165
North Carolina, 21, 22, 23, 25, 26, 27, 33, 38, 39, 40, 41, 42, 58, 59, 60, 61, 68, 72, 74, 75, 76, 79, 84, 93, 97, 98, 109, 119, 120, 121, 123, 132, 142, 143, 144, 149, 156, 157, 160, 166, 167, 172, 173, 174

O'Connell, Daniel. *See* Irish nationalism; Repeal Movement
O'Connell, Maurice, 89
Ogeechee uprising, 101–103. *See also* African Americans, land
Ohio, 57, 158
Old Guard, 35
Omaha *Republican,* 129
O'Mahoney, John, 45, 55, 171
O'Neil, John, 1, 46, 63, 67, 115, 171
Oregon, 56
Orr, James L., 37

Paine, Thomas, 152
Parnell, Charles Stewart, 172
Parsons, Lewis, 132, 134
Pearce, Charles H., 84, 96
Peeler, Anderson J., 75

Pennsylvania, 57, 96, 125, 152
Perote, Ala., 4
Perry, Benjamin, 97, 98
Petersburg, Va., 32, 150
Philadelphia, 52, 152
Philadelphia *Public Ledger,* 65
Phillips, Wendell, 148
Pinchback, Pinckney B. S., 137
Pineville Democratic Club, 32, 36. *See also* Democratic Party
Pittsburgh *Catholic,* 47, 77
Poland, 129–30
Political associations, 35–37
Pollard, H. Rives, 147
Pope, John, 122
Populism, 105, 173
Potter, David, 7
Powderly, Terrance V., 172
Powers, Ridgely, 39
Pratville, Ala., 99
presidential election of 1868, 39, 159
proto-nationalism, 21. *See also* nationalism
Pulaski, Tenn., 60, 72
Purman, W. J., 38

race, 114, 131–36. *See also* ethnic nationalism
Radical Reconstruction. *See* Reconstruction
railroads, 28, 38, 98, 114
Raleigh, N.C., 111, 117, 119
Raleigh *Daily Sentinel,* 32, 135
Raleigh *Tri-Weekly Standard,* 26, 78, 144
Randolph, Edward Ryland, 35, 75
Rawlins, John A., 154
Readjusters, 173
Reconstruction, 18, 23, 48–49, 155; diplomatic issues of, 47–48; and Irish Americans, 43–48; land question during, 90–108; problems with sources, 16, 91; and southern whites, 30–34
religion, 120, 131
Repeal Movement, 88. *See also* Irish nationalism

Republican Party, 40, 43, 53, 69, 75, 90, 91, 92, 124, 135, 137, 140–142, 154, 158, 159, 170, 173; and American nationalism, 140–42, 148–50; civil rights, 8; and Irish Americans, 43–48; and land question, 93–99; and Reconstruction, 18–19; and Union Leagues, 20–29, 57–58
republicanism (political philosophy), 10, 33–34, 52, 78–79, 86, 91–92, 131, 140, 152, 169, 175
Richardson, Alfred, 38
Richardson, Heather Cox, 9n11
Richmond, Va., 118, 147
Richmond *Daily New Nation,* 40
Richmond *Dispatch,* 134, 135
Richmond *Enquirer and Examiner,* 35, 74, 133, 146
Richmond *Independent Republican,* 161
Richmond *Whig and Public Advertiser,* 24
Ridegway, Battle of, 1–3, 171
Roanoke Guards, 36
Roberts, William R., 1, 45, 46, 125, 126, 130, 151
Robinson, William E., 47
Rome, Ga., 40, 67
Rubin, Anne Sarah, 7
Ruffin, Edmund, 36
Rural Carolinian, 106, 109

San Francisco, Ca., 56, 127, 128
Savannah, Ga., 100, 123, 137, 145, 159
Savannah *Daily News and Herald,* 24, 101, 102, 109, 122, 134
Savannah *Herald,* 92
Savannah *Morning News,* 102, 103
Savannah *Republican,* 102
Saxton, Rufus, 101
Scanlon, Michael, 14, 44, 45, 46, 83, 127, 138, 151, 153
Schenck, David, 41, 75, 132
Schurz, Carl, 92, 100, 158
Scott, Robert K., 26, 106

secret societies, 12, 50–52, 72–80; as antirepublican, 78–79; association with night, 75–78; as countersubversive, 77–80. *See also* Fenians; Know-Nothings; Ku Klux Klan; Society of Ribbonmen; Sons of Liberty; Union Leagues
Seibels, E. W., 60, 91
Seward, William Henry, 44, 45, 162
Seymour and Blair Club, 36, 154. *See also* political associations
Shelbyville *Republican,* 97, 158
Sheridan Circle, 66
Sherman, William T., 92, 95, 100
Shorter, George, 4–5
Shotwell, Randolph A., 79
Simmel, Georg, 70, 79
Simms, James M., 137
slave patrols, 67. *See also* Ku Klux Klan
slavery, 118–20
Smith, John R., 173
Smith, Thomas, 65
Smith, William H., 26
Smithfield, N.C., 75, 149
Society of Ribbonmen, 50. *See also* Ireland
Society of United Irishmen, 54
Sons of Liberty, 50
South Carolina, 26, 34, 36, 37, 39, 41, 58, 59, 60, 85, 90, 91, 92, 95, 97, 99, 100, 101, 104, 106, 107, 118, 123, 136, 137, 144, 157, 159, 160, 167, 168, 169, 174
South Carolina Leader, 101, 119, 121
South Carolina Republican, 93
Southern Argus, 108, 133, 165
Southern Field and Factory, 106
Southern Homestead Act (1866), 95. *See also* land
Southern Opinion, 147
Southern Republican, 107, 165
southern rights associations. *See* political associations
Southern Standard, 76
Southern Watchman, 23, 30

southern whites, 6: on African American citizenship, 164–65; and American nationalism, 146–47; comparison to Fenians, 12–14; and ethnic nationalism, 131–36; on immigration, 108–10; and land, 101–8; on race, 110; on Reconstruction, 30–34
Special Field Order No. 15, 95, 100–101
St. Simon's Island, Ga., 103
Stanton, Edwin M., 90
Stanton, Elizabeth Cady, 15
Steedman, John, 100
Stephens, James, 55
Stephens, John W., 40
Stevens, Thaddeus, 96, 97
Stone Mountain, Ga., 174
Strong, George Templeton, 158
suffrage, 154–163. *See also* Union Leagues; Reconstruction; Republican Party
Sullivan, D.O., 150
Sumner, Charles, 149
Spartanburg, S.C., 37, 41
Swayne, Wager, 4
Sweeny, Thomas W., 1

Tallahassee, 25
Tallahassee *Sentinel,* 76
Taliaferro, John B., 60, 67
Tammany Hall, 53. *See also* Democratic Party
Tax Resisting Association, 168
taxpayers' conventions, 168–69
Tennessee, 39, 110, 142, 158
Texas, 31, 32, 35, 46, 95, 105, 109, 144, 168
Thomas, General H. H., 22
Thomas, J. P., 13
Tilden, Samuel J., 167
Tillson, Davis, 120, 165
Tone, Wolfe, 54. *See also* Irish nationalism
Tourgée, Albion, 84
Treaty of Washington, 163
Tri-Weekly Austin Republican, 94

Troy, N. Y., 44, 66, 87
Trumbull, Lyman, 93
Turf, Field, and Farm, 107
Turner, Henry McNeill, 29, 98, 117–18, 126, 137, 143, 145
Turner, William V., 59
Tuscaloosa, Ala., 94, 141
Tuscaloosa *Independent Monitor,* 35, 75, 98, 110, 133, 134, 135, 147, 159, 165
Tuscumbia, Ala., 122
Tuskegee, Ala., 38
Twitchell, Marshall, 174
Tyler, Warren, 5

Union Leagues: decline of, 172–73; and ethnic nationalism, 121–22; and initiation rites, 70–71; organization of, 58–59; origins of, 57–58; as paramilitary organization, 69; and Republican Party, 20–29; as secret societies, 73–77; similarities to Ku Klux Klan, 59; and voting rights of African Americans, 25. *See also* Deep River Union League; Enfield Union League; Green Creek Union League; Hamburg Lodge; Maryville Union League
Union Reform Party (South Carolina), 91
Union Springs, Ala., 106
Unionists, 41, 121, 138, 144, 160
Unionville, S.C., 37
United Irishmen, 88
Utah, 56, 152

Virginia, 26, 36, 59, 79, 95, 107, 133, 135
Virginia and North Carolina Land, Immigration, and Colonization Society, 109
Virginia State Agricultural Society, 107
Vorenberg, Michael, 2n2
Vrignault, M.H., 73

Walker, Gilbert C., 161
Wappinger Falls, N.Y., 86

Warmoth, Henry Clay, 22
Warner, Willard, 22
Washburne, Elihu B., 123
Waverly Emigration Society, 109
Weed, Thurlow, 77
Weekly Panola Star, 134
Wells, David, 167
Wells, Henry H., 161
Wetumpka, Ala., 59
Whig Party, 53, 63, 77, 107
Whistler, Ala., 154
White Draymen's and Cartmen's Democratic Club, 36. *See also* political associations
White Leagues, 174
white supremacy, 37
whiteboys, 50. *See also* Ireland; secret societies
Wide Awakes, 35. *See also* political associations
Wilcox County News, 110, 133
Wilder, C. B., 169

Williams, Henry Llewellyn, 89
Williamston, S.C., 106
Wilmington, N.C., 27, 165
Wilmington *Daily Post,* 93, 94, 141, 149
Wilmington *Herald,* 132
Wilmington *Journal,* 109, 135
women, 102n34, 163. *See also* Anthony, Susan B.; Stanton, Elizabeth Cady
Wood, Fernando, 53
Woodward, C. Vann, 115
Worth, Jonathan, 33, 97, 160
Wright, Ambrose, 91

Yorkville *Enquirer,* 106
Young Ireland, 54, 130. *See also* Irish nationalism
Young Men's Democratic Club, 36, 154. *See also* political associations
Younger, J. J., 72

Zionism, 82

www.ingramcontent.com/pod-product-compliance
Lightning Source LLC
Chambersburg PA
CBHW070337240426
43665CB00045B/2141